TWO IN ONE

TWO IN ONE

E. MARTIN BROWNE
WITH
HENZIE BROWNE

For by your leaves, you shall not stay alone
Till holy Church incorporate two in one.
Romeo and Juliet, II, vi

CAMBRIDGE UNIVERSITY PRESS

CAMBRIDGE
LONDON   NEW YORK   NEW ROCHELLE
MELBOURNE   SYDNEY

Published by the Press Syndicate of the University of Cambridge
The Pitt Building, Trumpington Street, Cambridge CB2 1RP
32 East 57th Street, New York, NY 10022, USA
296 Beaconsfield Parade, Middle Park, Melbourne 3206, Australia

First published 1981

Text set in 11/13 pt Linotron 202 Baskerville, printed and bound
in Great Britain at The Pitman Press, Bath

British Library cataloguing in publication data
Browne, Elliott Martin
Two in one.
1. Browne, Elliott Martin
2. Theatrical producers and directors – Great
Britain – Biography
I. Title   II. Browne, Henzie
792'.0233'0924   PN2598.B72/   80-41288
ISBN 0 521 23254 6

Contents

Illustrations

Preface

In 1971 Henzie and I had been married for forty-six years. Our life contained a great variety of work and experience. We decided to start writing it by each doing a prologue to our meeting, in the expectation that this would show us how to go on from our marriage. She died in 1973, having finished her chapter (though there was a gap in the middle). There was in addition the short book *Pilgrim Story*, in which she had described our war-work, and quite a large collection of letters and accounts of particular happenings.

I have worked much of this writing into the pattern of *Two In One* and indicated where it occurs. The main part of the story I have written myself. Some of its events may have a place in the history of the English theatre, especially its religious and poetic aspects, but I have set them in the context of the partnership out of which they developed.

I should like to dedicate this book to all those many friends and colleagues who are not forgotten though their names are not in these pages. Audrey Browne has taken a lively and perceptive share in the editorial work, and also in making the index.

E.M.B.

September 1979

The author died on 27 April 1980, while this book was being prepared for publication.

Acknowledgements

The publisher acknowledges permission to reprint copyright material as follows:

extracts from *The Acts of St. Peter* and unpublished letters by Gordon Bottomley, reprinted by permission of Roger Lancelyn Green;

extracts from *This Way To The Tomb* by Ronald Duncan, by permission of Mr Duncan and David Higham Associates Ltd;

extracts from T. S. Eliot's *The Rock, Murder in the Cathedral* and *The Cocktail Party* by permission of Faber and Faber Ltd and Harcourt Brace Jovanovich, Inc.; copyright 1934, 1935 by Harcourt Brace Jovanovich, Inc.; copyright 1950, 1962, 1963 by T. S. Eliot; copyright 1978 by Esme Valerie Eliot;

extracts from *The Elder Statesman* by T. S. Eliot, copyright © 1959 by Thomas Stearns Eliot; from *On Poetry and Poets* by T. S. Eliot, copyright © 1951 by T. S. Eliot; by permission of Faber and Faber Ltd and Farrac, Straus and Giroux, Inc.;

extracts from *A Phoenix too Frequent* by Christopher Fry, by permission of Oxford University Press;

extracts from *George Bell* by Ronald Jasper, by permission of Oxford University Press;

extracts from *The Old Man of the Mountains* by Norman Nicholson, by permission of Faber and Faber Ltd;

extracts from *The Shadow Factory* by Anne Ridler, by permission of Mrs Ridler;

extracts from an unpublished letter of John Westbrook, by permission of Mr Westbrook;

extracts from *Thomas Cranmer of Canterbury* by Charles Williams, by permission of Oxford University Press and David Higham Associates Ltd, and for extracts from an unpublished sonnet of Charles Williams, by permission of Michael Williams and David Higham Associates Ltd;

The Making of T. S. Eliot's Plays, published by the Cambridge University Press in 1969, is complemented by the relevant passages in this book. *Pilgrim Story* by Henzie and E. Martin Browne, from which chapters 6 and 7 are condensed, was published by Frederick Muller Ltd, London, in 1945.

Where it has proved possible, the publishers have obtained permission to reproduce the illustrations, and in these cases acknowledgement is given with the illustration.

Prologue by Martin

I came out of the back door into a large space surrounded by a high circular wall of old brick. A forest of purple flowers with bright yellow stamens, taller than my 4-year-old self, filled the whole centre of the garden. I was being gloriously drowned in a purple sea. My father had put in potato-plants to clean the ground.

That's my first memory, on my first sight of Fifehead House. A square stone building with a pillared portico, it had three storeys plus 'cellar' which, besides housing my father's billiard-room and a row of huge cupboards, became our favourite place for 'hide-and-seek'. I believe it was built about 1815, but it had the internal grace of an earlier period, with ample sash-windows and broad fanlights over the front door and between outer and inner halls. From the latter, two flights of shallow stairs spiralling round a well led to the upper floors. A hexagonal lantern, hanging from a brass chain fixed in the ceiling, contained an oil lamp to light the hall and stairs at night. There was strong brass netting above the mahogany stair-rail where it reached the top landing, to prevent one from doing what I imagined with fascinated horror – flinging oneself down onto the flagstones far below.

Nursery life on the top floor was self-contained. My father, who had been colonel of the Yeomanry in the Boer War, was master of foxhounds, had a large stable full of horses and led a full social life with my mother as well as managing a thousand-acre estate and taking seriously his responsibility for everyone on it. So I didn't see much of him; nor of the brothers seven and six years older than I who by now were sharing his life when not away at boarding-school. My next younger brother was born just before we moved (when I went back recently to our birthplace at Zeals, over the Wiltshire border, I didn't remember it at all); and the youngest, eighteen months after we reached Fifehead. So I spent my first two years there with Nurse and the baby taking daily walks along 'the Gillingham road' or down 'Trill Lane'.

This lane was very dear to me. It had steep banks in which grew a profusion of wild flowers – 'lords and ladies', wild orchids, cowslips and primroses and harebells, meadow-sweet and cow-parsley, and dozens more. There were bird-nests to be found, and butterflies. If the walk was long enough we would get to the river Stour and stand on the stone bridge looking into the weedy stream to see the fish, from stickleback to the occasional trout and, if one was allowed to go down the steep bank, finding the frog one had heard croaking from above. The river would flood from time to time, and I remember when I was older, shuffling along the upper railings of the fence just above the swirling flood-water, to the patch of dry road on the hump of Trill Bridge, where I stood triumphant in the midst of the surrounding sea.

The village consisted of a single road with cottages dotted along it, the post office, the laundry (quite a large house, which during the first world war became a convalescent hospital), two farms, the vicarage and of course the church. This was a focus of my life as far back as I can remember. My father restored it from a half-ruined state, employing a little group of craftsmen to lodge in 'the laundry' for months, like the itinerant craftsmen of old, while they rebuilt it, re-roofed it with stone tiles, and furnished it with oak. It remains a good solid job; if the original date was, as the style suggests, fourteenth century, there are no positive marks of identification left, but there's also no reason why the church of St Mary Magdalen, re-dedicated on 22 July 1905, shouldn't last another five hundred years.

Our vicar was a lazy man, who employed delaying tactics against the demand of our High Church governess for an 'Early Service' once a month, and was said to have been found in bed by the bishop on a surprise morning-visitation. But he was the right kind of man for the villagers: a good fisherman, a good shot, a first-class carpenter, full of country lore; and they felt safe with him. Indeed, this whole way of life felt safe in a way now unbelievable.

I must, very early, have become an enthusiastic churchgoer, and soon my great delight was to walk, or later bicycle, to evensong in the church on the other side of the river. The living of Stour Provost was in the gift of the Provost of King's College, Cambridge, and to it he had presented the Rev. E. Capel Cure. Here was a preacher whose oratory thrilled me, and whose congregation obviously came because it wanted to. But although Sunday Matins was to most a feudal duty, we had a pride in our own church; and to decorate it for the great festivals was everyone's pleasure. I had a plot, on the far side of the round garden, next to a grassy bank: and up this I would train vegetable-marrows. When a marrow was small, I would inscribe, say, GOD IS LOVE on it with a pin, and then feed sugar-water into its stem from a jar to make it swell. For Harvest Festival, I would carry it in my arms to church, to ornament one of the window-embrasures or lie at the base of pulpit or lectern.

When I was 6, came a resident governess and regular lessons both morning and afternoon. (I had already taught myself to read by plaguing Nurse to interpret the names on the gates of the houses at Bournemouth during our seaside holiday.) But there was plenty of time to spare for the delights of the country. To make a 'house' in the space between the double hedges was an enchantment to my little brother and me: we evolved a whole life-style for it. I made a passable collection of butterflies from the fields then full of them, whites, browns, blues and yellows, tortoiseshells and red admirals, the painted ladies and the peacocks which loved the flat, pink heads of sedum in the round garden. A bicycle was a great help in all my ploys, allowing further exploration both of the deep clay country, the Blackmore Vale, on the edge of which we lived, and of the lighter soil to the east leading up to the chalk escarpment of Shaftesbury, seven miles away.

My father had inherited an estate in Australia. His father and uncle had, as young doctors, taken ship's surgeons' jobs because they found England slow in the 1830s and wanted to try their luck abroad. Both must have been men of great courage and enterprise. My great-uncle did a famous exploratory trek across the hinterland of South Australia in 1844; and my grandfather introduced merino sheep into the province, with profitable results. So my father would go out, every few years, to visit his 'station' which was run by a relative by marriage. In 1909 he took with him a 17-year-old niece of my mother's who had suffered a 'nervous breakdown' (I can remember her in a darkened room at home), 'for the sea air'. They started the return journey in a new ship on her maiden round-trip voyage, the *Waratah*. Between Durban and Cape Town, she disappeared. Ships did not yet carry wireless, and when she didn't arrive a prolonged search was made over hundreds of miles of ocean. My mother clung determinedly to the belief that on some uncharted island survivors would be found, until, two years later, part of a ship's boat with 'SS *Waratah*' on it was washed up on the South African coast where, in a great storm on 26 July 1909, she must have foundered with all hands. It is one of the mysteries of the sea.

At the time, it made very little impression on me. My mother must have shown great fortitude in not breaking down under the long strain, and in not involving us in her grief. My father had always been a remote figure and I was hardly aware of the difference between his temporary and permanent absence. We children were much less close to our parents than those of subsequent generations: the people we saw most of were the staff of house and garden and stables. And in the autumn of 1909 I went to boarding-school at Heatherdown, Ascot.

I am grateful to the young headmaster for the extent to which music was a part of the school's life. The assembly hall had an organ with pictures of his twelve favourite composers. Bach was disallowed as dull; Handel and Beethoven held the places of highest honour; Spohr surprisingly scraped in as twelfth man. We sang a great deal, it seems to me, and once a party of us were taken to *Elijah* at the Albert Hall. The effect of that evening has never worn off; though I have been in it hundreds of times and done a show in it myself, the Hall still has for me a peculiar grandeur.

We also read Shakespeare. Sitting round the long table in the library, we took parts in his plays under the headmaster's keen tuition. I had never seen a play so I didn't imagine Shakespeare on the stage, but I was completely captured by his poetry. By the time I was 11, I knew *Hamlet* by heart without learning it.

School life had its miseries, of course. I was subject to fits of temper, and it was one of the school sports to 'bait' me till I lost control and then stand round in a ring and laugh at me. The most surprising thing to me in retrospect is that I don't remember being mocked as 'pi'.

For 'pi' I certainly was. The chapel, a raftered attic room, was like the church at home a natural delight. I don't remember having a personal 'religious experience': I just felt a sense of completion in worship. The second master was a parson, a huge man who was very proud of his Oxford rowing blue. I gravitated towards him, and he was sensible in just letting me follow my bent.

Somebody took me to Edward VII's funeral. We were in a window in Oxford and Cambridge Terrace and the sombre pageantry of it all was after my own heart. I had never met death at close quarters, so for me it was a procession of coffin and kings with musical accompaniment in the minor keys. George V's Coronation we spent at school, or rather schools. Next to us was Heathfield, a very high-class school for girls up to 18. We spent that hot day playing cricket against each other on our field, and the evening dancing in their hall. Though I had a number of girl-cousins who were friends, I had never experienced adolescent girls *en masse*; I was hopelessly clumsy (and remained so) on the dance floor, but the strange tingling sensation of that contact has remained in my memory.

In September 1913 I moved on to Eton, where each boy has his own room. The first night alone in an attic room, among strangers almost all larger than myself, led to a period of increasing loneliness as I found that I didn't make friends easily nor share the interests of most of my fellows. It was a rather dreary period, soon overshadowed by the first world war.

Four of my five years at Eton were war years. Many boys lost fathers and brothers: my eldest brother was severely wounded late in 1914 and my mother went out to his hospital in France. Such happenings are swept along, though, for a child at boarding-school, with the tide of daily life: classes, games, cooking your fagmaster's tea and then your own before prep gives you no time to think, and the system is devised to that end. When you get higher up the school and are encouraged to think, it is a fencing-match of wits: emotion is kept out of it, or kept under the control of style. This period can be happy: it felt to me like coming out of a tunnel several years long.

In April 1919, after a few months in the army, I went up to Christ Church, Oxford and found myself in a new and enchanted world. In those days Oxford was a civilised city; one could walk or bicycle about it, and the traffic moved in a gentle flow. One's freedom, after Eton and the army, was so complete as to be frightening. I had to learn quickly how to use it, for I set out to get an honours degree in seven terms – History first, so as to have two years for Theology. I was particularly lucky in that half the undergraduates of 1919 were four or five years older than I and had fought through the war. The subject was hardly mentioned. They were eager to put it behind them and cram into their shortened degree-courses all the knowledge they had time for. I started a Shakespeare Reading Society in my ugly turret room in the Victorian Meadow Buildings, which produced a memorable Othello from L. A. G. Strong.

Eastertide saw the college gardens golden with spring flowers and fresh leaf: and in one of them I fell in love. It was at a tea-party at Corpus: the girl was a relation of the then Master. Incredibly she was 15; but she was much more self-assured and experienced than I was. I doubt if she knew any more than I did about modern art, but her chosen nickname was Fauvette. I don't doubt she was a virgin; but she knew a great deal about the subtler arts of young love-making. In the summer, I took her to stay at Fifehead. My mother always reacted violently, and with surprising crudity, against any girl her sons were interested in. But Miss Fifteen was quite equal to the feminine conflict (and Master Nineteen was dotingly helpless). We had a lovely time, in a little stubby punt on the Stour, walking over the countryside, sitting under the cedar trees. For a year-and-a-half I was possessed; but it was a possession progressively less interesting to her, who was growing up so much faster than I.

On my 21st birthday (29 January 1921) I took her to Granville Barker's production of *The Betrothal*. I had still seen very few plays, but one of them was Barker's *Dream* in 1914. People always talk of his 'golden fairies', but the magic it left in my memory was that of brilliant light: such shining contrasts between the cleanly defined life of the court and the mysterious shimmer of the woodland. The poetry was spoken fast and with agile expressiveness, the opposite of the deliberate pace in the only other Shakespeare play I had yet seen, Forbes-Robertson's *Hamlet*. So even for me it was revolutionary, and liberating. The only production that had a comparable effect on its contemporaries is another *Dream*, Peter Brook's of 1970. And in both cases, one's first thought was how well the director had served the poet.

The war had prevented my seeing any more of Barker's work before he retired from the stage, so it was a shock that he should emerge to spend his gifts on a sentimental piece of whimsy. But the magic was reborn, with the substantial help of Charles Ricketts who surrounded the deep stage of the Gaiety with a trellis bearing great swags of blossom – wistaria, I think. It was a successful evening; but no betrothal was in prospect – Fauvette was soon busy in other fields while I was left alone in mine.

I had joined the college rowing club, having got as far at Eton as stroking my House Four, but I soon found that the Oxford standard was both technically and physically beyond me. I was also put off by the arrival of Dr Frank Buchman from America. He stayed in Christ Church and I think actually founded the Oxford Group there: certainly some of his chief allies were the rowing men. He had apparently heard of my bent towards religion, for I was well canvassed; but I was repelled by him and his methods and fought my way out of his net.

I had always taken it for granted that I should ultimately be ordained. I used to possess an Illustrated New Testament inscribed 'To Martin from his godfather who does not remember a time when he did not mean to be a parson'. But it was at Oxford that I discovered the sacramental aspect of religion. Although the Fifehead governess had ultimately won her point, that did not affect me for one did not attend the Holy Communion service until one was confirmed. And when I was, at Eton aged 15, it remained a private, if deeply cherished, early morning mystery. But the Oxford Movement, born in 1833 and still going strong, had established the Eucharist as the main service of the day, the central act of worship in which 'young men and maidens, old men and children, praise the name of the Lord'.

My mind is cast in a sacramental mould, looking for 'the outward and visible sign of an inward and spiritual grace', needing the specific action to express the impulse of faith. So when I found anglo-catholic worship I was eager to take part in it and to learn all about this new and richer expression of Christianity. My centre for both instruction and worship became Pusey House; and there I met Charles Gore. He had been Bishop of Oxford when I was at Eton and had confirmed me; but we boys used to mock his favourite phrase in the pulpit, spoken in his deep voice from within his beard: 'I am profoundly convinced.' But now I came to realise how true it was: and after his retirement, when he celebrated at Grosvenor Chapel in London, to know the humility that went with it.

He never shared the militant intolerance, perhaps an inevitable concomitant of a missionary impulse, which anglo-catholicism certainly had. I was an arena steward at the first Anglo-Catholic Congress in the Albert Hall (one heard every word from the platform twice in those echoing days, before the miracle of the inverted saucers), and can remember the fervour. Some of it was marred by the gulf that it opened between 'catholics' and 'prots', and by the fissure within the movement between those who aped the Roman use and those who sought to rediscover and maintain an English catholic tradition. Having now for a generation felt at home in St Mary's, Primrose Hill, where Percy Dearmer brought both art and practical sanity to the latter task, and watched Rome lead its own revolution, I see the tumult of the twenties from very far off. But I recognise that it brought me an inestimable religious gift.

I realise that it helped to bring out also another latent power in me. The Eucharist is an action: 'Do this'; and it is action in a ritual form. I was deeply attracted by catholic ritual, and simultaneously by another kind of ritual which grew out of religion, the theatre. It was strange, since I had no theatrical forebears; I didn't get to the theatre much in my wartime adolescence at Eton and no play was ever produced there. But at Oxford I went almost weekly to the New Theatre (the old friendly building, not the present barn). And by February 1920 I was a member of the Oxford University Dramatic Society.

The OUDS had then its own rooms in George Street with a good cheap restaurant. The leaders were the older men back from the war. Maurice Colbourne was president, and determined that the first post-war production in the theatre should be on a grand scale. He got A. E. Drinkwater, who had stage-managed it for Barker, to direct Hardy's *The Dynasts*. The scale could not have been bigger – it is a huge chronicle of the Napoleonic wars – and it was a resounding success.

In the summer, *As You Like It* was the customary pastoral production. Nigel Playfair had staged it (and played Touchstone) at the Lyric, Hammersmith in April, with decor by Lovat Fraser and Athene Seyler as Rosalind. I have never forgotten the enchantment of her performance (nor her laughing feet in *The Mask and the Face* four years later). Dennis, under Playfair, was my first appearance on any stage – two lines, and I was worth no more.

Maurice Colbourne, as Nelson in *The Dynasts*, died in *Victory*: his successor, as president, Charles Morgan, as Sir John Moore, had his death-scene at Coruna. Charles was determined to emulate Maurice; and as 1921 was the year in which the authorities required us to do Shakespeare in the theatre, Charles chose the largest of his plays, *Antony and Cleopatra*. In those days, the OUDS invited professional actresses to play the female leads, and Charles scored a triumph by securing Cathleen Nesbitt for Cleopatra. She already had a fine record: leads with the Irish Players, in London and New York, Perdita in Barker's *Winter's Tale* and many other parts, including my first seeing of her as Jessica at the Royal Court. I can still hear her voice in the first lines to Launcelot Gobbo:

> I am sorry thou wilt leave my father so:
> Our house is hell . . .

W. Bridges-Adams, since 1919 director at the Shakespeare Memorial Theatre, Stratford-on-Avon, found time (how? I could never guess) to direct this and some subsequent OUDS shows. He came and looked us all over. 'You haven't got an Antony.' 'Oh surely,' said Charles, and named some of our best actors. 'They all look wrong.' said Bridges. 'Go and find an Antony. Doesn't matter whether he can act – I can teach him – but he must *look* right. Otherwise, you can't do the play.'

Charles was doggedly determined to do the play. He went out into the highways and byways and compelled the president of the Union to come in. Cecil Ramage, who had been through the war with the Scots Guards and won the MC, was now reading for the Bar. He had a fine voice and oratorical style, he looked like a Roman emperor, and he had never been on a stage in his life. I was sitting in the club-room after lunch on the Sunday of the first reading, when Cecil came in with uncertain steps. 'I haven't been to bed, I breakfasted on five double whiskies, and now Doc Counsell [our beloved club-doctor] has given me beer for lunch.' But it was love at first sight on both sides; and I have never seen Shakespeare's most difficult female rôle played as Cathleen played it:

> Give me some music: music, moody food
> Of us that trade in love.

It was all there, music, passion, guile, sorrow, fury, dignity, exaltation.

As sweet as balm, as soft as air, as gentle –
O Antony!

This play is another of my complete, magic memories.

I was Curio in *Twelfth Night* that summer, with Robert Harris singing of the wind and the rain in the scented darkness at the close: and Diomedes in the *Rhesus* which fulfilled our obligation to do a play in Greek every third year. That's all – I never played in the New Theatre, but was on the business or the stage staff. Not a promising beginning; but I was hooked all the same. In the long vacations we lesser lights were able to shine more brightly in a garden at St Leonards-on-Sea. Gerald Vernon, a Magdalen friend who was afterwards vicar of very 'high' Christ Church there and then Bishop of Madagascar, organised productions of *As You Like It* and *Twelfth Night*. He was well cast as Jacques and Malvolio, and we were luckily and happily directed by the OUDS stage manager, Oliver Bell.

In a long vac, too, Gerald and I went to Italy. I had had no contact with the visual arts at home or school until a young master who came to Eton in 1917 gave some talks on Italian art, with black-and-white lantern-slides, in the evenings. The Italians, from Giotto onwards, filled my mind with light; for me the Renaissance actually happened then. I plunged into J. A. Symonds, even into Crowe and Cavalcaselle's *History of Italian Painting*. During August, very hot, mostly in Florence, we drank in a great deal and later visits, with Mark Gambier-Parry, who left his grandfather's collection to the Courtauld, enhanced my intoxication.

I had been warned, when I chose to read for honours in Theology at Oxford, that it was the best way to lose one's faith. It didn't have that effect on me, but it did make me aware what a 'closed shop' the professional Church then was. How could I be any use to a parishful of people faced with everyday problems if I went straight from school (except for the few army-months) to university, to a year in a theological college and so into a dog-collar? First, I must find a way out of the Church enclosure onto the rat-race-course of life. In fact, I had already, though I may not then have recognised it, been presented with the opportunity.

One day in my first term, I met De La Warr in the High. I hadn't seen him since we had had several long discussions on the social and political problems which were already exercising his mind at Eton. (He became president of the Board of Education in

1938.) 'Look at this,' he said, 'it's just up our street and I wish I could go, but I can't. Why don't you go in my place?'

It was an invitation to attend as an observer the conference of the staffs of the educational settlements, newly formed into an Association. There were a round dozen of them – centres both for classes, especially of the Workers' Educational Association (WEA), and also for lectures and study-groups which the members asked for or were attracted to. They subscribed a tiny sum, but most of the funds came from the great Quaker families – Cadburys, Rowntrees – and in fact the conference was to be held in the house of old Joseph Rowntree on the hill above Scarborough, with Arnold, his eldest son, as host.

I arrived in considerable trepidation in this totally strange world, but was welcomed as the new baby. I was by far the youngest person present, and for most of the week they had their specific concerns to discuss; but they all took time to let me see life with their eyes, and encouraged me to join in the discussions of principle as well as in the silence of the Quaker meetings which formed the staple of their worship.

On the Saturday, England was celebrating the Treaty of Versailles. A beacon was lit on top of the hill, and we all climbed up to it. In its glow, my companions spoke to each other of the Treaty's unchristian harshness, and prophesied those things that indeed came to pass. To me this was an amazement: I saw politically for the first time. Then I saw socially: for several of my new friends invited me to visit them at work. A Baptist minister called Brown, a magnificent figure of a man, had the settlement in Hull, and there I went with him into slum houses. I had never been in an industrial city before, though my mother's family had made their money in Oldham. I went to Liverpool, then to York, where the centre was run by an eccentric who called himself 'Brother Richard' and dressed as nearly Franciscan as possible; he had a Yorkshire countryman, Wilfred Crosland, as colleague to keep him down to earth. York was for me a potent mixture of back-to-back housing (the settlement was then in St Mary's by the railway) and soaring Minster. I was never to escape from its spell.

I kept up these contacts throughout my time at Oxford. It must have been in 1922 that I went back to visit York, believing that this settlement work was the way by which I should get into real, as opposed to ecclesiastical, life, if they would have me. There was a new warden, working with Crosland, and he would have me as a trainee – number three – when I 'came down' next year. His name was John Hughes.

John's Welsh blood showed itself in passionate feeling and in glorious voice. He had been precentor at the Minster until the secure aloofness (and sometimes cynicism) of the ancient establishment became intolerable to him and he asked for a parish job. They gave him a mining village: it broke his faith in the efficacy of established religion, and nearly broke his health as well. Luckily he was married to the sturdy daughter of a Harrogate business family, who shared his poverty and his convictions but laced her compassion with enough Yorkshire common-sense to spice his Welsh indignation with realism. They became Quakers, and John found the outlet for his creative energy in teaching, especially speech and drama.

Robert Speaight and I had become friends during this time, though he was still at school and would only be coming up to Oxford as I went down. At New Year 1923 I stayed with him at Hatfield, in a fine Georgian house which his father had filled with antiques (his business, and what a showroom!). The family lived in the top flat, and in the basement was a tiny theatre, a raised alcove providing a ready-made stage. Most of our talk was of Shakespeare, about whom we were both besotted. Constantly on our lips was the name of William Poel, the crusader who dragged the theatre back from its obsession with scenery to the actual texts of the plays and their unbroken continuity. We revered him, with Barker, Robert Atkins at the Old Vic and Bridges-Adams at Stratford as his disciples. And suddenly came a proposal that I should join Bobbie and his family in following their footsteps.

In the previous summer, the Speaights had established with a successful *Merchant* (Bobbie aged 18 as Shylock) a summer festival at Angmering-on-Sea, a newly developed estate of private houses with a Sports Club as its focus. Now they planned, besides reviving *The Merchant*, to produce *Hamlet*. Could I persuade some OUDS actors to join the company? Yes, I thought I might. And would I direct it for them? Would I not! I had never directed a play before: but if they were rash enough to entrust themselves to me I might as well start with the biggest of challenges, which was also the most familiar. I had by then seen Forbes-Robertson, H. B. Irving, Martin-Harvey and (for the first time) Ernest Milton in the part, and was full of ideas both about Shakespeare's play and his stage. We talked and talked. This was the month to look forward to: before starting at York in September, there would be August at Angmering.

Prologue by Henzie

A semi-detached house in Hampstead, new when I was born in it at the turn of the century, was where I lived till 20 December 1924. It was entirely without beauty or excitement. The drawing-room was not a large room, but as a girl I thought it grand. It was only used when there were visitors, and to prepare the room there was a great untying of tapes to remove the faded cretonne which protected the velvet seats of chairs and settee, and the satin corduroy of piano stool and armchair. There were two bronze Art Nouveau ashtrays – one gilt and one green – both had very undressed ladies on them. The gilt one, naked, knelt on a leaf, the other appeared in Ophelia-like draperies swooning or drowning on a wave crest. I dusted them on Saturday mornings, with interest.

Memories are vivid and isolated, like leafing through old snapshots. For instance, kissing Mother's friends when she had a tea party. My sister, older and therefore mysteriously superior, and I were in our best pinafores. Hers was white cambric trimmed with valenciennes lace, with a pale blue bow on the yoke. We whispered outside the door: 'Who do we *have* to kiss?' – 'You go in first, you're the eldest' – 'No you, because you're younger.' So taking a deep breath I went and kissed the *lot* and landed behind Mother's chair. Murmurs of 'How affectionate the child is!'

The front doorsteps were hearthstoned daily by Cookie, Eliza Hocking, as she gossiped on her knees with the next-door maid similarly engaged. The black-and-white tiles only needed wiping, but 'step over the steps now', or I'd be lifted over and down, dolls' pram and all. Hours were spent in our street 'walking up and down' pushing the dolls' pram, alone, with sister, with neighbours; just as far as the lamp post (within sight of the windows), then further to 'the little road', and for a very long time the limit was the top of the hill where the main road crossed ours. When I was a little

older, and allowed further afield alone, I would be sent by my sister
to the 'Coffin Shop'. It scared her, but fear has always attracted
me – the desire to test the blade of a knife, the terror of acting. I
would go to the 'Coffin Shop' because my sister was making a
needle-case as a present and the leaves of cream flannel had to have
three edges pinked. They had a pinking machine, I tried not to
think why. It was just endurable if there was no hammering going
on.

Noise: its dictionary definition is 'a sound of any kind', but its
derivation, 'Latin, probably from nausea, disgust, but possibly
from noxa, hurt'. Today, many people seem not to be able to do
without it. I shrink from it in my older years. In my childhood,
'children should be seen not heard'. But how nostalgic are certain
sounds! Clop-clop of horses, the new noise of the car, the motor
horn with its rubber bulb that one squeezed. On Thursday night a
German Band played in our road, and at Christmas, carols were
sung through the letterbox. Then the hush between wheel-sounds
when straw was laid down before three houses; somebody was
seriously ill in one of them. The hurdy-gurdys, sometimes a clothed
monkey perched on the instrument. Pennies dropped out of
windows: either 'Give them something,' or it could be 'Give them
something to go away.' Once I knitted a pair of mittens and
wrapped a penny (my week's pocket money) in the palm of each,
and gave them to a pavement artist. I remember the awful
embarrassment of the giving. I do not know why I felt shame, nor
why shame as a memory endures. 'You must *say* you're sorry.' Why
so difficult, so painful? To feel it is easy.

In high summer 'Uncle' and 'Aunt' who lived next door took a
house at Westbrook, between Herne Bay and Margate. Twice my
sister and I shared part of that holiday. After breakfast Uncle took
himself off to the harbour where he kept a sailing dinghy, and the
rest of us went on the sands, until – I don't know how it came
about – he began taking me sailing. We had a fisherman as crew,
and there was no talk, only obedience and bliss. I loved it rough.
The sea – how I adored it. I had a private idea that if I were just
put into boy's clothes quick enough, I might become a boy – I
wasn't very sure of the difference – and then I could become a
sailor.

A daily governess was installed for years. My sister had over two
years' start of me, and I was kept out of the 'sitting-room' every

morning till I was 6. When Father had gone to business and the household was busy I would come down from the nursery and crouch outside the door and listen. By the time I started lessons I knew the *First Reader* by heart. The governess was staggered. How could I read without learning? That was easy. But not this: 'Good morrow Hubert.' 'Good morrow little prince.' 'You are sad.' 'Indeed I have been merrier.' Very mysterious: it never dawned that this was *dialogue*. I knew it was 'Shakespeare', nearly holy, like the Bible not to be questioned. Relief came years later when I read *King John*. Then, I was not given Shakespeare but Lamb's Tales to read.

My first real play was *The Tempest* at His Majesty's. The opening storm was magnificent. My elder sister, who was terrified of thunder and lightning and even of crackers being pulled at parties, was promptly led out screaming. I was in a glory. The setting of the 'Yellow Sands' was just like the seaside. High rocks to the left; a disconsolate young man weeping for his father. Viola Tree as Ariel looking like a beautiful tall angel on an Easter card, sang 'Where the bee sucks, there suck I.' I learned the words and sang it, out of tune, for years. This magical play, when I became involved with it as director, was to transform my life.

One afternoon an elderly American called – much of our mother's youth was spent in New York. We told him our mother was at a concert at the (late-lamented) Queen's Hall. Mr Bry said we would go 'down town' and meet her at the end of the concert. We arrived and sat in the foyer. As the last number approached its end, the attendants passed through the curtains and opened the double doors at the centre back of the grand circle. I left the other two and slipped through the curtains and heard the last third of Tannhäuser's Overture – Venusberg raptures – cooled by the Pilgrims' March. I drowned in sensuous bliss till I was nearly knocked down by applause and the departing audience. Music had entered my life.

My mother. I was close to her, and until the day of my marriage, I wrote to her daily whenever I was away from home. She was tremendously vital, attractive, good-looking with marvellous chestnut hair which fell, all her long life, in loose curls below her waist, though she wore it done up in Edwardian style. She was short and rather stout, but carried herself well and wore her clothes with a natural elegance; rarely well-off enough to be fashionable, but always soignée. And how decorous! She was an actress manquée; intensely self-willed, a passionate puritan.

I am amazed how I managed my life – my varied friendships with men, armed only with mother's powerful warnings, admonitions, but practically no explanations. I attracted men. When I was $12\frac{1}{2}$, we had a family summer holiday abroad, sailing up the Rhine in a small steamer. I only remember one other passenger: Albert Gould. He was quite old, 19 I think, on holiday before Oxford. He treated me as a person; and he was a man. ('Men, to me, are a world to themselves,' says Alizon, straight from her convent, in *The Lady's Not For Burning*.) We had 'talks'. I was for my years well read. I was devoted to Dickens, Kipling and had begun on Wells, and I knew a lot of poetry and had a splendid memory. One day that autumn he came to tea with us in London, gave me a book, and I escorted him back to the nearest underground station. Just before he left he kissed me on the cheek. He left me standing dumbfounded. I rushed home, told Mother, and asked if I could be going to have a baby. She laughed, reassured me – and told me nothing.

I think I may have been 13, when a 19-year-old son of family friends took my arm to pilot me through a milling crowd. The contact produced the sensation of *soda water*! I found it delicious but extraordinary.

School brought much that was welcome, and among the many doors that opened was one that showed me the road I was to travel, in one way or another, for always. Once a fortnight there was 'elocution'. Miss O'Neill took our class of a dozen or so for fifty-five minutes. The poem we studied was 'Curfew shall not ring tonight'. It is a story of the time of Cromwell. From the church belfry, the curfew is rung at sunset. At that hour, Bessie's lover is to be executed. She, the heroine, pleads with the sexton not to ring the bell of doom. He refuses and

> She with quick step bounded forward,
> Sprang within the old church door,
> Left the old man coming slowly
> Paths he'd trod so oft before.

She climbs the spiral staircase to the bell chamber, hangs onto the tongue of the bell and so prevents it clanging:

> Out she swung, far out, the City
> Seemed a speck of light below,
> There 'twixt heaven and earth suspended,
> As the bell swung to and fro . . .

Cromwell appears over the hill and Bessie falls before him:

> At his feet, she tells her story,
> Shows her hands all bruised and torn . . .

And the poem ends triumphantly:

> 'Go, your lover lives,' cried Cromwell,
> Curfew shall not ring tonight.

The method of direction was drill. We were ranged in a row and spoke simultaneously, trying to copy the teacher's inflections, suiting each action, hand and foot to the word:

> England's sun was slowly setting [it began]
> O'er the hill tops far away,
> Filling all the land with beauty,
> At the close of one sad day.

With raised and extended arm, wrist above hand, an arc was described to right, and slowly descended with fingers above wrist, only to turn palm upward and add similar gesture with left arm for 'filling all the land with beauty', and a final turn, lowering both wrists, fingers raised, so that 'at the close of one sad day' that gesture was completed, with hands at sides. For most of the class restrained giggles increased as, literally all together, we 'bounded forward' and looking over left shoulder, observed 'the old man, coming slowly'. I didn't giggle, I was enthralled, and gave Miss O'Neill all she asked for. Then the wonderful thing happened. I was told that on the day that we broke up I was to recite the poem solo, before the entire school. Quite unprepared to stand up alone – no private rehearsal – I faced the sea of faces: the big and little ones, the staff, seventy perhaps. I began obedient to the teacher's discipline. Soon I became aware, amazedly, of power and communication with the audience. Their excited reception, totally unexpected, reduced me to a flood of tears as I obeyed the hissed 'Bow again.' Now I knew what I had to aim for.

But how? There was no money, I had no stage links. But after Tree's *Tempest* had come an amazing contrast, a series of productions by Harley Granville Barker. *Twelfth Night* at the Savoy in 1912, his *Dream*, *The Dynasts*, *The Great Adventure* of Arnold Bennett, *Fanny's First Play*, *The Witch*. I knew where I wanted to be and with whom. Leaving school early, I heard that Lillah McCarthy, the enigmatic beautiful first wife of H. G. B., and his leading lady, had a sister Marion Huntley, who 'gave lessons' and lived near the

Quinneys.' I looked at my navy blue suit in dismay. 'Oh, we'll put you into Isobel's wine satin.' (Her daughter was a thin wisp.) I was packed, holding my breath, and fastened in. 'No time for supper,' said Marion, 'we'll each swallow a raw egg.' I implored my Maker to see me through this too. He did. The egg was pricked and swallowed and remained put!

The ardours of looking for work: interviews and auditions. It was nearly impossible to get started in those days. In the long vanished but distinguished St James' Theatre, I entered a sumptuous office feeling I was rather splendidly attired. The manager sat me down opposite his desk. Then he broke out suddenly 'What an extraordinary smell: [sniff sniff] – I know – it's moth balls.' 'I'm so sorry,' I said, 'it's me. I'm wearing Mother's furs.'

The Stage, which appears each Thursday, carried in its pages columns of 'Wanted' ads. I found an entire company required for a tour, heavy man, blonde ingénue – the lot! The play was A Heritage of Hate. It stated that one should write to Mr Sam Livesey at the Managers' Club, Wardour Street, for an appointment. This I duly did – and my name Henzie proved to be valuable. In wartime (now 1916) men were scarce, and he thought I was one. So I received a card asking me to come to the Managers' Club at 10.30 or 11. Much opposition at home – me still in my teens and hair not 'up'. (It was generally put up at 17 or 18.) Mother wanted to come too. Impossible. So in my nice dark-blue suit and blue hat – and gloves of course – I departed. A woman was on her knees scrubbing the doorstep – hearthstone, brush and clanking pail. 'Good morning,' I said, 'excuse me,' and was about to step over the wet area. 'Oh! you can't go in there, dearie, it's for the gents only.' 'But I have an appointment with Mr Sam Livesey,' I said, producing the card. 'All the same, you can't go up. I tell you wot, I'll take it up to 'im.' Which she kindly did, and soon down lumbered Mr Sam Livesey, now playing the Heavy Lead in Tiger's Cub at the Garrick opposite the enchanting actress Madge Titheradge. He boomed at me with a kind smile, 'But I wasn't expecting a young lady; I can't ask you in.' 'Could we talk here?' 'I'm sure I could play something – no, no experience yet, but a Gold Medal for Lady Macbeth, and a high comedy scene from London Assurance. Please try me in any part.' I prevailed, and he sent me to the stage door of the Garrick to collect the script. I was to come and read with him, during a long wait the next night, the virtuous young

now vanished Adelphi Terrace. That Terrace was a V
housed Barker, Shaw, Barrie, Galsworthy ... I fou
telephone book a Mrs M. Huntley who lived in Buckingh
far end, by the river. An unlikely person opened the
Marion Huntley?' 'Yes. What did I want?' I had hear
lessons and wanted to know if she'd take a student. Sh
perplexed. 'Thought I seemed young' with my long h
into a swinging plait. It seemed I had met the wrong M
'Walking the streets' not 'treading the boards' was her
did not know from what, but I backed away and flec
Strand to consult another telephone book.

I ended up with the right Mrs Huntley, in an encl
floor flat in John Adam Street. Marion was a miniature
did teach: in fact, after every Barker rehearsal she wo
sister who, though her performances were splendid, mu
leaden in rehearsal to Barker's quick-silvered direction
fine Helena, but I had it from Bernard Shaw's lips th
frenzy of impatience, Barker leapt on the hill which
Fairy Wood and cried out, in a dance of rage, 'God! F
fool!' Marion taught me a great deal, coaching me in L
so I was now in touch with my idol at one remove. I fin
for the first time in that flat in 1915 or 16. A brief m
remembered always. They were just home from a
season. I had come for an afternoon lesson. Marion wa
door was opened by Lillah – a 'tall personage',
dressed. She listened to what I had prepared, bore
encouraged me. Marion returned with Barker who
dining with Barrie tonight.' I nearly passed out.
Lillah, 'I must go and change', and the sisters left me
sat on the window-seat and leaned out listening to the
coming in from the Strand. I sat in my chair (
introduced) and prayed: 'Please, God, give me some
to say.' No answer! 'Something intelligent ... or
silent.' Barker drew in his head and said happily
always London.' I was lit up and replied 'Yes, oh!
when you come into the big railway stations.' 'Th
believe he said, and in came Marion, and Lillah in a
suit.

The Olympians departed. 'Now,' said Marion, 'nc
have a box at the Haymarket for tonight to see He

wife who had a big scene in a wood where she was thrown down
and murdered. I rushed to Marion Huntley, who was dubious: and
at home they said 'Out of the question'. But I had an appointment,
and I was going. To placate the parents I permitted Mother to
come and wait in the foyer.

Through the stage door into the dressing-room. Mr Livesey in
Esquimaux furs was waiting. I had put my hair up to dissolve the
schoolgirl image. We read the scene – next time through with
business, and I did a splendid fall. He was very impressed, but
amused and not certain. Not certain at all. Salary one pound a
week. I admitted I would have to extract permission from parents.
Was he going? 'No,' he said, 'and,' (inexplicably) 'just as well.'
Time was getting short. 'Well,' he said, 'we rehearse tomorrow at
10 a.m. at Hampton Court Palace.' I couldn't believe it. Hadn't I
gone there several times? At last I could impress Mother. 'You
know it?' he said surprised. 'First floor, the pub just by Elephant
and Castle Tube Station.' A 'pub'! I'd never been in one. 'Give me
your answer there!' Shaken, I said goodbye and went to collect my
anxious parent. 'Out of the question' – 'impossible' all over again
. . . Deep down I'd begun to think so too. However, next morning
we found the Hampton Court Palace and climbed up a side stair to
a room full of people from an unknown world. Rather elderly, down
at heel, and the ladies badly made up. Sam appeared, made it very
easy, and said to Mother 'I think she had better wait a bit.'

MARTIN FILLS A GAP

She didn't have to wait long. Within a year Henzie Raeburn made
her first professional appearance at the Theatre Royal, Bath, in a
war-play. It was followed by a tour of *Quinneys* which she had seen
at the Haymarket. Drab as the conditions were, she was in the
theatre! And at Birmingham, she caught another glimpse of the
kind of theatre she really wanted to be in. The Repertory Theatre
had been built and was largely financed by Barry Jackson, who had
not only money but also taste and judgement. The auditorium was
a single tier of steeply raked seats; the proscenium had therefore to
be very high, and the stage seemed marvellously near to every seat.
Henzie was invited to a matinée by Bache Matthews, Sir Barry's
business manager. She came out dancing for joy. This had the
same feeling as Barker's work. Each night of that week when her

own curtain had fallen she would rush round to see the last few minutes again.

A friend gave her *On the Art of the Theatre* by Edward Gordon Craig. 'After you have been an actor you must become a stage manager', ran one piece of his advice. Henzie made up her mind to act on it. The perpetual search for work took her in 1918 to Leon M. Lion, who was preparing *The Chinese Puzzle* for the New (now the Albery) Theatre in St Martin's Lane. All the parts (as usual) were cast; all the understudies filled. 'Have you got an assistant stage manager, Mr Lion?' Taken aback, he answered 'Well, no, we haven't, but . . .' (no woman had ever been on a stage staff). A pause – finally: 'What are the ASM's duties?' 'To hold the book, to check the setting of everything on stage, to get whatever the director asks for as quickly and as cheaply as possible.' And she was engaged – the first woman ASM. Her stage manager was beastly to her but it was a happy engagement, lasting to 1919. She made friends with Lilian Braithwaite, and later, for life, with Sybil Thorndike who took over the juvenile lead. After a matinée, Sybil would rush out in full war-paint, to get home for tea with the children. 'That girl will never get on' was Lilian's verdict.

Next year, Stratford-on-Avon. The old theatre, ugly and cramped (the amateur 'extras' dressed in the basement unless it was flooded) but friendly and intimate. On the last night, the people at the end of the dress circle held hands with those at the corner of the stage for 'Auld Lang Syne'. The atmosphere, for a young actress, was magic. Bridges-Adams was directing the 'New Shakespeare Company' formed the previous year to take over the Festival at the end of Sir Frank Benson's long reign. Benson had been the supreme trainer of actors, among them the leading man Murray Carrington. He was handsome and greatly gifted, then at the height of his powers as Richard II, Benedick, Henry V, Hamlet. But Henzie, going in to see him before a performance, noted a full bottle of port ('good for the voice'). 'It will be two by the end of the season,' he said ruefully.

She herself was playing Celia in *As You Like It*, Jessica in *The Merchant*, Margaret in *Much Ado*, and Alice in *Henry V*, plus some bit-parts and walk-ons. Six plays had to be prepared for the Easter Festival of four weeks, and another four rehearsed while on tour, for the six-week Summer Festival. Bridges was most interested in design; he spent much of the meagre rehearsal-time for *Cymbeline* (the 'Birthday Play') in making Cloten's head. He relied much on the group of Old Bensonians in the company, mostly character actors of fine quality. 'What did Pa do?' Bridges would ask, and would thankfully adopt most of Benson's 'business'.

To the rich and highly organised Stratford of today it would have seemed an impossibly makeshift way of working – and of course in many ways it was. But the essentials were there. The verse was finely spoken and the productions were full of life. And Stratford itself, still just a market town to which the Festivals were side-shows, was a place you could take to your heart – even if its mostly puritan inhabitants didn't take you (rogues and vagabonds) to theirs. Henzie's first lodging was near the railway station; here, after an all-night dress rehearsal, the landlady refused to admit her. She moved to Mrs Rawbones, a Baptist deaconess by the river. When the road was flooded, one of the actors carried her home. After this, 'no gentlemen callers' after dark.

Between Festivals they toured in the north. At Buxton, Henzie had her first heart attack. She had gone vegetarian and was enthusiastically walking in the Peak District on very little food; no one, herself included, took much notice of her collapse except to restore meat to her diet. At Manchester they were in Miss Horniman's Gaiety Theatre, the last 'live' show to occupy that most famous of early repertory stages. Their visit to Manchester coincided with those of two other Shakespeare companies, a *Julius Caesar* with Henry Ainley and Basil Gill from the St James', and H. V. Neilson's troupe headed by Sir Frank Benson. Of course the old master had to organise a cricket-match with all those past and present Bensonians in one city! Henzie took a snapshot of the moment when the ball hit his mouth, knocking out a tooth. 'It was worth it,' he said: 'I held the catch.'

After the summer season, *Henry V* played daily matinées at the Strand all autumn. This was good as well as joyful for Alice, and some offers came of it, but none could be accepted. She was 'off' for several months with a mastoid.

In 1921 she got, for more than a year, the sort of theatre she had seen at Birmingham. The Everyman was made out of a church hall close by Hampstead tube station: it is now a cinema. Norman Macdermott turned it into a theatre of 300 seats and ran it until 1926, producing a staggering series of plays. These attracted, at derisory salaries, most of the best actors then coming to prominence. Henzie went there as one of two ASM's and to play parts – she hoped not too small. Two of them were for Komisarjevsky, who directed Franklin Dyall in *The Race with the Shadow* (Henzie, as a German maid-servant, tying her apron higher in front than behind and wearing 'hospital shoes') and *John Gabriel Borkman* (little Frieda Foldal having her music-lesson). Another was for Edith Craig in *The Shewing-up of Blanco Posnet*; she gave Henzie hell all morning, then took her out to lunch and they became friends.

Macdermott did most of the direction himself, and since he couldn't count on a show running more than three weeks, the pressure was unremitting. He revived Ibsen, but especially Shaw, whom he brought back to the London stage after the neglect consequent on the war. Eight plays were staged with some brilliant casts. Shaw came to rehearsals, and was approachable even by the small fry.

There were new plays, some that failed, of course, others that succeeded and transferred to the West End – C. K. Munro's *At Mrs. Beam's*, Sutton Vane's *Outward Bound*, Noël Coward's first 'straight' success *The Vortex*. New ideas in production appeared as well: in *Twelfth Night*, the clean white 'permanent set' used by Copeau at the Vieux Colombier (where I saw it in 1920) and with Isabel Jeans displacing the then traditional matron as an enchantingly irresponsible young Olivia. Macdermott also learned from Appia the imaginative possibilities in stage lighting, and discovered the young electrician Veness who was only tempted away from the Everyman's primitive liquid dimmers by the new Schwabe-Hasait plant that Basil Dean imported from Germany for *Hassan* in 1923.

Always on the edge of bankruptcy, Macdermott kept up the highest standard with the smallest resources. If associates were uneasy at the shifts he resorted to, they could not but respect and value the quality of his work. It bound Henzie closely to the Everyman. When he tried to seduce her and she refused and said 'Now do I get the sack?' he replied 'Of course not.' Her instinct in casting was useful to him; and in that department she had discovered both a pupil and an ally.

At a dance given to raise funds for the Everyman she met John van Druten. He lived not far from her and they had mutual friends, but had never met till now. He was 21, obliged by his father, and after his father's death by care for his mother, to read law, but he was theatre-mad. The Everyman was already his Mecca; now he was meeting one of its company. His voracious appetite for theatre and his uncannily accurate memory soon led to lengthy critical discussions, on the telephone when not face to face, of plays that they saw, often together, and of the actors' performances. They would sharpen each other's wits by arguing out the ideal casting for a certain play. John himself had already written one, and Henzie took it to Sybil for a reaction to the prentice-work of a young man, in whom she saw great promise. Ten years later John wrote one of his best plays, *The Distaff Side*, for the star who had encouraged him in his beginnings. His next play, *The Return Half*, was directed by Henzie for a Sunday night show by ex-students of RADA (then the Academy of Dramatic Art) with the young John Gielgud in the lead.

HENZIE AGAIN

About this time came my next encounter with Barker. I *had* trod the boards – Stratford, tours – had known the mysterious bliss of being directed by Theodore Komisarjevsky – and was well acquainted with disappointments, 'resting', frustrations and some satisfactions too. In 1923 the Play Actors' society was to put on for a single performance Martinez Sierra's comedy *Wife to a Famous Man*, translated by Helen and Harley Granville Barker. (By this time, Barker had left Lillah, and the theatre, for his second, American wife.) Barker would oversee rehearsals and take them occasionally – always accompanied by his wife. The leads were to be Mary Clare and Milton Rosmer; she a star, a fine sultry actress, he a leading actor and a friend with whom I had played, and by whom I had been directed. His part was that of a Madrid aviator who had won a race and was to be fêted at a banquet. Mariana was an emotional devoted wife and mother who had kept the family of three generations by running a laundry. I was invited to play a young laundress and to stand in for the star, Mary Clare, who was about to open in *White Cargo*, and would be absent from some rehearsals.

Two incidents may serve to illuminate the character of this wonderful man: the first was in our rehearsal hall. H.G.B. and his wife sat in the balcony. His voice rang out from above. 'Miss Clare:

you are very embarrassed – your husband is out and this neighbour Señor Julian is making insinuating overtures to you. You are suffering justified jealousy of your husband, his success in the city, his success with sophisticated women: but what you are hearing outrages your modesty. You are disconcerted and you blush.' 'Yes,' said Mary Clare, and the passage was repeated. 'But,' called the voice, 'I said you *blush*.' 'I understand. I know what you mean, but I can't actually blush.' 'Just a minute – ' and down came Barker, sprang onto the stage and took a chair beside her, very close. 'You can't blush, Miss Clare?' 'I don't understand.' 'You can't do that?' and the chair came closer. She turned her head away in a misery, the cast daren't breathe. 'Look at me; don't you feel an intolerable heat at the back of your neck? Creeping up, under your ears, where can you look? Hotter and hotter'. Poor Mary Clare was now scarlet with mortification: 'Quick – speak the lines.' Near tears, came her voice, drenched, and that was IT. He thanked her, and next time she gave all that was asked for.

The second incident was in the theatre: for me, a peak moment – a small peak, but it has still a golden glow. The evening before the dress rehearsal I was telephoned to be told that Mary Clare would not be present, and would I please *read* Mariana 'from the book'. I knew the lines, but I must have the timing right and do the business. This was literally impossible with book in hand, for in Act I José Maria is being elaborately dressed on stage. Water and scented soap, Eau de Cologne for handkerchief, moustache and hair, cravat to be tied, shoes to be polished and put on, hair brushed and parted. A starched shirt so stiff that a hair pin is needed for the buttons – and dialogue for all throughout. Rosmer, naturally nervous, was anyway unsure on lines, and repeatedly we went back to synchronise words and business. The lines became less certain, and finally Barker became impatient. Rosmer, getting strung up, flared back 'Well if all I get at a dress rehearsal is an understudy what can you expect?' We had a small audience present. Barker clapped his hands for silence, ran to the barrier of the orchestra pit and addressed the house: 'Please accept my apologies for this ungallant remark. Henzie Raeburn has not given us a *reading* in this emergency, but a fine performance, and I would ask those present to acknowledge this and thank her.' Turning to the stage, he held my eyes as he led the applause. Rehearsal was resumed. Milton and I were able to feel right with each other.

If Martin had married another woman, he would, I believe, have had an utterly other career. Dog-collars and gaiters would probably have come into his wardrobe, and who is to know what shape his life would have taken? I was able to give him a varied accumulation of theatre knowledge, and many personal theatre friendships which directly and indirectly were to steer the course of our journey through the years.

We met because I am fascinated by words, their meaning, their derivations, their sounds. The dual juxtaposition of NG was irresistible. In 1921 my sister and I had a holiday. Should we go to the Wye Valley? Then I saw the name ANGMERING, and we had to go there. We actually went, not to the old village inland but to Angmering-on-Sea, a new estate of private houses on the West Sussex coast. There was one hotel, some ladies who took in summer lodgers (ours were called the Misses Shakespeare), a sports and social club with a hall, run by the owner of it all, Mr Hollis, who selected the residents he allowed to build their own homes.

On Sunday nights there was a concert at the Club, with a programme put together by residents plus any suitable visitors. Word got round that a young professional actress was among them, and I gave two numbers, powerful dramatic recitations which 'brought the house down'. Two years later, there was to be a week's Shakespeare Festival, *The Merchant of Venice* and *Hamlet*. Mr Hollis, wanting a finger in this pie, set up a bust of Shakespeare to be unveiled after a luncheon on the Monday. He also organised a 'Shakespeare Concert' for the Tuesday, and asked me to give two Shakespeare numbers. Out of work in high summer, I was delighted. I chose the letter scene from *Macbeth* and Katharine of Aragon's defence of her marriage, from *Henry VIII*. I got from Tom Heslewood, who had been Irving's stage manager, a marvellous dress which had been worn by Ellen Terry.

I had arranged to stay for the week with friends. On the first Saturday afternoon after lunch, I found a photo-call for *Hamlet* going on. As the stage lighting was only gas, it was out of doors, using the concrete esplanade and its parapet. A superb Viking Ghost (Gyles Isham) dominated the picture; Bobbie Speaight, looking very young in black tunic and tights, was under his spell; and a slim, darting young man in an orange cotton tunic was directing operations. He seemed to know just what he wanted. But an appalling condescension took hold of me. Amateurs daring to

1   Communing with Shakespeare: EMB at Angmering, 1923

present Shakespeare! Had I not already worked at Stratford? I was
introduced to the Hamlet and the director by Gyles who had seen
and met me at the Oxford Playhouse. I shook hands, immediately
liked something about the director, and found myself suggesting
that I would be glad if I could help. I winced as I said it, but 'Yes
please,' said Martin immediately, 'could you help me with Hamlet's death?' (He himself was playing Horatio.) Next day, we
worked on this; and on the Monday I saw the first night. I was very
surprised indeed at the quality of the direction and some of the
performances.

The Tuesday concert went well. On Wednesday afternoon I was
called on formally by Bobbie's father, the organiser, and Martin.
They were very disturbed: Peggy Zangwill, the 14-year-old Ophelia (daughter of Israel Zangwill) had a feverish chill. Had I played
Ophelia? No. Would I learn it, and play Thursday night? *Please*! I
sat up nearly all Wednesday night and learned the lines. At
rehearsal on Thursday morning the actress–director encounter was
entirely professional. I found Bobbie secure to work with but as I
remember could get nothing from him or the other players, good
professionals as some were to become.

In performance, at the second Mad Scene, something unforgettable happened. Ophelia gave her (imaginary) flowers to Laertes,
the King and the Queen. Then I turned to Horatio, downstage left:

'There's a daisy: I would give you some violets, but they withered all when my father died.' I found and took an alive sympathy: those eyes were aching with mute compassion and I was no longer on the stage alone.

In that exchange, our relationship was surely conceived. Is this part of the mystery of acting? or is it that 'at the first sight/They have changed eyes'? It took some time – if you can measure time by the calendar – to know:

> only in retrospection, selection
> We say, that was the day. The critical moment
> That is always now and here.

The summer of 1924 was to bring another Festival. The intervening period was a peculiar time of preparing the ground, with no pattern which was apparent then. Martin had his first job, which like so much in the story has significance 'in retrospection', at York. He was entering a world very different from that familiar to him, most of all when he was sent once a week to Doncaster to help the Folkhouse (as the educational settlement there was called) get itself born. As letters came and went between us, his recalled the shock I had received when, after living all my life in London, my first tour took me to the north.

From our meeting on 25 August it took till 14 November for Martin to write: 'by the way, don't be afraid of my Christian name, as you see I am of yours'. That letter was signed 'Yours ever, Martin Browne'. My reply on 26 November began without personal address: I again hadn't the courage to write 'Martin', but I signed it 'Henzie', suddenly, at the end of a sentence. On 7 December he replied to 'My dear Henzie' and signed it 'Yours ever, Martin'. It was not until after we had met two or three times at Christmas, and I had heard him actually *say* my name, that I set down 'My dear Martin'. Forty-nine years on, how 'period' these slow measures of intimacy sound! But from my heart I feel that, in the directness and honesty of today, a treasure has evaporated. To hear one's name spoken by the desired voice for the first time! It is the first caress, a memorable shiver.

I was aware I could be falling in love. I decided I must find out before any sign was given. During the late spring we met at the Knightsbridge Hotel to spend most of a day discussing the plays for Angmering, now settled as *Richard III* with Bobbie and *The Tempest* with Martin as Prospero, and I to direct with help from him and from a line-by-line study of Quiller-Couch's new edition in the Cambridge Shakespeare. In the morning we plunged into casting, setting and costumes. At lunch, when we put away our notebooks and queries, I privately decided that our table-talk should provide the challenging moment for me to consider him. But he was shy and it was all very halting and unsatisfactory. I, a chatterbox, found the ball always in my court. As my flow began to slacken, I divided anything I could think up to say into two parts. By the time coffee came I had rejected the non-offer, cleared my mind, and sat down again to work with my co-director; and to suggest that for *The Tempest* blue-green should be the colour to symbolise invisibility.

I

Marriage into Doncaster

Dingy grey London, only just light at 9.30 a.m. The wedding was so early because I insisted on a nuptial Eucharist and the last train to St Ives for our honeymoon left at noon. It was the Saturday before Christmas.

Who would come at that hour? My mother had offered me a trip round the world if I would not marry Henzie, and the two families couldn't meet so a reception was impossible. But mother came to the Savoy Chapel, supported by her sons and a few specially beloved relations. On the bride's side, behind her parents, sat a galaxy of young theatre people. They came for love of Henzie, at an hour when, with two shows to play, most actors are in bed. What they thought she had landed herself with, I can imagine from John van Druten's question when Henzie told him she was engaged to me. 'What will you do about laughing?' Henzie taught me that.

The service itself had elements of absurdity. Gerald Vernon was conducting his first wedding, and true to catholic form had brought a medicine-bottle of holy water to sprinkle over the couple. He had forgotten to find out my first name and asked 'Will you, Edward . . .' I, '*Elliott* Martin', snatched a service-paper from someone in the front row so that he should have Henzie's names right. We had chosen music from the *Tempest* production at Angmering, during which we had got engaged in August: but the organist, fuddled, I suppose, by the manuscript copy, fell back on Mendelssohn. As we walked out to his infuriating strains my younger brother thrust a packet into Henzie's hand – 'for Marty (that hated diminutive!) from Muth'. The contents were smelling-salts and sal volatile for her fasting son.

But laughter dissolved it all into happiness: and to compensate for our long fast until after the mass we had breakfast at the Savoy – *real* breakfast with grapefruit, fillets of sole, bacon and mushrooms – with the maid-of-honour (Henzie's sister), the best man (my youngest brother) and the clergy. Then the going away, in a taxi. The best man had a dentist's appointment in Wimpole Street – would we please drop him there? We arrived at Paddington at 12.01. 'I won't go home to Mother,' said Henzie. But there was a relief-train at 12.03 – and our reserved seats were on it. The whistle blew and we were alone – not physically alone for many stations, but alone with each other. In the Cornish darkness we changed at St Erth into a little local train and found ourselves in a carriage with two sailors who were discussing the fate of the *Waratah*.

Doncaster. It was to this that we returned after our Christmas fortnight, for this that Henzie had given up London and the prospects of her theatrical career. This dreary town; we used to walk one each side of the streets and count the aspidistras: 'You have forty-six?' 'I've only forty-three.' Did anyone ever smile there? Henzie took as a private pupil the dumpy daughter of a publican. 'You must *smile* at me when you say "good afternoon".' Once she arrived while Henzie was busy and our little maid came to ask her to wait a few minutes. The smile, put on as the door opened, dropped with a clang on the floor: 'Oh, I thought you were Mrs Browne!' (the maid told us afterwards: it had puzzled her).

But our home was something different. I had started living there in September, taking the two floors above a sweet-and-tobacconist's shop in the High Street (Georgian buildings here at least, however disfigured by modern shopfronts). The big room on the first floor for the Folkhouse, with a seminar-room behind; above, our quarters to be made into a home from dereliction. Henzie came with me after Angmering to plan it: money was very short, but colour and gaiety could be as inexpensive as drabness if you had her flair. Our bedroom, on the half-landing, with a line of waterdrops from the always damp walls along the lintel, would be a blue-and-green extension of Prospero's island. The study–dining-room primrose-yellow with royal blue paint (when she first saw it, the fireplace was out, and in the middle of the room was a sheet of iron to stop anyone falling through a hole in the floor). Her sanctuary (called Number Eight because that number was on the door – could it formerly have been a brothel?) had orange walls (an expensive paper, to get a good colour, was our one extravagance), peacock-blue paint, a picture-rail of the same, and down to the rail a yellow ceiling. The decorator couldn't believe it: but it was St Leger week and perhaps the spirit of that annual fête helped to persuade him to carry out the mad plan. Doncastrians called, observed the week-end joint under a wire cover in the passage (we had no larder), came into the rooms and gasped: in course of time some smiles crept onto their faces. It was a happy place. Henzie cried a lot, at unexpected moments: she had so huge an adjustment to make. But she made it – perhaps the biggest of many to come.

Doncaster is the centre of the south Yorkshire coalfield, and we were determined to spread our work through the mining villages. We didn't go down a pit until much later, but miners came in to WEA lectures: one from Bentley was, the lecturer told us, the foremost authority on Herbert Spencer. And the principal lure was theatre.

Already, before we were married, I had done a triple bill: Yeats' *The Land of Heart's Desire*, Brighouse's *The Price of Coal*, Clifford Bax's *Square Pegs*. Henzie, 'the distinguished London actress' (the poster said), came to play in the Yeats with me. From this and from our programme of classes in the *Doncaster Herald* it was evident that theatre was to be alive here, and some miners wanted it enough to mix with the faithful band of tradesmen and professional people – schoolteachers, a doctor, a Presbyterian minister, a baker, a chemist, a nurse etc. – who had founded the Folkhouse and asked us to come there. And if the miners were coming to us we must go to them. Tours were essential. Were we allowing the Folkhouse, which was supposed to be an educational settlement, to be swamped by theatre (not accepted then as an educational activity)? The secretary of the Educational Settlements Association, who came to inspect us every three or four months, was worried about that (and shocked by our frank happiness): but the eaters, of all kinds, wanted that sort of pudding, and he accepted the proof. I kept a lot of other work going: we had John Hughes on Beethoven, Oliver Bell (now League of Nations Union secretary in Birmingham) on international affairs and many more, as well as my own classes. But in an area totally without theatre, this was the clamant need.

We started with *Candida*, surprisingly well received by snooty Doncaster, and took it to several mining villages. Shaw was safe, but our next venture was a wild gamble. Henzie had a speech and acting class, and used passages from *Hippolytus* as exercises. It was Gilbert Murray's translation, which didn't sound *vieux jeu* then (and, in passing, isn't it worth notice that Murray is the only translator of Greek drama who with play after play took big money in the professional theatre?). The class got lit up: couldn't we produce the play? We did, between us; and it was in the mining villages that it made the strongest impression. We began to understand that what was of value to them was a play which spoke out of experience common to all men.

Sybil Thorndike always had a profound influence on us, as an actress and as a person. A few weeks after she opened as Saint Joan, she played for the Stage Society Ernst Toller's *Masses and Man*. He wrote it in prison, after the fall of the people's government in Bavaria at the end of the first world war. It is an abstraction from the story of Rosa Luxembourg, who led the pacifist revolt against the Kaiser's war, split from the militant communists, and was executed by the reactionary government that defeated them. It was written at white heat:

It literally broke out of me and was put on paper in two days and a half . . . The laborious and blissful work of pruning and remoulding lasted a year.

This was vibrant theatre, in the (then) avant-garde Expressionist style, but comprehensible to anybody in an area of industrial turmoil. Heads were shaken, but we had no difficulty in getting a cast. Henzie was the Woman, I the Guide, and for the Nameless we had an active communist. He was most interesting to talk to, a widely read man whom the Party had ordered to stay at the coalface rather than climb the educational ladder because he could 'do more good' there. He was married to a South African, but they only met occasionally at a week-end because his wife, after a training period in Russia, was posted elsewhere and they were only free when neither was at a party meeting. This dedication we had never met before; it reminded us of the early Franciscans but with hate substituted for love. The part, of course, was 'straight' for him.

During the last rehearsals, Henzie's father had an emergency operation and was dying. We were sent for on Friday night; he died on Saturday at noon. A quiet good man who asked very little of life except love, and Henzie had loved him warmly. But 'the show must go on': we shuttled up and down between Doncaster and London, coping with the funeral and finding a way for her mother, with very little money, to go on living in the same familiar street.

Looking back, it seems odd that we took so little notice of what happened to Henzie that summer. We had bought a very used car, with a bonnet like a Rolls-Royce in miniature. His make was 'Albert' so we called him Albert. We learned to drive on him (no tests in those days) and perhaps it was as well that his top speed downhill was 30 m.p.h. But it was also very tiring on a long journey. For our holiday, I planned to introduce Henzie to my belovèd Dartmoor. On the way, we would stop in London to see Henzie's mother, and spend a few days at Box Hill near Dorking, of which Henzie was fond. Albert was loaded – too heavily, perhaps – and I let in the clutch. Bang – the back axle broke. It took several days to get and fit a new one: meanwhile, we had lent the flat to my 'little' brother and his coach for Responsions, the entrance exam to Oxford, and they had already arrived, so we were very redundant. Accordingly, when the car was ready we didn't wait another night but set off at 5.30 p.m. We reached London at 2 a.m., slept a little and made a quick visit to Henzie's mother, and went straight on to Box Hill. As we arrived, Henzie collapsed. The doctor said 'heart failure due to exhaustion: two weeks in bed'. They were spent in the hotel. Albert was meanwhile exchanged for something younger; and we proceeded to Dartmoor which we explored, by car only, as best we could. When we got back to Doncaster we plunged into all that I have described and never gave the heart another thought. The shadow had crossed our path: to forget it when the sun shone again was the healthy reaction and, repeated over and over again, enabled Henzie to live very fully for forty-eight years more with a hole in her heart.

At Christmas, we did the Coventry Mystery Play of the Nativity in a church so hidebound that the vicar would not allow Henzie to play in it because she was a professional actress, of the devil's brood. She acted as prompter to the amateurs, in a nun's habit. The play was lit entirely by candles – two racks of 'footlights', twenty-six in each. Very hot for the actors; but the light was alive as the candles flickered. The fire authorities took no notice, if they knew. After the last performance, a man with one arm asked for a word with me. He was the Governor of Wakefield Prison and was pioneering an experiment in progressive self-government with young prisoners sentenced for between six months and two years.

The men in each block at a different stage, a wider range of activities, meals at tables for four instead of at one long table ('they have stopped throwing the bread'). He would like us to bring the show and play it in the prison chapel. I was delighted: he gave me a long look. 'Don't be surprised, whatever reaction you get: just go on playing.'

The date was set for a month ahead, at the end of January. This had one big snag. Bobbie Speaight had done us the great kindness of coming up for a few days to play the famous boastful Herod (who 'rages in the pagond and in the strete also'). By the Wakefield date he would be in another show. The only alternative was for me to play it myself. Neither my shape nor my voice could have been more unsuitable, especially as Barry Jackson had lent us the costumes of his musical version (Rutland Boughton's *Bethlehem*) and the designer, Paul Shelving, had gone to the limit of oriental exaggeration in Herod's costume. It was huge and flowing, topped with a colossal crowned turban.

The whole Wakefield experience was unforgettable. The terrible gaunt building with its resonant iron passages radiating from the 'watch-tower' hub, contrasted with the lively young men, full of resource, who were allotted to us as stage-hands. The chapel seating was steeply raked – again for observation and control. We cleared an area before the altar, and the play began. It was punctuated with carols, no scene was very long, and it seemed to be going pretty well – keen attention, laughs for the shepherds, and only the occasional snigger in the wrong place. Then, enter Herod. A great gale of laughter, full-throated, that went on for several minutes. In my inexperience I had no idea if I could stop it, or how: but I did at least stand still. As it began to subside, I started my boasting. Repeated laughs at the absurdities; and as the scene with the Kings drew to its end, I was wondering whether such laughter, the like of which none of us had ever heard before, could possibly be subdued for the gentle little scene of Joseph, the angel and Mary which followed and ended the play. The response was perfect. Afterwards, the governor said 'You see what I meant? I didn't want to tell you because I wanted it to happen. Some of those men haven't laughed for six months.'

Meanwhile, the tension among the miners was growing to breaking-point. When we went on tour we would find, on identifying the number on one of a blackened row of industrial houses and going in, a welcome not only warm but deeply intelligent: the shelf of books would comprise philosophy, history, literature, drama, and they had been well studied. The conversations this provoked, often revealing to us our own immaturity, revealed also a sad, burning bitterness, born of the neglect of the miner by the community, his exploitation by owners of royalties and those who ran what was then a private business. Even to people so inexperienced as we were, it was no surprise when in 1926 the strike began.

There followed the tragedy of the General Strike; a tragedy most of all for the miners, since after its abandonment they were left to carry on alone. We saw privation steadily overtake them. The fur coat that a miner working much overtime had bought 'on tick' for his wife went back to the shop. So many pianos went back to the hire-purchase firm that they had not storage-space and left them to rot in the yard. Soon food was getting short. It was clear that the Folkhouse could not survive after the five months' strike: subscriptions lapsed and classes were given up: this youngest of the educational settlements was doomed. We must look for other work. For us, as well as for the miners, there was then no social security, and in 1926 jobs were hard to come by. And we were expecting a child.

We decided that until the child was born we would go back to Angmering, where we could rent a little furnished house very cheaply. Denis was born there on 12 August, and in the autumn we moved to a tiny cottage in Hampstead. All this time I was applying for jobs: the ESA offered us one at Letchworth but we couldn't face the 'precious' atmosphere and foolhardily turned it down. Interviews took me all over the country but to no avail. We got a little evening-class work in London to earn a pittance; but a better, if temporary, job came from Geoffrey Whitworth.

He had founded in 1919 the British Drama League. Its aims were

to assist the development of the Art of the Theatre and to promote a right relation between Drama and the life of the community.

He had gathered into this 'supporters' club' most of the people whom Henzie and I revered as practitioners of that Art. The League's early work reflected their ideals, with Geoffrey, and a secretary who had gone through the fire of apprenticeship to Lilian Baylis, to implement them.

The League's foundation had coincided with the first 'great leap forward' of the amateur drama movement. Although Geoffrey at first focused his attention on the professional theatre, he welcomed amateur members and soon found that they were in the majority. Quite a few of these amateur groups were eager – more eager than some professionals – to walk by the fresh light which Granville Barker (who was chairman till 1932), Gordon Craig and others were shedding on the theatre. As a focus for this amateur activity the League started a National Festival of Community Drama. Each team presents (for it still flourishes) a one-act play of its own choice before an adjudicator appointed by the Festival Committee. If he knows his job, and is frank without being sarcastic, he can provide not only useful instruction but the climactic entertainment of the evening, leading up to the announcement of Third, Second, First. Henzie and I were to do a great deal of this later. Geoffrey began by sending me to Scotland, where I saw thirty-six teams between the Border and Aberdeen. It was the first venture of what soon became the Scottish Community Drama Association (SCDA).

Our cottage was up the road from the Everyman, now run by Raymond Massey (who had made his first stage appearance there in Henzie's time), George Carr (her boss as stage manager) and Allan Wade. Henzie could not ask for work, being tied to her baby, but we saw shows there and sometimes further afield. 'Komis' was doing Chekhov at Barnes – the first public performances in England of some of the plays. We saw all three: *Uncle Vanya*, *The Cherry Orchard* and *Three Sisters* with a screen-scene full of flickering shadows as the girls long for Moscow.

Hamlet recurs over and over again in my theatre-going memory. I had seen Gyles Isham play it under J. B. Fagan at the OUDS in 1924: the soldier ('Sound all the lofty instruments of war!' he had said as Hotspur in my last OUDS show), but not the dreamer. The next year came John Barrymore from America, speaking meticulously a part he had studied rather than lived, in a setting by Robert Edmond Jones that supplied the missing magic. Barry Jackson, indomitably enterprising, put on (with Colin Keith-Johnston in the part) the first *Hamlet* in modern dress. We saw it twice in one day, first to absorb the shock (which was hardest on the ladies in their twenties frocks) then to look for new light on the play. Most of this shone on the court, with Frank Vosper as a superbly smooth seducer of Dorothy Massingham's sullenly sensuous Queen, and Bromley-Davenport as a neatly bearded diplomat showing Polonius' mistakes as stemming from the worldly man's inability to understand Hamlet's other-worldly experiences. But most significant of all the Hamlets was Ernest Milton, back at the Vic: mannered and exotic, he revealed the full emotional depth of the character and the full horror with which he felt himself confronted.

Here I got one of the two small parts by means of which I slid, in a manner now rightly deprecated, onto the professional stage. The Old Vic gave each year a matinée of 'The Entirety', the uncut text of *Hamlet*, which was always a sell-out. I was Voltimand; and so was lucky enough to see at close quarters how Milton developed the overwhelming sweep of emotion in key with the high poetry of the play, while allowing harsh brutalities also to escape from Hamlet's overcharged heart.

Just before that, I had made my very first professional appearance in a Sunday night production for the Stage Society. This was the oldest and most important of the bodies set up to produce plays the commercial theatre wouldn't attempt. They played Sundays because they could thus use actors playing in West End runs, and 'for members only' to evade the Lord's Day Observance Society and the censor. The play was D. H. Lawrence's one dramatic excursion into scripture, the untidy but undervalued *David*, which concentrates on the friendship with Jonathan but also evokes the dark tribal mysticism of Samuel and the bacchic frenzy of Michal. I was the Elder.

It would have been natural to use professionally the name by which everyone called me – Martin Browne. But just at this time a thriller called *Cobra* was enjoying a successful run, and its author's name was Martin Browne. So I stuck the 'E' of 'Elliott' in front of mine.

Professional acting, however, was not a promising career for me, and was at the moment impossible for Henzie. My search for a more regular job had so far proved futile. Now occurred two events, apparently unrelated, which were to change both our lives as 'NG' had changed Henzie's. What Jung calls 'the extremely indirect methods of creation' were at work.

I described one of them for Marion Cole's *Fogie* (Peter Davies 1967):

I first met Elsie Fogerty in a church schoolroom in Folkestone in April 1926. I was on the staff of an Amateur Drama School as Producer, though still pretty inexperienced myself. So, in the interval between the morning sessions, I walked in to enrol as a student in the class of the famous teacher of speech. I saw a big, lively woman in a brown coat-and-skirt and velours hat, eating from its skin a banana which she had taken from a paper bag. I was frightened and yet fascinated by her personality: this was the reaction, as I later came to know, of almost every one of her students. But the fascination soon overcame the fright, especially as she communicated in vivid teaching and conversation a great store of knowledge on those subjects which meant most to me.

While at Folkestone we received a cablegram from America. It was signed 'B. Iden Payne', and offered me the post of Assistant Professor of Speech in the Drama Department of the Carnegie Institute of Technology at Pittsburgh, to start in September. We had learned that this might happen from John van Druten, who in fact was responsible. His next play after *The Return Half* had been

2   Elsie Fogerty and GBS at her Malvern Summer School Garden Party, 1934. Photo by permission of the British Drama League

Young Woodley, which, absurdly banned by the Lord Chamberlain as casting aspersions on a public school, had been produced in New York with huge success. It was now touring the 'number one' theatres of the USA, and John had joyfully thrown up his law-lectureship at Aberystwyth to give lectures as advance publicity for his play. Pittsburgh was one of his dates.

Memories are short in the theatre. John was in the first rank of naturalistic playwrights from then until the Second World War and even after it, but I find that very few people now know his name. To Iden Payne the English theatre's debt is even greater. He formed and directed the first repertory company, Miss Horniman's at the Gaiety, Manchester (1907–11), which was the model for all the hundreds that have followed it. Besides giving audiences outside London their first opportunity to see Shaw, Galsworthy, the Greek translations of Gilbert Murray, and to experience the new light thrown upon Shakespeare by William Poel and Granville Barker, he established in Manchester a school of native playwrights of whom Harold Brighouse and Stanley Houghton became the best known. He has been forgotten in England largely because he discovered in America his great gift of teaching, and so stayed there (except for a few years at Stratford-on-Avon) until his recent death aged 94.

When John went to talk to the Drama Department at 'Carnegie Tech' Iden Payne confided to him that he needed a junior faculty-member to teach speech and do some directing; and he would prefer to have an Englishman since at that time American speech teaching was doctrinaire and to his mind not the best preparation for actors. John suggested me – in effect, suggested both of us, for there was parallel work in evening classes. It was a kind act, if a rash one – because I had no formal speech training. But the sound of us appealed to Iden – only he felt he must have a second opinion. John suggested Sybil, who had been Iden's leading lady in Miss Horniman's company. He cabled to her and received a characteristically enthusiastic reply. So his message reached us at Folkestone.

We had not asked ourselves whether we could tear up all our roots: we had learned by bitter experience not to count our chickens on either side of the Atlantic. So the actual offer was a 'facer'. We expressed great interest and promised a definite answer in a week's time. About the teaching of speech, for which I had no proper qualification, I appealed to Miss Fogerty for help, and she found time to give me an intensive course of private lessons. No one else, I am sure, could have enabled me to acquit myself even as well as I did for the next three years in a strange land: she not only taught me speech-technique, but, quite as important, gave me an insight into my own character, and illuminated the relationship of speech to personality. For Elsie Fogerty speech was never an end in itself.

When we got back to London we went to see Geoffrey Whitworth: he had given me the only substantial work in that barren winter, and had since conveyed the impression that it might lead to more. But we could not live on adjudication or short courses, and he couldn't foresee anything more, still less prophesy the further future. With fatherly kindness he sent us away from the British Drama League's beautiful rooms at 8 Adelphi Terrace to make our decision. We descended to the Embankment Gardens and sat for a long time on a bench, silent. The decision, of course, was already made. We had only to recognise it.

2

America: the first time

On Labour Day (the first Monday in September, a national holiday) we arrived in what Henzie's mother had called 'the American Sheffield'. That conjured up to us the impenetrable yellow fog through which we had groped our way on winter tours from Doncaster. In Pittsburgh's summer the sun penetrated it with what seemed to us prodigious heat; but the sulphurous smell associated with steel-mills was the same, only more so, since the city was bigger. (Everything, we realised, was going to be bigger.)

Iden Payne was back in town, though the semester didn't start for another two weeks. He was at once a friend, quite without the grand manner that his record in the theatre would have justified. He became also a master. He was 46 two days after we arrived, slight and smallish, very agile, with a mobile face of great charm. On stage, his broken nose could be an asset in 'character' comedy but was handsomely built up with nose-paste for a 'straight part'. He confesses in his delightful autobiography *A Life in a Wooden O* that he always thought of himself as primarily an actor, and indeed he was a most attractive one; but the strength of his convictions about the theatre as an art, coupled with his meticulous care for its professional standards, inevitably made him a leader and director. He was a professional to the bone, and it seemed extraordinary that he could bear with the ineptitudes, and still more with the half-heartedness, of some students at what was after all, despite its high reputation, a department in a middle-western College mainly devoted to industry. But he was a natural teacher, and hope sprang eternal in him as the endless flow of young people in Pittsburgh, Iowa, San Diego, Oregon, Banff and Texas passed under his spell.

The faculty was not a well-matched team and Iden didn't drive it with ease. Naturally a modest man of sensitive disposition, he had not, and could not even assume, the hardness which the

faculty, as well as the students, needed from the head of department. And a duodenal ulcer was sapping his strength.

I am incredulous when I recall our beginnings in this set-up. As
we ascended for the first time the flight of broad steps that led to
the remotely pseudo-classical portal of the College of Fine Arts, two
students passed us and one said to the other 'A ga fa dallrs.' By the
time we had interpreted it to each other as 'I've got five dollars,' I
knew I had my speech-work cut out. At my first class was an albino
boy who seemed sleepy. I tried to discover whether he was
listening, but all I did find out was that he couldn't understand a
word I said – nor could I understand him. He came from southern
Texas. With the potent, though to them utterly strange, aid of Miss
Fogerty's principles and exercises, I gradually made useful contact
with most of my freshman class, and a bit more than that with the
sophomores (second-year students) who had had a year of pretty
hard experience. Besides a full schedule of classes each day and one
major show during the year, the freshman (or woman – it was a
completely co-educational institution) had to act as 'crew' on the
technical side of the productions, set-building and setting, lighting,
costume-making and dressing. In those days dress rehearsals were
allowed to go on till 3 and 4 in the morning (just like the real
theatre), so it was not surprising that quite a few people slept in
class.

The major productions of the department were given a run of ten
days to a fortnight. There was quite a large subscription audience,
who paid a fee that just covered mailing expenses and got the
chance to see a lot of plays which would never come to Pittsburgh's
two commercial houses. Iden encouraged, therefore, a diverse
programme of interesting plays. But even he was startled when he
asked me what I would like to do as my first major production and
I replied *The Tidings Brought to Mary*. This was Louise Morgan Sill's
translation of Paul Claudel's *L'Annonce faite à Marie*, which since it
was written in 1910 had been seen briefly in Paris, fleetingly in New
York and on a Sunday night (directed by Edith Craig) in London.
The poet was at that time French ambassador in Washington.

Iden agreed and I started casting-readings. Many of the students
were fascinated by this strange play. I began to realise – and found
it even more apparent when the audiences came – that something
which we in Europe have in our blood does not enter into the
American past. They never had the Middle Ages. Claudel's play is

set in the fifteenth century in and around a farmhouse, both practically as well as mystically connected with an enclosed order of nuns. This was something old which was completely new to Americans, and which in the play exercises a compelling power. To Claudel, the religious instinct expressed in Catholicism is an absolute: you can fight it, you can deny it, but you can't kill it, nor in the end evade it. So when you see his plays on the stage you may be repelled, but you cannot be indifferent.

I have a copy of the letter which the earnest young director wrote at the time to the distinguished author, and I quote some of it:

> *Department of Drama*
> *Carnegie Inst. of Tech.*
> *January 23rd, 1928*

Dear M. Claudel,

It is a matter of very deep regret to us all that you did not see the production of *L'Annonce faite à Marie* which closed here last Wednesday, for we should all have valued most highly your opinions and criticisms of our interpretation. It is thought that you may nevertheless be interested by as full a record as we can give you of the production, and in that hope I am writing an 'account of my stewardship' as director.

First, let me say how happy an experience the whole production has been. As I told you, the students loved the play – as much to my surprise as yours. Throughout our preparation it has increased its hold upon the actors. Everyone has bent to the difficult task of doing the play justice, with a willingness which has resulted in a representation acclaimed by many as the most beautiful seen here for years, and played to houses packed to the last seat every night. The depth of emotion and intensity of thought in the play have made it, both to performers and to auditors, a satisfying experience.

Now to pass to the details by which I want to try to give you an idea of how we treated the play. You will imagine that, for a very small stage with little capital or equipment, I had to devise means by which the many scenes could be easily built and quickly changed, and I also felt that, for an audience strange to medievalism, it was necessary to unify the visual ideas of the play as far as possible. I revolted against the 'architectural' type of setting which suggests no special time nor place. Finally I arranged with the scenic director to enclose the whole play within a painted picture-frame of Gothic shape, with an 'Annunciation' as the curtain; and to place permanently at the back a great built piece representing corn-land, rocky hills, and upon the summit of the highest, in the centre, Monsanvierge. The influence of the monastery seemed to me to pervade the play so deeply that I felt it was the 'common chord' upon which all the modulations of light and darkness, as of joy and sorrow, should be played. You will see from the photographs how the different apertures through which it was seen altered its appearance: I wish they could also convey the very remarkable lighting changes, which made so moving a picture of many a scene.

Certain details in the photographs, being alterations of your original ideas to fit this scenic scheme, need explaining:

(1) In the prologue, we found double doors both too heavy to construct and too bulky for our stage-space, so I altered them to what I have sometimes seen in medieval English barns, a rough portcullis wound by a winch.

(2) In the kitchen, we placed the windows at the back to give us the view of the mountain, and the table broad-wise because the stage was not deep enough for it long-wise! Many people commented on the resemblance of the end of Act I to a Quattrocento 'Last Supper', and indeed it was just such pictures that I had in mind throughout the play.

(3) The 'fountain' scene I removed to an open garden; and at the beginning of this was heard 'Salve Regina'. (In the little 'orchard' scene before it, Monsanvierge was hidden from view) . . .

In the 'scenic director' referred to I was supremely lucky: and into the bargain Henzie and I made two lifelong friends. Frank Stout was a painter of distinction. As a young man, he had trained in Paris for three years, in the period of the great Impressionists. Back in the USA, he had supplemented his inadequate income from painting by working for Tiffany; then, becoming interested in theatre-design, had taken courses and worked at the Neighbourhood Playhouse (not so unlike the Everyman in Hampstead) where he had met and married a student of acting and direction, Helen Rosenthal. Iden Payne had directed there, and so offered Frank the job at Tech.

Until now, I had never known from the inside a theatre which could produce a work of visual art. Henzie used to say of me in our Doncaster days that I depended entirely on screw-eyes: and in those primitive conditions all one could hope for was that the curtain-surround would stay up! To have had a vision, as I had of *The Tidings*, and see it brought to a life finer than my imagination, was a totally new experience. I watched Frank building, with papier-maché applied to a cut-out, the surfaces of the cornfield below, the craggy rocks of the mountain and then the outline of the convent building to be seen against the sky.

Before *The Tidings* was on stage the friendship of us four was cemented. Frank was usually a silent person: both our wives talked a great deal; but that didn't prevent the foursome being emotionally balanced. We often wondered at the quick sprouting of friendship in America: somehow you seem to know at once that you belong together, when in Britain it dawns on you gradually. But though the growth is quick it does not follow that it will wither 'because it has no root'. This friendship (like not a few others) could always be taken up, even after years, as if no interval had occurred.

The friends we had very soon had their adoption tried. Early in November, Henzie developed what we and the doctor took to be 'flu. We had found a small apartment in a new building, the cheapest because on the ground floor but still costing a third of what, from England, had seemed a good salary. For three weeks she was in bed there with a slowly but steadily rising fever. Her natural gaiety and wit seemed to be increased by it, as Helen Stout and John van Druten (who was passing through on a second *Young Woodley* tour) tried to give her some care while I coped with her work as well as my own. The doctor, finally baffled by the lack of any symptom save the persistent fever, ordered her into hospital. There, the tests showed up soon enough – typhoid. She was the only case in the city and none of us caught it. With the fever at 106° she was very near death. On Christmas Day, she was normal: Tidings of great joy.

As soon as classes started again came the opening of *Tidings*; and Henzie came home a few days after. Since the tests did not pronounce her free of infection she could not go to see it. By the end of the run I collapsed with tonsillitis and we were lying in bed side by side. Enter Chester Wallace, second-in-command of the department. Iden had to go at once to Chicago for an operation. Next semester, that is at the beginning of February, I must take over his projected major production of *King Lear* (his Shakespeare play was of course the event of the year) and Henzie must undertake my *Midsummer Night's Dream* with the freshmen.

We were both to use Iden's 'modified Elizabethan stage', which he had designed to fit into the Tech theatre. It was the result of many years of study and experiment beginning in 1907 when he had asked William Poel to direct *Measure for Measure* as the opening production of Miss Horniman's Gaiety. Poel had begun in the 1890s a single-minded campaign to reinstate Shakespeare's own texts on the stage, to get actors to speak them as clearly and as fast as the author intended, and to restore his flowing rhythm of scenes which the Victorian use of representational scenery had destroyed.

Granville Barker might be called Poel's disciple; and while Poel remained an eccentric genius, Barker was so powerful in the theatre that he succeeded in awakening it to Poel's vision. Iden Payne, in his quietly persistent way, had a like influence in America, which is evident in many buildings (Ashland, Oregon and San Diego, California, for instance) and most of all in the Guthrie–Moiseiwitsch Festival Theatre at Stratford, Ontario, which is to me the most exciting theatre in the world.

His stage was a modification for a roofed auditorium with artificial lighting of the type of stage for which Shakespeare himself wrote. It had a 'penthouse' roof supported in front by two tall columns and covering about two-thirds of the total stage depth – leaving the other third as fore stage, which was especially useful for soliloquies, street scenes and 'comics'. A pair of tall curtains could be drawn between the columns. At the back of the main stage were two shallow, curtained inner stages, which Iden called 'inner above' and 'inner below'.

This was by no means all new to us. Bobbie Speaight (who later wrote Poel's biography) and I had been assiduous students, and Poel had even come to see our *Tempest* and *Richard III* at Angmering.

They were directed by those who had dramatic intelligence, and the method of production adopted was obviously Elizabethan, embodying, as it did, a simple and direct action, with a spontaneous delivery. In a wooden shanty by the sea, playgoers were brought close up to the poet's work, and this was mainly due to the skill and intelligence of the performers.   (T. Werner Laurie, *Monthly Letters*, 1929)

But the 'shanty by the sea' had not allowed of even a modified Elizabethan stage. So we got Iden, before he left, to explain to us how both the actors, and we as directors new to it, must change our points of view when using his stage.

The actors, he said, would instinctively gravitate to the columns – they felt naked in the open. The director must stop them: and must stop himself using the inner stage whenever the action seemed to happen in an enclosed place. To get the actors out, as near the audience as possible, was Shakespeare's aim: the actor when alone should talk directly to them, and the main stage was an open space with the audience looking down on the pattern of movement. For the upper stage, don't think of it just as a balcony but as an upper stage, and use it both for small scenes (such as the

Edmund–Gloucester scenes in *Lear*) and for giving two levels to a full-stage scene. Make the play move fast: if you use some scenery in the inner stage, keep the front occupied while you change it. And even more important, let there be *no gap at all* between scenes: as one group goes off let the next come on, *speaking*. Barker and Payne both aimed at this continuous flow of speech: no bits of music between scenes: if there's applause, let the oncoming actors learn to time their entrance *into* it as it diminishes, as you time the next line or movement into the end of a laugh.

When Iden came back next year we were to see the master do it: meanwhile, we had to learn the hard way. Both our tasks were equally taxing. I had Shakespeare's most colossal play, with a Lear competent but physically 'o'erparted' and, as usual, a double cast of women to train (I had had *three* Violaines in *Tidings*). Henzie had a cast of freshmen who, after one semester's speech-training, had to

3 Garlanding Shakespeare: HB at Carnegie Institute, Pittsburgh, 23 April 1929

speak Shakespeare's most stylish verse, and a bunch of middle-western kids to introduce to the manners of courts, human and fairy.

Shakespeare himself might have been better entertained by the celebration of his birthday at the museum, also founded by Andrew Carnegie, which was Tech's next-door neighbour. It fronted on a big main road, and on either side of the portal was a seated statue. The director decreed that each year an ode written by himself should be spoken to the seated Bard. Henzie, crowned, undertook, by the strength of her voice aided by watchful timing, to beat the traffic, including the trams:

> O Shakespeare, on this joyous natal day
> We come with garlands, crowned, to own thy sway

she declaimed, and popped the garland over his head.

I don't think either of our results won, or merited, any great acclaim. But the jobs were done: and may serve to introduce one more personality. Abe Feder was a powerful bull of a boy from a midwestern Jewish family. I don't know how early in his career he gravitated to the lighting-switchboard, but I suspect it was in the first week. By the time I was working out the complicated light-plot for *Tidings* (Monsanvierge had to be seen at every hour from dawn to sunset, in every season from Christmas to hot summer) he was already doing the job: and when I started on *Lear* the cues multiplied from scene to scene with added frustrations – one of the columns would be in the way of a spot, you couldn't get enough light under the penthouse roof to light the inner stage, and so on. It was, I think, the most exhausting dress rehearsal of my career. Abe's comment was: 'I like you, you set me big problems.'

At the end of the academic year comes the question, does any student have to be dropped? The decision rests with the dean of the faculty. I heard from Abe that because he had not the requisite grades in the academic subjects (History of Civilisation, History of Theatre etc.) he was threatened with expulsion, and junior as I was, I marched in to the dean's office. 'You can't drop Feder no matter what his grades are, he's a genius.' Some formula was found and Abe stayed on. He was grateful to me – not that it mattered, I'm sure, to the career of the American theatre's top lighting man whether he got a degree or not, but because of the blow it would have dealt to his parents, who had sent him to college with so much sacrifice, if he had 'flunked'. I am eternally grateful to *him*: in our three years together he taught me not only how lights work but how to make them speak to the imagination of the beholder. He has been called a wizard: the wizardry is in the feeling quite as much as in the technique. The theatre is a hard mistress, and at the end of a long session under the lash of Abe's tongue students would feel rebellious – until they came out in front and looked, wondering, at the result.

I think it was a good thing for Abe, and for those in other departments too, that our theatre's equipment was limited and was constantly being stretched beyond its limits. That's how you learn ingenuity. You've got to solve the 'big problems' with what doesn't appear to be there. It's a mistake, I'm sure, to give students 'the perfectly equipped theatre', as some American colleges do. It is in one's student days that one needs the challenges to invention which most graduates will constantly meet again in the 'real' theatre.

In the spring we made our first trip to New York. In the twenties, the city was at its most thrilling: the very high buildings were few enough to seem fabulous, and the air was still pretty clear, so that the vertical contrasts, especially in sunlight, were a perpetual amazement, and at twilight innumerable jewels appeared in space. Here too we made friends, mostly through *Theatre Arts Monthly* and its editor and founder, Edith J. R. Isaacs, a big, capable, motherly woman who with her lawyer-husband was supporting this magazine. Finely produced and illustrated, it was scholarly but not academic; the purpose was to open up every avenue towards achievement for the theatre as a performing art. Edith Isaacs and her colleague and successor, Rosamond Gilder, not only became our friends themselves but linked us to the like-minded theatre-people of the time. Examples of our own work were published in the issue annually devoted to 'the Tributary Theatre'.

Broadway had more than twice as many theatres as it has now, and the first (and perhaps still the most significant) wave of American dramatists was breaking upon it: O'Neill, Sidney Howard, George Kaufman, Marc Connelly. The outstanding management was the Theatre Guild; and we were grateful to them not only for Broadway shows but also for tours which came to Pittsburgh, bringing such treasures as Reinhardt's production (in curtains and set-pieces) of Tolstoy's *Resurrection* with Alexander

Moissi, and an English play, *Wings Over Europe* by Robert Nichols and Maurice Browne, set in the Cabinet Room and dealing with the splitting of the atom by a Shelley-like young scientist.

In the fall, Iden was back, and though he had to carry a carton of milk about with him to comply with his dietary instructions, was in something near full vigour. He played for Helen Stout at the 'Y' Playhouse, A. A. Milne's *The Dover Road* with Henzie opposite him, and *Around the World in Eighty Days*. Here we saw his powers and his methods as a creator of character. His production of *Cymbeline*, of which we were able to watch some rehearsals, was another revelation. Casting, as William Poel used to do, with a pattern of sound in his mind, he would explain, coax, bully, persuade the actor into a conviction that *that* was the sound that expressed the thought and feeling. The verse of *Cymbeline* is some of the most complex in Shakespeare, and some of the most profoundly expressive. Iden's mastery of its tiniest detail astonished and shamed us. We also learned from his use of his stage. I particularly remember the scene in which Posthumus overhears Iachimo's boasting 'the

4   *The Trojan Women* (Euripides/Gilbert Murray), Carnegie Tech, 1929: Hecuba holding the dead Astyanax.

morning after'. Iachimo and his little group were in the 'inner below', with Posthumus only a foot or two outside it. As they left he came straight down to the very edge of the fore stage and assailed us with

> Is there no way for men to be, but women
> Must be half-workers? We are all bastards.

My own major production was *The Trojan Women* (Gilbert Murray's translation). This came before *Cymbeline* and also used the fore stage. The set consisted of a ruined temple-front – a flight of steps and three columns broken at different levels (the lowest could be stood on), against the forty-foot sky-cloth which was Abe's 'big problem'. Irene Tedrow, who as a junior (third-year student) was one of my Violaines, played Hecuba as her chief senior assignment, and for a young actress produced great dignity and strength of feeling. It may be well to remark here how many graduates of Tech have, like her, attained eminence or at least respect in theatre, movies and television. To set against what I have said about the

5   *The Virgin and the Clerk* (A. Kingsley Porter), Carnegie Tech, 1930

crudity of background is the far more important fact that here has been a school which through fifty years has insisted on the best professional standard as an aim which you must work with all your might to attain. *Godspell* was created by Tebelak and Schwartz from the drama department as a joint Master's thesis, and first performed by the students at Carnegie Tech. (It is now called Carnegie–Mellon University, but when I met Tebelak I found that he at 24 was as riled as I at 73 by the change of name. It's still Tech to the drama department!)

In this second year when life was not dislocated by quite so many crises, the church again exerted its gravitational pull. In the small episcopal church we attended, I staged the Coventry Nativity Play during the week 26–31 December (no Boxing Day in America). Next Christmas we did the York Nativity in a bigger church, and Easter plays in a still bigger one; and Abe was pulled into the act. This was another challenge he enjoyed – finding ways of fixing theatre lights in church, then an unheard-of thing to do, and discovering how few instruments you need, because the building itself supplies the distances and the atmosphere. I have used and refined on this knowledge in literally hundreds of churches.

Our younger son, Christopher, was born on 14 October 1929. This meant that I was again doing Henzie's teaching as well as my own, so I did less direction. I gave *After All*, a family comedy by John van Druten, its first American performance; and with a freshman year of unusually high standard I was able to cast an unpublished play by A. Kingsley Porter, professor of medieval studies at Harvard, on the original legend of Theophilus. Gustav Cohen's revival at the Sorbonne of the medieval *Miracle de Théophile* was a recent landmark. Porter's *The Virgin and the Clerk* is a far subtler treatment, in a witty, clipped style reminiscent of Greek *stichomythia*, and with a Jungian ambivalence which the Virgin's final line expresses in the image

> Does an artist paint snow-mountains solid white?

The author sent me the printed text with

> Deep gratitude to Mr Martin Browne for his poetic staging of *The Virgin and The Clerk*, a realisation of all I could have hoped the play might be.

After Christmas, Henzie was confined to bed for two months with heart trouble. We were quite exceptionally lucky to meet through friends Jennie Anderson, who came to live with us and look after house and babies. And when this worked out well, we planned to go with Denis to England for the summer. It would be the first sight of home in three years. Jennie would keep Christopher in the Stouts' apartment so as to take some of the load off Henzie who was still pretty weak. We were of course contracted to Tech for another year, which I had preferred to a job at the University of Washington; there was no thought of a future other than in America.

3
Religious Drama: George Bell's call

We had been home two weeks when Sybil Thorndike bade us to a meeting on Religious Drama. She was a vice-president of the newly formed Religious Drama Society (RDS), founded by Olive Stevenson, widow of a leading Congregational minister. She had interested Sir Francis Younghusband, the explorer of Tibet, who had been impressed by the power of Hindu drama and felt that the Church could present Christianity in this medium. He became chairman with Mrs Stevenson as secretary. The Society aimed at raising the standard of religious plays and their performance, and was embarking upon training courses, the formation of a library with advisory service, and the critical encouragement of good playwriting.

Its president was the new Bishop of Chichester, George Bell. As Dean of Canterbury, he had in 1928 presented the first play to be seen in the cathedral since the Middle Ages – *The Coming of Christ*. This was specially written by John Masefield, with music by Gustav Holst and costumes by Charles Ricketts. At the meeting were Elsie Fogerty, Lilian Baylis of the Old Vic ('*and* – in a year or two – Sadler's Wells') and Geoffrey Whitworth, of whose British Drama League (BDL) all of them were keen supporters. After it was over, Geoffrey told me that Bishop Bell would like me to go and see him. Here is my account of this call, which Ronald Jasper printed in his *George Bell* (Oxford 1967):

The Lambeth Conference was on, and I found that George Bell had a flat in Lambeth Palace. Feeling rather frightened, I climbed the stairway of Lollard's Tower and knocked at his door. The man who opened the door surprised me. He seemed incredibly young: he was forty-seven at that time, which is young for a bishop, but this was a kind of youthfulness which had nothing to do with years, and which never left him. His slightly protruding eyes seemed always ready to laugh, and behind a slight

56

primness in the mouth lurked a glee which again I can only call boyish. He held out his hand and I took it: another surprise. The handshake was very soft, so gentle that one expected it to be flabby. Then one felt under it the pressure that denoted his secret strength and his tremendous warmth of heart. It was like no other handshake I ever knew, and I shall always remember it. We started talking about America, and I became aware of that rare thing . . . the real and intense interest in the person he was talking to. He really wanted to know what this completely strange young man felt about America. But this, I discovered, was the result of a tremendous breadth of interests, and a breadth of mind too, which operated in every direction. After a little while we got round to the reason why he had asked me to come. He wanted the diocese of Chichester to have the first Director of Religious Drama. In those days religious drama was a new thing, frowned upon by the considerable puritan element remaining in the Church. . . . He believed in it. He believed that the drama should once more be the valued servant of the Church; and as for his own diocese, he was determined that the standards set for drama should be worthy of the subjects it was to portray. He had many visions, like this one, of the way in which other aspects of human life could be brought close to Christianity, but he was always firm and realistic in making sure that the view of God they expressed was the Christian view. He wanted to encourage the use of the church building for drama – but the drama must be good enough.

This was 30 June. Two days later we were to leave for a holiday in Germany ending at Oberammergau, and the decision we had to make was not simple. The salary Bell could offer (raised, I believe, by some quiet begging from sympathetic friends, since no church funds could be called on for such a purpose) was that of a junior curate, with no accommodation or expenses and no contract for the future, other than his word that the experiment would last three years. We should be back to a Doncaster level of budget. Furthermore, we were doubly committed in the USA. I had signed another year's contract at Tech; and we had left Christopher at Pittsburgh. I could only accept subject to Chester Wallace (who had taken over from Iden) being willing and able to find a replacement during the summer vacation; and if he agreed, Henzie would have to go over and bring the baby back. Despite all this, we don't seem to have hesitated. On 14 July I received Bell's confirmation of his offer; and Chester's cable releasing me reached us at Oberammergau.

My memory of the Passion Play, confirmed by photographs which I still have, is vividly equivocal. At such a moment, one would have expected to find it a fount of inspiration. I went to Mass at 6 a.m. in a packed church with the whole cast present – and this was in fact the highlight of the day. The performance began at 8 a.m. in the newly opened theatre which the play's international success had made possible and which is still in use: a hangar-like auditorium, a severely classical stage-building with three openings, the centre one having a pair of bronze sliding doors revealing the glass-roofed inner stage, a huge forestage open to the sky, and the panorama of mountains behind it all. The pace was very slow, the music matched the Victorian text with its wealth of lamentation, the crowds and the elaborate still tableaux were perfectly drilled. It was only at a few moments, such as the washing of the disciples' feet, that a surge of emotion occurred. For the most part, the strength one had felt in the church was regimented into pious conformity. I was rebelliously determined to get away from this pietism in the work ahead of me – however inept and crude most of it would seem compared to this perfect precision, it must be free to grow into our own century, free to find its own life.

I should admit that our fellow-members of the vast audience didn't give the play the best of chances. We were staying in a player's house (admirably clean and kindly run) with an American package-deal tour 'doing' nineteen countries in sixty days (and this before aeroplanes). A lady just in front of us at the play looked up from her programme and said to her companion, 'Jesus? I thought that was a swear-word.' But this was probably better for one's judgement than being in one of the clerically guided tours. After the lunch interval a mountain rainstorm engulfed the village: one saw the point of the glass roof – for the Crucifixion, for instance – and appreciated the doggedness of the twenty-four singers on either side of Anton Lang, chanting away with their long wet hair lashing their faces.

The next night was to provide a startling contrast. We had booked seats on the Sunday night train from Munich to Paris. In Munich we found posters of a show *Totenmal* to be given in a specially built theatre on the outskirts of town. Albert Talhoff, the Swiss poet, had written, created and directed this 'dramatic chorale for speech, dance and light'. *The Call of The Dead* from the World War was expressed in choral speech and music, in abstract patterns of light, and in the modern dance that stemmed from the work of Rudolf Laban, performed by a troupe led by Mary Wigman, the greatest performer in this medium. In the earlier part of the play, letters from the fallen of every fighting nation were relayed from various points in the auditorium, so that we were surrounded by these living voices of the dead. The anti-war message was being punched home with (once more) German thoroughness; and looking back one can see that the emotional power so generated could all too easily be turned in another direction than that of Peace and Light. But we were being introduced to new and thrilling aspects of theatre: light as an abstract medium, orchestrated choral speech, dance of a kind we had never seen before.

Quickly we set about finding somewhere to live. It must be in the centre of Sussex, which is over ninety miles from east to west, or some of my journeys to parishes would be impossibly long. We settled on an old flint cottage, which had once housed the chief coastguard, on the cliffs between Rottingdean and Newhaven, next to the Brighton sewage works. It was unmodernised and minimally, scruffily furnished. But we brought our own things into it, we got electricity after three months – and we loved it. To walk straight out onto the cliff, or cross the road to the gorse-covered Telscombe Tye, was always exhilarating even when you couldn't stand up against the south-west wind. That sea air blew us through three years of extremely hard work.

We were also lucky to be near Brighton, then hardly touched by the big developer, though his threat was already audible. Particularly, we loved the Theatre Royal which, then as now, showed a high proportion of 'try-outs' or London companies on tour. John van Druten, at the height of his success with two or sometimes three plays running in London, would take Edward Knoblock's house, 20 Regency Terrace, as a quiet place in which to write. He would use us as 'guinea-pigs' to read or listen to scenes and give reactions – he had a respect for Henzie's judgement in particular; and he would ask us for titles. One came by chance: he rang up to talk about an idea he had for a play in which a girl falls in love at first sight. But did it ever really happen? 'There's always Juliet,' I replied. 'Thank you: that's my title.' Another was *Behold, We Live* – my biblical training coming in useful. Auriol Lee, who by now was directing all John's plays, was often around too; and we went up to their first nights and to other shows from time to time.

Among them was *Le Viol de Lucrèce*, one of the first offerings to London of La Compagnie des Quinze. Henzie saw it first, and insisted on taking me. How dare I single out, from all the hundreds of shows I have seen, this as the most perfect? Yet that is how it still seems to my memory. I saw several of the Quinze shows afterwards. and I think the unique thing about their work was the completeness of the ensemble. Here were fifteen players already of the first rank when they left Paris with Michel Saint-Denis to gather round his uncle, Jacques Copeau, at his house in the country, with a dramatist, André Obey, to work with them. So the play, its direction and its performance were made together; a single work of art was carved out, refined and polished. The image was clean, spare, inevitable. In *Bataille de la Marne*, group after group after group of refugees fleeing in orchestrated terror . . . a long, long pause . . . heavy boots tramping . . . enter a single German soldier. Curtain of Act I.

The work in Sussex, or most of it, was very remotely related to such theatre. Bell was the wisest of employers, because he left me free to create my own job but wanted to be kept in touch with what I was doing, to be asked to advise and encourage those of the clergy who would co-operate with me, to attend performances I thought significant and discuss questions on which I was in doubt. He started me off by writing in his diocesan Newsletter and having me speak at the Diocesan Conference (16 October, the day after Henzie got back with Christopher). He introduced me to Francis Hughes, the Vicar of Eastbourne and I managed in the few weeks available before Christmas to put on the York Nativity Play in St Mary's, the beautiful Norman church of the original village. It won over some of the Parochial Church Council who were still strongly prejudiced against drama in church. Hughes took the firm line that the experiment should, under his watchful eye, be tried and those who disagreed should suspend judgement till they saw the result. 'It couldn't have been done anywhere else' was the verdict given by one such opponent.

I arranged the church with small platforms at the head of each side-aisle as well as the main stage at the entrance to the choir. These I used singly or together, to fill the whole building with the action so that every person present felt involved. Even if one of the thick Norman pillars blocked his view of some scenes, he had a clear view of others. The movements through the congregation from stage to stage would sometimes be interrupted in mid-career by an actor speaking from another position, so that a few lines were played *en route*. I published acting editions of this and similar texts to show how the plan worked. It was a natural development of the procession, which has always been a feature of Christian liturgies. Many problems are posed by playing in church – sight lines and acoustics are the worst: but the processional opportunities are a great compensating advantage.

Christmas was of course the busiest time, since many parishes had got as far as accepting a nativity play but most of them didn't know how to go about it. I administered the bishop's rule that no play might be done in church without his licensing the script. I had to read scripts and report to him, and this usually gave me also the chance to visit rehearsals and do some rescue work where necessary. Not by any means all the promoters, especially the clergy who are a stubbornly independent profession ('the parson's freehold'), welcomed this interloper from diocesan headquarters, and I had to learn a good deal of tact. All too rare was the vicar who would stop a play in rehearsal because the standard wasn't high enough. All too common was what the Americans call 'bathrobe drama', which may be translated into English usage as 'dressing-gown Palestinian'.

Many of these efforts were directed by people without training, sometimes without experience; and I had at the same time to shore up their sagging self-confidence and show them how to get a decent result. Of one such incident, repercussions still reach me. At Petworth, the vicar's wife had been enlisted to create and direct a nativity play, which must be in dumb-show because (as in many country places then) most people were so fearful of the sound of their own voices that they would only take part if they didn't have to speak. She proposed to take refuge in the dismal expedient of still tableaux. I sat down in the vicarage before the rehearsal and worked out a play in dumb-show with movements timed to bible-readings from the pulpit or to carols which allowed of the processional use of the whole church. Since I found that her problem was a constantly recurring one, I wrote it up and published it the next year as *The Story of Christmas in Mime*; and I am still meeting people who use it as a framework which they can adapt to the needs of their own building.

Most parish plays have to remain simple if they are to be the natural and direct expression of the players' feelings. Dr Jasper quotes an example which the bishop and I saw together:

the nativity play given by the children of a tiny country parish near Chichester which the vicar had written in the pantomime-doggerel and idiom which they understood. Bell was particularly delighted by the boy-innkeeper who, before refusing the Holy Family a room, searched through the hotel booking-register for vacancies!

I wanted at the same time to produce plays of quality and show them throughout the diocese. This meant assembling a group of chosen actors willing to tour – I looked for ex-professionals, people who had trained for but not gone on the stage, amateurs of talent who wanted more interesting work than their local society was doing. The group changed, of course, from play to play, but a core of capable people remained with The Chichester Diocesan Players. The bishop was enthusiastic and held a special service of blessing for us in the cathedral. He also persuaded the Vicar of Brighton to house our opening production in the parish church. This gave it prestige, which was brilliantly exploited by our honorary publicity man, Leonard Neville, a high official in a national insurance company who lived in Hove. He achieved queues round the church for free entrance to three performances, and was doubtless helped to get capacity 'houses' by the protest-procession (too mild to be called a 'demo') of the Protestant Truth Society.

The play was *The Marriage of St. Francis* by Henri Ghéon, a disciple of Copeau who had felt the obligation to provide Christian plays for a popular audience. Until we had English authors of his quality writing for us, he was the dramatist whose work we most frequently borrowed from a Catholic country where the drama-tradition had never been broken. The four scenes show, first the rich Francis Bernadone deserting his boon-companions to marry the Lady Poverty, then the poor Brother Francis rebuilding the ruined church, preaching to the birds, and receiving in his body the marks of the Lord Jesus. One critic, comparing Ghéon's treatment with others, points out that

The Marriage of Saint Francis gives us a picture of the saint which clearly accounts for his abiding influences upon Christians. It is a normal man that we see, though not, of course, a usual or an average man. He is the truly developed type of redeemed humanity.

He was acted by the vicar of a small church on the upper slopes of Hove, a transparently genuine man whose movement was rather ungainly but whose speaking was strong and direct:

The people who walked and talked on this stage in the Brighton Parish Church wore, as was necessary, the costumes of twelfth-century Italy. But they walked, and talked, pretty much as people walk and talk in Brighton today.

Neither the Francis nor any other of the players was named: we hoped that this anonymous offering of their gifts as actors would lead people to understand the spirit in which it was done. I may illustrate the need for such understanding by reprinting a leading article from *The English Churchman* of 2 April 1931 which quotes a 'pro' description to state an 'anti' case:

THE DRAMA IN CHURCH

With the approval and in the presence of the Bishop of Chichester, performances of the Mid-Lent play, known as 'The Marriage of St. Francis of Assisi', were recently given in the Parish Church of Brighton on three successive week days. A correspondent sends us a highly apprecia-tive description of the proceedings, which appeared in 'The Brighton and Hove Herald' of March 21, and in which we are told that 'a cycle of history has come back,' and that the reconciliation between Church and Stage 'has been made in the fullest possible degree by the presentation of this play about St. Francis, with the chancel of the Parish Church as background and the body of the church as auditorium'. The report informs us that 'a stage was erected. Flood lighting was used. Suitable symbolic scenery was set up. The right period costumes were worn. Use was even made of such theatrical devices as thunder and lightning.' We are assured, however, that 'this was no entertainment. It was an act of worship.' Four scenes were presented: in one of them 'it was a little curious at first to hear the laughter and noise of mocking boys echoing down the dark pillared spaces of the parish church'. But 'prejudice soon disappeared, conquered by the sheer simplicity and earnestness of the whole'. In the final scene of the Stigmata, 'a single pillar of the chancel stood out from the darkness like a shaft of light. The figure of the saint, in ecstasy, agonised at the base. A voice cried three times, "Francis". At each call a soft nimbus of light glowed about the sacred Figure above the altar. Francis submissively followed the gracious apparition of the Angel into the darkness. Each splendid pain of the Stigmata was signalled by a roll of thunder and a lightning flash that lit up the great east-window and the golden reredos.' And so on. The producer, Mr. E. Martin Browne, has been recently appointed to a post as director of dramatic work in connection with the diocese of Chichester. We may assume that the display in Brighton Parish Church is but the prelude to similar perfor-mances in other churches in the diocese, and that they will soon be regarded as integral features of Church 'life' throughout the Church of

England. We can well understand the enthusiastic approval which this development will receive in many quarters. But, for ourselves, we cannot regard such performances as 'acts of worship', and we cannot agree that they have any legitimate place within the walls of our churches. We have spoken of them as a 'development', and this they are in truth. The demand for 'ornate' services has prevailed for many years to change the simplicity and purity of common Prayer and Praise and the ministry of the Word and Sacraments into spectacular and sensuous ceremonial, a fit stepping-stone to the further advance which has now been staged in Brighton Parish Church. Passion plays, miracle plays and the like make their appeal to the emotions, but we believe that they have no warrant of Scripture and that their introduction as 'acts of worship' in our churches is a retrograde step and one which will prove to be detrimental to the true progress of the Gospel and the preparation of a people ready for the Lord's return.

I add a few notes on the methods used and the experience gained in this production. The stage was a platform stretching right across the head of the nave, the centre section dipping to allow of the altar remaining in view, and the side sections were approached from it up gentle slopes. Backstage, steps led up to these side stages, and a ramp led from the chancel on to the centre stage. Indications of place were given by pieces carried on and off by actors: a well in the town square for Act I, the arch of St Damian's, in pieces used by Francis and his helpers to rebuild it, for Act II (the 'mocking boys' were deriding the Saint's efforts). The birds in Act III were dancing children appearing in the open countryside, while one of the great pillars at the side of the stage made the background for the stigmata. These dispositions conformed to my belief that a church building should be used without altering or shutting off from view any essential, feature, and that this is not only an obligation on the director but an advantage to him. In this very large building I was able to capitalise fully on what Abe Feder and I had learned about lighting, and the impression made by a spotlit area in a great surrounding darkness. The music, too, written by Muriel Talbot Hodge who had composed for our Angmering *Tempest* and lived at Worthing, benefited by the placing of performers at different distances behind the stage. Monteverdi made use of such opportunities in St Mark's, Venice.

The St Francis play had been produced in mid-Lent, and Passiontide was very near. The Passion was far less often dramatised by parish groups than the Nativity, since the acting demands are much greater; so I toured *The Passion of Christ in the Soul of Man* by Margaret Cropper, a twenty-minute dramatic meditation for three actors, which could be fitted into a service. Edith Harley, who had been Henzie's colleague at the Everyman and now lived at Lindfield, joined Henzie and me to make the cast. I was also asked to take over direction of R. H. Benson's *The Upper Room* at Holy Trinity, Hastings, a centrally situated church which had ventured, on Good Friday of the previous year, to give two dramatic performances for the throngs of visitors, and had attracted large crowds. This was obviously a 'growth-point' at the eastern end of the diocese. Benson's play 'worked' but seemed very old-fashioned: it is written in the blank verse of the turn of the century, and centred on devotional ideas and symbols rather than on the actual happenings of Good Friday. Since the appearance of God or Jesus on stage was forbidden by the Lord Chamberlain and, though his writ did not run in church, was thought by many to be unfitting there also, the nearest one could get to Jesus was the tip of his cross passing outside the window. So for the next year, I substituted the

6   *The Marriage of St. Francis* (Henri Ghéon), Brighton Parish Church, 1931: St. Damian's arch. Photo: Pollard Crowther

mystical approach. Margaret Cropper, in *Christ Crucified*, set some historical scenes in the framework of an angel-chorus who, using the words of the Bible, linked the Old Testament expectation with the New Testament story. The angels witnessed Gethsemane and the Crucifixion, as do the agonised angels in the skies of Giotto's pictures.

Giotto's frescoes in the Arena Chapel at Padua had made an indelible impression on me, and the next venture was influenced by this. I had been studying the medieval Mystery Plays for some years and had already brought the Coventry and York Nativity Plays to production. I had worked also on the cycle wrongly called *Ludus Coventriae* and most probably belonging to Lincoln. It contains the legendary stories of the birth and early life of Mary, dramatising the exact scenes shown by Giotto. I conceived the idea of presenting these beautiful scripts in settings and costumes by Giotto as the Diocesan Players' summer show. The Annunciation play, which is the only one to contain the actual moment of the Conception, would be the final scene. *The Play of the Maid Mary* was first produced at Alfriston.

(Thirty years later, for St Mary's College, Notre Dame, Indiana, I made a full-length script called *The Mystery of Mary*, using the material which I had prepared for Alfriston as the first part. The second part began after the Conception, and included the more 'rugged' portions (as the Americans well use the word) such as the Trial by Ordeal of Joseph and Mary on the accusations of Slanderer and Backbiter, and Death's assault on Herod as he celebrates the massacre of the innocents, which bring the Mystery Plays down to the earth they sprang from. Simeon's vision in the Temple 'flashed forward' to the sword piercing Mary's soul at the Crucifixion, followed by Jesus' appearance to Mary (unique to this cycle) at the Resurrection.)

Alfriston church, built of squared flints in the form of a Greek cross, has been called 'the cathedral of the Downs'. We were lucky enough to find Alfred Clark, a fine character-actor from Henzie's Everyman days, living at Worthing, and got him to play Joachim to her Anna. And Mary Casson, Sybil's elder daughter who at Christmastide was the current Wendy, spent the summer with us to play Mary. I had bought for £60 an old Wolseley touring car, and built to fit into the back seat the little houses which Giotto depicts: so with the three of us in front and the costume-trunk on

7   *The Mystery of Mary*, scenes of Mary's birth and early life from
the Mystery cycle (Lincoln?), here produced at St Mary's
College, Notre Dame, Indiana, 1960

the luggage-rack, we toured the show. Visits to Brighton and
Horsham churches and to the Pier Pavilion at Worthing (which,
like the rest, was packed), culminated in two performances at
Chichester. In the afternoon, the scenes were set in the bishop's
garden, and there followed a service of thanksgiving in the cathedral for the first year's work.

The poetic quality of the fifteenth-century writing was a joy to all and a revelation to many; but some questioned the value, in the twentieth century, of reviving something so remote from 'real life'. If I had attempted to show 'real life' on the Sussex stages of the thirties as we show it today, people would have been deeply shocked; but it was right to demand that Christian drama should concern itself with contemporary affairs, and our next production focused on the first Disarmament Conference. This was announced for February 1932. Now that we have seen these discussions drag on for forty-five years, with an interval for a second and more devastating World War, we forget them most of the time or treat them with cynicism. But at the beginning there was a surge of hope: and I was determined that we should try to meet it with a play recalling the carnage of World War One, dramatising the Conference itself and stating its aim in Christian terms.

One morning, Henzie woke me: she had dreamt our play. I wrote desperately to set down what she told me before the memory faded. When it was done, we saw that we had a good scenario, and some bits of dialogue as well. Its protagonist was a young man, who had come through World War One but lost his memory, entering the church crying out for his friends. The Guide (shades of *Masses and Man*) shows him the war memorial: and this leads to flashback scenes of the war culminating in one between two dead soldiers, English and German, who talk to each other as they watch their women coming to their graves, try to speak to them and find they cannot hear (neither of us at that time knew Wilfred Owen's *Strange Meeting*). So to the hope of a better future; the Conference round the green table (the Jooss ballet's influence here) which becomes an altar of offering.

Who was to write it? An obvious opportunity for a poet. George Bell urged us to try Robert Nichols who was living at Winchelsea. I rang up and asked if we might come and see him. 'It's no use. My wife is leaving me tomorrow and I'm having a nervous breakdown.' Various other approaches followed with negative results: time was getting on. George had passed the scenario: Henzie must write it herself. *Disarm!* was completed in October with substantial help from Oliver Bell, who from the knowledge gained in his League of Nations post was able to summarise for Henzie the points of view of the various nations. Muriel Talbot Hodge was asked to write the very important music, a cast was assembled headed by W. Earle

Grey as the Man, performances were arranged in Brighton for the last week of January and in St Anne's, Soho during the opening week of the conference. As this coincided with the Church Assembly, the vicar, Basil Bourchier (brother of Arthur the actor, and quite as much an actor as he), succeeded in inviting a different bishop to each of the eight performances. These were followed by a Sunday night at the Duchess Theatre and two performances in Birmingham Town Hall.

In the summer, I was asked to provide a play for a Missionary 'Garden Meeting'. Remembering Sir Francis Younghusband, I chose *Sacrifice* by Rabindranath Tagore. A young temple servant gives his life to open the eyes of priest and people to the cruelty of the goddess they believe in, and to show them a better way. F. Yeats-Brown, the author of *Bengal Lancer*, was living at Rye, and helped me to make dress and behaviour authentic. It was a small but significant contribution to the reversal in our time of the rôle of missions. We showed it in several parts of the diocese.

8　*Disarm!* (Henzie Browne) in St Anne's, Soho, February 1932.
Photo: Pollard Crowther

All this varied experience continually pointed up, to the bishop as well as to myself, the need for good new writers. There was a plethora of poor ones, many producing not plays at all but opportunities for devotional dressing up. The long Puritan ascendancy had made good authors fearful, not only of the minuscule financial return (the clergy and other religious persons had a particular strong distaste for paying royalties), but also because they feared that any exercise of the imagination would be misunderstood or even attacked as blasphemous. But unless we got them, the revival of Religious Drama would peter out. Up to now, almost all the plays available, even those of quality, operated within the accepted framework: they were celebratory rather than exploratory. If our drama was to speak to our own time we must find fresh voices.

The bishop's concern about this was unceasing, and his contacts in the world of letters were wider than mine. He made a special

9   *The Acts of Saint Richard* (E. Werge-Oram), Chichester Cathedral, 1933

10 *The Acts of Saint Richard:* Death in the Doorway. Photo:
Malcolm McNeille

effort in a week-end conference at the palace in October 1932. Dr Jasper recalls that

He invited a number of prominent poets and dramatists. The company included Laurence Binyon, Lascelles Abercrombie, Charles Williams, Margaret Cropper, Geoffrey Whitworth, Mona Swann, Kenneth Ingram, and Martin Browne and his wife. The discussions covered a wide field, in particular the purpose of religious plays; the conditions and possibilities of their production in churches; the use of the Bible in drama, the relationship of religious drama to drama as a whole; and the approach of the modern poet to religious subjects. It was agreed that the Authorized Version of the Bible was especially suitable for text as well as subject of religious plays; that the Old Testament was notably rich in dramatic possibilities; and that authors must be allowed freedom of interpretation and treatment. With respect to plays written specifically for production in churches, they regarded the most appropriate form as the masque accompanied by music and ceremonial; but they felt that great reserve should be exercised in representing the Deity. Bell was delighted with the week-end, writing that 'our Religion and Drama conference went excellently'.

The author we had wanted most had been unable to come: but we had met him at an earlier week-end. In December 1930 Mrs Bell invited Henzie and me for the first of many visits. Her hospitality was warm and unfussy, and she was adept at noticing when young visitors needed a hint. The house (now split up for a variety of uses) is beautiful and restful. In the Early English chapel with its famous round Madonna, the bishop would speak with quiet conviction the words of the Book of Common Prayer while the five maidservants, who enjoyed the direction of his chaplain Colin Dunlop, would sing plainsong psalms and hymns. This regular simple worship was the core of their life.

Among the party of ten was T. S. Eliot. It had not escaped Bell's notice that in 1927, after a journey from a Unitarian upbringing through an ironic agnosticism, Eliot had been baptised into the Church of England. His interest in the drama had long been manifested not only in critical writings but in the recent 'fragments' called *Sweeney Agonistes*. It seemed to Bell that this small creation might be the forerunner of bigger things. Mrs Eliot, already becoming chronically ill, had excused herself; Eliot, as usual at this time, was a very silent guest. Henzie and I were somewhat awestruck by our surroundings. The party must have been heavy going for the host and hostess.

Meanwhile, the Religious Drama Society had been working hard to provide instruction, for producers and directors especially, and because of my new position I was at once enrolled. In December 1930 the British Drama League conducted with the RDS a five-day school at Bournemouth with Henzie and me heading the staff; in June 1931, another of the same length was held at Salisbury. In Sussex, we constantly did one-day courses in different parts of the diocese. By 1933 it was possible to give this study a specific objective, by devising a show in which a number of groups would each work with me, its peripatetic director, on one scene, the whole being brought together, round one or two central figures, for final rehearsals and performance. I agreed with the bishop and the dean (A. S. Duncan-Jones) that this play should celebrate the centenary of the Oxford Movement and its subject should be Saint Richard, the thirteenth-century bishop who is buried behind the high altar of Chichester Cathedral. I got E. Werge-Oram (the pen-name of two women-writers who had created a play on Rahere for St Bartholomew's, Smithfield) to script *The Acts of Saint Richard*, and design for it costumes of great beauty as well as historical accuracy. For once we had enough money to make them as full as they should be (so many costumes fail for lack of enough material). The play was an episodic biography of the Saint, using many of the medieval carol-tunes brought to light by Martin Shaw in the *Oxford Book of Carols*, of which I made constant use in my work. It ended with a procession of cast and audience, singing 'Jerusalem, my happy home' (in the full sixteenth-century translation from St Augustine), to the shrine in the cathedral where the dean said a dedicatory prayer and gave a blessing.

The *Guardian* paid tribute to the priest who took the part of Saint Richard: 'to his strength, his reverence, his humour and his entirely convincing and unsentimental loveableness'. His performance was the natural focus of a great gathering which showed the vitality the Church still had in the English countryside. The production was also to prove the starting-point of a development in a different area of her life – and of ours.

4
Beginning with T. S. Eliot

While I was preparing *The Acts of Saint Richard*, we were visited by the Reverend R. Webb-Odell. He had the colossal task of raising a 'Forty-Five Churches Fund' from which new parishes in the fast-expanding suburbs of London Diocese (that is, north of the Thames) could be provided with buildings and endowments. He decided that a major demonstration of the aims of the Fund must be given, and came to ask me to create a pageant. Fortunately, Webb-Odell himself had already ruled out this wearisome idea without realising it. He had engaged a theatre for two weeks in the spring of 1934. It was Sadler's Wells, which Lilian Baylis had recently reopened to duplicate in North London the work of the Old Vic. A passionately keen churchwoman, she was delighted to let the theatre to him at the end of her regular season. Immediately I heard this good news, I pointed out that a pageant in a theatre is impossible – you can't have processions, you can't have horses, you can't have large crowds, in fact all the necessary elements presuppose the outdoors, or an arena. We must find a form suitable to a theatre; it must have a voice, and that voice must be the voice of a poet. The voice I wanted was that of T. S. Eliot.

Since we met at George Bell's house in 1930 I had scarcely seen him, nor heard from him until just after Webb-Odell's visit, when he wrote to ask my opinion on the script of someone else's play. In replying, I said I wanted to see him 'on a definite matter', but – fortunately as it turned out – he was just off to Harvard and the meeting was postponed. By the time it finally took place, Webb-Odell had come to agree with my view, had convinced his committee, and had persuaded them to forgo the older-established poets to whom they first thought of turning and risk the 'difficult, modern' T. S. Eliot. I have told in detail the story of *The Making of T. S. Eliot's Plays* (Cambridge University Press 1969), and *The Rock* occupies Chapter One. Eliot and I met frequently from the time when he accepted the commission (September 1933), and friendship as well as collaboration steadily developed.

Meanwhile, I was becoming close to a poet of an older style and generation, Gordon Bottomley. I had seen a number of his plays as adjudicator, especially when I spent a snowy February working in and from Edinburgh. Bottomley had moved on from his earlier extensions of Shakespeare – *Gruach* (Lady Macbeth) and *King Lear's Wife*, which were seen in London – to concentrate on the Celtic legends and history of Scotland, like Yeats in Ireland. Like Yeats also, he was powerfully influenced by the Japanese Nō. His play *Ardvorlich's Wife*, produced by Duncan Clark of Falkirk, one of Bottomley's best interpreters, came before me in the 1932 festival, when I sent it on to win the Scottish final and the National Festival of Community Drama. Thus we had bonds of sympathy when we met that summer at the Scottish summer school at St Andrews. The quotations in what follows are from his letters to me.

He was a picturesque figure, like most of the pre-Raphaelites whom he so much loved, blue-eyed and bearded – Henzie was enthralled by the gesture with which the first and second fingers of his left hand parted his moustache from his beard to admit a spoonful of soup. His courtesy was as exquisite as his kindness, but he was as firm as he was kind. Suffering from lung-trouble which kept him in constant danger of haemorrhage, he yet managed to see a lot of plays, and to adjudicate regularly in Masefield's Verse-Speaking Festival at Oxford.

Later in 1932 I reviewed his volume of *Lyric Plays* for the *Scottish Stage*. He wrote (10 December 1932):

I could not elsewhere receive such valuable support as you can give, with the reputation you have made in Scotland as an understanding adjudicator of wide vision. And all this reputation you have put at the service of my book, my offering to the constitution of Scottish drama – and so unreservedly that the fight is going to be easier henceforward because of it, and poetry surer of its place on the stage being recognised again.

Poetry's place on the stage has had an importance for me parallel with that of religion. Eliot is regarded as the man who put it back there. Bottomley had no share in the results of Eliot's breakthrough; but he prepared the way for it, and helped me to prepare myself too. He was the Georgian poet who took most trouble to understand the practicalities of the stage and determinedly stood out for the kind of theatre which his work demanded. His book *A Stage for Poetry* (privately printed by Titus Wilson, Kendal, 1948) is an almost unknown treasure-house of thought and pictures on this subject.

His 'fight' is to 'relieve poetic drama from the present requirement of representing daily life'. He calls his *Lyric Plays* 'the new handful of my secular ceremonies'. He writes about the report of the Chichester conference:

I cordially accept the distinction drawn between 'ceremonial' and realistic plays and their functions. It takes one straight back to the Greek theatre, which was always a 'ritual' theatre with the idea of worship behind everything else – perhaps the only really religious theatre there has been yet. Which need not keep one from longing for another one.

So he was writing plays with a Chorus, consisting sometimes of the two or three Curtain-Folders already introduced by Yeats or else of speakers representing forces of nature: Snows, Winds, Waves, Trees.

The Chorus is *never* my chief character: it is *ever* my scenery. It also acts as a distancing device; for if it is involved in the story that is only with the detachment of natural forces or as the agent of memory.

Bottomley is deeply committed to 'the Oriental retrospective method' of telling a story:

it is one of my greatest assets – for it frees me to handle a large amount of subject-matter that has always been thought impossible in the European theatre . . . it makes one able to put poetry first all the time. (You can see how keen Shakespeare is to use it, though his convention did not foster it: look at the advantage it is to him in presenting the murder of Duncan and the death of Ophelia. He knew that narrative has a greater part in poetic drama than in realistic drama.) If one wants to present the action consistently and at first hand, poetry is an encumbrance and prose is *much* better.

In his letter of New Year's Day 1933 he tells me

a piece of news that I ought not to let you hear from anyone else. After a good deal of thought I have accepted an invitation from the Dean [*W. R. Matthews, afterwards of St Paul's*] and Chapter of Exeter to write a play on their patron, St Peter, for performance in the nave of the Cathedral daily during the Octocentenary celebrations in June. It will be in front of the Choir Screen, and there will be a stage of four levels. I shall be going to Exeter soon to see how and where the building will help me, before I let the play begin in my mind.

It was finished by April and he sent it to us to read. It was – and I think remains – a major achievement. It makes Peter a convincing central character without either glossing over his weakness or losing focus at Christ's Crucifixion, the climax which comes much too early in Peter's story. We corresponded in detail about it, and about the progress of the production which the author made sadly laughable:

There is a County Committee at Exeter which is settling the Festival programme. It has altered the time-table because there must be a Masonic service – which comes at (say) 6 o'clock on a day when my play is at 4 o'clock. The stage has to be taken down for that, which occupies half an hour. So I was asked to cut that much more out of my play. Then it appeared that another twenty minutes must be allowed for the Freemasons' processional assembling; and they want *that* much more off the play. Of course I am doing all they want: the producer assures me he means to give as much as 70 minutes to the play.

And so it went on:

I think I can say with confidence that there will be something to be seen at the performance if you honour me by coming all that way to see . . . but *what* it will be I have not very much idea.

When we had seen *The Acts of St. Peter,* he wrote:

Your indignant sympathy goes straight to my heart . . . I was rather expecting something of the sort, you know, and from the first I found myself wondering WHICH would happen, rather than WHAT . . . I can't claim any credit for 'meekness', when all the time one was wanting to sit down and laugh helplessly at the extent to which one's premonitions were coming true . . . Everybody, except the new Dean . . . was probably thinking of a side-show for a county function . . . Everyone says the play is going extraordinarily well: but I don't know where to.

Maimed as it was, the play proved its stature. And the very next week, another Bottomley play was shown near by, at Dartington Hall, Totnes, where the Elmhirsts, as part of their experiment in the re-creation and enrichment of English country life, had built – not yet a theatre, but a dance-school. Ellen Van Volkenberg, a well-known *avant-garde* American director, was putting on for Mrs Elmhirst's daughter, Beatrice Straight (already an American star), with a cast of dance-students excellently trained to add choral speech to their accomplished movement, *The Woman from the Voe.* This is Bottomley's Shetland version of the myth, universal among peoples who live close to nature, of the shifting frontier between human and animal life. Rona is both woman and seal; she has a human family and a chorus of seal-friends. The inevitable tragic choice is not only hers but her daughter's. The Dartington production reminded us of the expressionists – *Totenmal* returned in memory. It satisfied Bottomley, whose vision had been based more on historical records, but who had a wonderfully open mind and eye. (He was a competent draughtsman, and his quietly witty guardian–wife Emily was a good painter.)

I was determined that *St. Peter* should be done in London. Soundings had been taken for a theatre production, but the Old Vic, which would have been the only suitable (and probably the only interested) management, could not fit it in to a Charles Laughton season. So this was the chance for the Religious Drama Society, which sponsored the play under my direction in St Margaret's, Westminster.

'The first complete production' was given there on 21–4 March, five performances of the first play ever housed in the church of Parliament. Its acoustics are excellent, and allowed us to play fast enough to include all of the text that the author wanted. He uses a chorus of women worshippers as living curtains closing in upon the action and providing the bridge to the next scene. This was done by Marjorie Gullan's London Verse-Speaking Choir, a group of poetry lovers rather than actresses, but trained by a fine teacher to instinctive unity and a wide range of vocal expression. Some of the best moments were theirs, especially in creating the Crucifixion 'by poetry alone'. Bottomley begins with what he describes as 'a dead march, with three strong beats in each line, like a knell tolling.' The next section, in contrast to this and to the hammer-blows offstage, is in long lines of five stresses:

> Along the long street
> Now, now He comes:
> Men's pulses beat
> Like deep quiet drums . . .
>
> Up the hard hill
> They drive Him now
> The men ready to kill
> Wait on the brow.
>
> *On Calvary. Four deliberate blows are heard, as of a heavy hammer*
>
> He has power in Heaven and earth, and they take away His clothing:

He does not lift His eyelids, lest He should look and be known.
If He should look, their minds would fail them and become
nothing;
And the evil that they must do would never then be done.

They wounded His right hand first; they have torn His left hand
now.
He is white and clean and they injure Him with dirty hands.
They have barely begun, and His life from His hands begins to
flow . . .

A SINGLE VOICE
O, Pitiful Friend, pity them: none of them understands.

None of them understands what Life could flow from these
fingers;
Or whither these feet would lead them if they could get free.
They are fastened with a nail; and the man who drove it lingers
To see if it will hold when they raise up the rootless Tree.

*A single hammer-blow then a long shout 'Hai!' as of sailors hauling on a
rope, followed after an instant by a long falling sick sigh.*

A VOICE
Now get down from the cross and save Yourself!

ANOTHER VOICE
He saved others: He cannot save Himself!

The two lines shouted offstage by the soldiers are typical of the
verse in the dialogue scenes. Bottomley keeps it firm and easily
speakable by the prevalence of 'end-stopped' lines and by the use of
the stress as an *impetus*. I have found, in a long and varied
experience of the speaking of verse on stage, that this is the greatest
help to an actor. If the stress is the motive force of the syllables that
follow, the speech has the character's vitality. Here is a passage
from the scene of Peter's denial in the High Priest's house:

THIRD WOMAN
entering with a faggot for the fire and throwing it down near Peter
There's for your fire, my man: look after it . . .
But who are you – you are not one of us?
Have you come here with Jesus? I believe you have.
What is the smear on your hand? Are you the man
Who cut off my cousin's ear when Jesus was caught?
I heard of it only now . . . And Jesus healed him!
Aha, no one would catch me healing an enemy.
You are certainly one of them.

PETER
Whom do you mean, woman? I have not seen Him . . .

FIRST MAN-AT-ARMS
Do you hear a foolish cock?
It has seen a lantern and believes it is sunrise.

SECOND MAN-AT-ARMS
How can a cock be wise with that size of a brain-pan?

I had become able to undertake jobs of this magnitude outside Sussex because I had drawn upon the best of my associates there to set up a Diocesan Drama Council with regional workers. Most of the short courses and advisory work in the parishes was done by experienced volunteers in their own neighbourhoods. One of them, Wyn Bruce Williams of Crowborough, who played in the London *St. Peter*, was ready to take over my job when I left, and carried it on well until 1939. The Council was revived after the war and is still in existence as a branch of the Religious Drama Society.

By the end of March the London pageant-play had been entitled *The Rock*, and both script and production plans were far advanced. Eliot and Webb-Odell had accepted my scenario at the end of November. It centred upon an outcrop of living rock (suggested by that in the War Memorial Chapel in Edinburgh Castle) centre-stage, on and around which a group of workmen were building the sanctuary of a new (1934) church. On this rocky eminence also appeared the Rock and his attendant group of chorus-speakers male and female, who related the Church of today to the eternal. 'In every moment of time you live where two worlds cross,' they said, and the modern builders found themselves involved in a free movement of time from the far past of Mellitus (first Bishop of London, 602) or even the Old Testament Nehemiah, to the more recent past of Bishop Blomfield who built two hundred Victorian churches (he overdid it, as we now see) and to the present of an Agitator, Redshirts, Blackshirts and a Plutocrat.

Eliot was called upon to write 'the words' (as he said) for all these groups. Already on 7 December he sent me the draft for the workmen's first scene. This group gave him the most trouble, because its leading actor, an Old Bensonian turned East End vicar, insisted on re-writing Eliot's cockney into a cockney of his own. The latter appears in the published text, with Eliot's admirably phrased disclaimer:

11 *The Rock* (T. S. Eliot), Sadlers Wells Theatre, 1934, designed
by Stella Mary (Pearce) Newton. Craftsmen decorating the
newly built sanctuary. Photo: Pollard Crowther

The Rev. Vincent Howson has so completely rewritten, amplified and
condensed the dialogue between himself ['Bert'] and his mates, that he
deserves the title of joint author.

A sample of Eliot's original script for these scenes is printed in my
book, and the whole may be studied in the Bodleian Library. The
comparison shows Eliot as the better workman. But the exper-

ienced actor was indispensable to us. This was one of many frustrations which Eliot accepted for the sake of seeing for himself how a stage production comes to life.

I had introduced scenes of past and present history, not in chronological sequence, but as the arguments or difficulties of the modern workmen evoked them. Those of the past were parallels; those of the present showed forces now engaging the Church. The most effective scene was Eliot's own invention. It was to fill that danger-spot in 'revue' – as both *The Daily Telegraph* and the *Morning Post* rightly called *The Rock* – the finale of the first half, which Noël Coward says 'should essentially be the high spot of the evening'. It presents in satirically varied verse-forms the warring ideologies of the thirties: communists, fascists, and the materialists of big business. The Redshirts' *vers libre*:

> Our verse
> Is free
> As the wind on the steppes
> As love in the heart of the factory worker
> Thousands and thousands of steppes
> Millions and millions of workers
>   all working
>   all loving . . .

and the Blackshirts' jingle:

> We come as a boon and a blessing to all
> Though we'd rather appear in the Albert Hall.
> Our methods are new in this land of the free
> We make the deaf hear and we make the blind see.
> We're law-keeping fellows who make our own laws –

are answered by the Plutocrat in establishment blank verse:

> I have a great respect for Mother Church –
> She is the bulwark of society,
> The great maintainer of stability –
> Her ceremonies, too, are very fine . . .

and he presents the materialist solution:

> I have had a little image cast,
> And I must say, you'll find it very neat,
> Something, I'm sure, that all of you will like –
> It looks like Gold, but its real name is POWER.

> *All struggle for and dismember the Golden Calf as they rush out. Suddenly The Rock is discovered standing brooding on the pinnacle.*

> I have known two worlds, I have known two worlds of death.
> All that you suffer, I have suffered before,
> And suffer always, even to the end of the world.

It was in the Rock and his Chorus that Eliot had scope: the stage time allotted to them totalled forty minutes. While Eliot allowed the rest of his script, as purely a *pièce d'occasion*, to go out of print, he preserved the choruses in his *Collected Poems*. The choral writing inaugurated a new style which Eliot developed in *Murder in the Cathedral*. It owes little to the Greek chorus, still less to the abstract Nō: it is inspired rather by the Hebrew prophets, whose direct address it adopts, whether in scathing denunciation or earnest exhortation of the people of God, or in prayer or praise to God himself. The versification also recalls the Hebraic parallelism:

> Why should men love the Church? Why should they love her laws?
> She tells them of Life and Death, and of all that they would forget.
> She is tender where they would be hard, and hard where they like to be soft.
> She tells them of Evil and Sin, and other unpleasant facts.

One chorus begins:

> The Word of the Lord came unto me, saying:

and another:

> Son of Man, behold with thine eyes, and hear with thine ears.
> And set thine heart upon all that I show thee.

The last chorus, and the most carefully wrought – having met all my other deadlines, Eliot asked for six weeks to perfect this – is inspired by the *Gloria in excelsis* of the Christian liturgy.

But all this depended for success on its executants. If I had not known where to look for speakers equal to the task of delivering Eliot's verse I would not have urged him to write it. Elsie Fogerty's Central School of Speech and Drama had for nearly thirty years supplied both stage and classroom with a stream of finely trained actors and teachers, which still flows as strongly from it today. I knew that, in her care and that of her colleague and successor Gwynneth Thurburn, Eliot's choruses would be heard in their full power and range of sound and meaning.

Their chosen group of students, seven men and ten women, had a task quite different from the *St. Peter* chorus. They had to act with their voices. Eliot's verse had an immediacy which demanded choral *speaking*, based on the actual speech-patterns in use when he wrote. I asked Miss Thurburn to recall for me how she and Miss Fogerty approached the task he had set them:

Voices were chosen for ability to blend and also to contrast sharply when necessary. No voice was ever forced out of its natural range, but adaptations of quality *were* expected. In general, deeper-toned voices were used as bass or background and lighter voices for a treble effect. Those with special characteristics or tonal quality were used for individual lines, words or passages.

The effect of 'orchestration' was sparingly used and the analogy with instruments never pressed far. The 'orchestral' effect of the human voice stems from personal and individual harmonic qualities rather than the difference in *kind* as between, e.g., strings and wind in an orchestra. A certain voice may have an 'edge' which makes it appropriate to a particular idea, or to cut across another voice. This kind of contrast is balanced with the use of voices which blend in tone, producing a concerted effect.

To 'build', one may first use a single voice and add one, two, three or more. This can be done with either men's or women's voices, or both if a big cumulative effect is needed.

To illustrate her points, I asked Miss Thurburn to indicate how some of the lines were distributed and delivered:

CHORUS VI (*Collected Poems*)
[*steady tempo, not too quick*]

TUTTI
It is hard for those who have never known persecution,
And who have never known a Christian
To believe these tales of Christian persecution

TWO MEN
It is hard for those who live near a Bank
To doubt the security of their money.

TWO WOMEN
It is hard for those who live near a Police Station
To believe in the triumph of violence. [*gradually faster*]

ALL WOMEN
Do you think that the Faith has conquered the World
And that lions no longer need keepers?

ALL MEN
Do you need to be told that whatever has been can still be?

WOMAN LEADER
Do you need to be told that even such modest attainments
[*slightly scornful*]
As you can boast in the way of polite society

+ 1 WOMAN
Will hardly survive the Faith to which they owe their
significance?

ALL WOMEN
Men! polish your teeth on rising and retiring: [*peremptory*]

ALL MEN
Women! polish your fingernails: [*clash*]

TUTTI [*suddenly merging*]
Your polish the tooth of the dog and the talon of the cat.

The most difficult thing with any chorus (she concludes) is to get
all its members to *think together*.

My job in setting up the spectacular scenes was a much bigger
one than in *St. Richard*. There were fifteen groups each from a

12   The Rock and his Chorus. Photo: Pollard Crowther

different parish in a semicircle of twenty miles' radius. Each one
had a local director, with whom I cast the parts and blocked the
movements; and I visited each periodically to check and encourage
its progress. The actors, who could not envisage the final result,
found it hard to sustain enthusiasm for their small parts. But few of
them were capable of more: the acting of the scenes was on a low
level, and the show was sustained by the choruses, the little group
of workmen (one ex-professional, three university actors), and by
the work of the two gifted artists who collaborated with Eliot and
me.

Martin Shaw wrote the music, the first of two jobs we joyfully
did together. He was like Ghéon, an artist who wanted to make
ordinary people do extraordinary things; and he was willing to
accept the limitations of amateurs so long as their hearts were in
the work, to pour out upon them his seemingly inexhaustible flow
of melody, and to galvanise them with his own vitality. He was
extremely well organised, and would take my detailed notes for the
dumb-show of each scene, tailor the music to fit the actions, and
demonstrate it to the local pianist and director. The notices testify
to the appropriateness and beauty of the result. The music had its
best opportunity in the one scene of pure mime when the craftsmen
adorn the sanctuary of the new church. This was directed by
Doreen Woodcock, who was on the staff with us at St Andrews.

From the same association came the designer, Stella Mary
Pearce. I asked her to create a visual unity by giving each scene its
own colour-scheme and building these up to a final display of the
whole spectrum, thus expressing in visual terms the theme which
Eliot put into words. She achieved this with costumes made under
her direction by the amateur groups, whose very ignorance perhaps
made it easier for her to get them to follow her designs. Those who
were accustomed to 'historical costume' in Wardour Street terms
might have found it harder to go along with her bold formalisation
and symbolism. The groups met her challenges because she told
them exactly what she wanted and how to do it, including the
making of wigs and the use of special make-up to match certain
colour-schemes. Of many striking effects the best remembered was
the dressing of the craftsmen in every shade of white. Eric Newton,
whom Stella married during the preparatory period, designed the
sanctuary which they decorated, the huge archangels which they
painted on its walls, and the rock on which the altar finally stood.

This was earlier occupied by the figure of the Rock and his Chorus, whom Stella dressed in stone-like robes of stiff hessian. The severity of this costuming did not stop the audience laughing at Eliot's satirical sallies, while it gave the appropriate power to the prophetic utterances.

The first night, 28 May, arrived, the audience came, Eliot was recognised by *The Times* as having 'created a new thing in the theatre'. After the last night we supped with the Newtons in their mews flat and drove home to Rottingdean in the dawn.

By this time we had moved from our house on the cliff (which its owner wanted back) to one at the top of Rottingdean village. It was on a road that led straight up onto the Downs. This was like coming home. The chalk downs had always exerted a pull on both our hearts, and indeed they were joined on one – we got engaged on High Down, Angmering, in August 1924. This summer was to be our only one in Rottingdean, and we took full advantage of it – many picnics with the boys, who were at a little day school in the village, many bathes from the as-yet-not-too-crowded beach, many walks including some visits to Glyndebourne, a few miles across the downs, where John Christie (who had taught me elementary science at Eton) was launching the Opera with that first, magical *Figaro*.

In the autumn I was approached from York by Seebohm Rowntree. He was chairman of the Citizens' Theatre Trust which was buying the Theatre Royal. This famous house had received its Royal Patent in the eighteenth century, when it had been the centre of theatrical life in the north under Tate Wilkinson. In the nineteenth century it was extensively rebuilt, and flourished until, with the advent of the 'talkies', it fell on evil days and was threatened with demolition. The Trust was formed to save it, but was then faced with the task of running it. A Civic Theatre was a new and strange idea; shocking, too, to some people whose puritanism still made acting smell of brimstone, and certainly not to be supported out of the rates paid by canny Yorkshiremen. There were experienced businessmen on the Trust, to be sure, but none who had any part in the theatre's management (which in recent years had not been of the best). The only strength lay in the considerable band of amateurs who had kept on doing good plays which the professional theatre had failed to provide.

John Hughes was the prime mover in this. While I was at the

MAY 28th—JUNE 9th, 1934.

SADLERS WELLS THEATRE

13   Programme cover by Eric Newton. Reproduced by permission of Stella Mary Newton

settlement ten years before, he had founded the York Settlement Community Players, and I had directed one or two of their early efforts. He concentrated on basic training, especially in speech, and carried with him in this regular study some actors of very fine quality, the men quite as good as the women. They had become one of the leading companies of the north, recruiting also dress-makers and property-makers and building up a good wardrobe. Other groups in the city were stirred to emulation. All this gave the Trustees the idea of a week's production in the Theatre by the combined amateurs: and I was asked to direct *The Rose Without a Thorn*, Clifford Bax's romantic play about Katharine Howard. I chose John's daughter, Barbara, to play her, with Leonard Picker-ing as Henry VIII. The show was very successful, and led to the confirmation of an offer which had already been provisionally made, that I should be the first director of the professional company to be formed at the Theatre Royal in the new year.

Looking back on it, I see my appointment as a mistake and the result as a near-disaster. I had almost none of the experience required. I had done a few professional productions under the care of experienced managers who had found actors for me and were running their theatres as going concerns. In York there was a vacuum: a stage stripped bare to the walls, a company and staff to find, the whole machinery of management to be re-created. The Trust, notwithstanding its high ideals, had to face a sceptical public (and no city has one more difficult to convince). Seebohm Rowntree, becoming aware of all this, seized upon Roy Langford who, he realised at a first chance meeting, had the 'know-how'. He was running the pantomimes at Golders Green and Streatham, two large suburban theatres under the same management. So Langford and I were to create the York season together.

We each contributed our quota to the company: mine included Christopher Casson (Sybil and Lewis' younger son), Guy Spaull, Henzie, Edith Harley, Hal Burton (later of BBC/TV fame) as young actor and designer; Langford's was headed by Robert Morley, even at 27 not one to suffer inexperience gladly. From the first day it was evident that the two groups were not going to 'jell' and that I was out of my depth opposite Langford. The first two plays, *The Queen's Husband* (Robert Sherwood's milder *Apple Cart*) and Noël Coward's *Fallen Angels*, were fairly well received: but I could see the Civic venture being wrecked before long if the deep rift continued. I gave a month's notice, to leave Langford in possession of the field. Rowntree was relieved and grateful. I was relieved too and glad that the next week's play was one of high quality, *Wings Over Europe* which we had seen in Pittsburgh, with Christopher Casson giving an inspired performance as the Shelley-like young scientist. Leaving York, to which we had become still more deeply attached, was painful, as was the acute uncertainty about both our own future and that of the Civic Theatre. The latter was shortly resolved by the Trustees calling in a more experienced management from Coventry, where a good rep. had been running for some years, with Anthony John as a director who knew these ropes; and though the intervening period has never been free of anxiety, I was happy in 1975 to take part in celebrating forty years of Civic Theatre.

Our own future looked bleak when we left York on 22 March. Neither of us had a job, and with one son already at boarding-school, we had very little money. Having no home, we must for the moment depend on the hospitality of relations. There was only one thing in prospect, the production, for a fee of £60, of a play for the Canterbury Festival.

5

Canterbury: the first *Murder*

The Canterbury Festival of Music and Drama had been the creation of – need I name him? – George Bell. When one considers how much he achieved, it is hard to believe that Bell was dean for only five years. I first visited Canterbury in 1920, and I remember its cheerlessness. It cost sixpence to go into each part of the building then, only the nave being open. Notices said 'Do not touch' and 'No admittance'. One entered The Precincts through a grubby Tudor gateway with a truncated top. There was no colour outside the cathedral or inside.

By 1925, within a year of Bell's arrival, the attitude had changed from negative to positive. Every feature in the cathedral bore a notice identifying and explaining it, and suggesting an intention for prayer in relation to it. Every visitor was admitted free to all parts except the crypt and Bell Harry Tower. An altar stood once more at the head of the nave, and as the process of restoration, which in all great buildings is continuous, was carried on under Bell, brightness and colour began to reappear.

Late in 1926, Bell conceived a new idea, the Friends of Canterbury Cathedral. Bell saw them as 'a body of supporters who are prepared to take some share in caring for it and in preserving it for posterity'. A few months after their inauguration the Friends acquired a new (voluntary) executive officer. At their 1929 annual gathering they discovered that the festival manager and their steward and treasurer were one and the same person, Margaret Babington.

There are certain 'characters' who remain lovingly etched on one's memory. She, like Miss Fogerty, was one of those – the opposite in shape but the same in quality. She was tall and very, very slim, correct in her behaviour as a vicar's daughter – but one who had in fact run his large parish of Tenterden in west Kent for him for seventeen years. Now retired with him to the cathedral precincts at 45, her energy must have been bursting its domestic bonds when George Bell called her to serve the cathedral. Such an object for her love and care fulfilled her completely; and when one of the cathedral craftsmen told an enquiring stranger, on the day of her burial in the Cloister Garth, 'she gave her whole life for the cathedral', he was speaking the literal truth. She gave it, not passively, but in ceaseless activity: persuading, cajoling even bullying the cathedral's friends (small 'f' as well as big) and guardians to support its repair and beautification. At my first Festival, 1935, Christ Church Gateway was blazing with heraldic colour, and at the Annual Gathering she announced the gift of money to restore its turrets, which were duly in place for dedication the next year.

Perhaps I make her sound (again like Miss Fogerty) a formidable person; and so she was in one sense – nothing would stop her. But other facets of her character were quite the opposite. Henzie used to recall her voice on the telephone: 'It's Margaret speaking,' what teenager called Margaret did we know? Her enjoyment of life and of people was always young, and her humour twinkled and bubbled. Canterbury's most familiar picture of her is mounted on a bicycle very tall and upright like herself. Henzie once saw her ride through The Precincts, down the ramp provided for wheelchairs into the cloisters to the door of the Chapter House, where in what seemed a single movement the bicycle was parked and the steward seated at her box-office table assuring a distinguished visitor that he would find his seats reserved at the front. Bell continued to act as the moving spirit of the Canterbury Festival, the much valued power behind Miss Babington's throne. He had kept the £800 surplus from *The Coming of Christ* as a fund for commissioning authors. His local ally was Laurence Irving, grandson of the great actor, and a fine designer who lived at Whitstable. It was these two, after Bell had satisfied himself by seeing *The Rock* that his 'hunch' of 1930 had been correct, who invited Eliot to write the first new play for the Festival.

Irving says that, in accepting, Eliot stipulated that I should direct, and I had evidently agreed to do so. How this was to be squared with the job I undertook at York I do not seem to have determined. Clashes of this kind constantly threaten a life so uncertain as that of a worker in the theatre, and can only be resolved when they actually occur. This one, of course, actually didn't. Meanwhile, Eliot and I were working on the play by correspondence: the letters are all in the Second Impression of *The Making of T. S. Eliot's Plays.*

I asked Robert Speaight to play Becket. We had not worked together since Angmering 1924, but we had remained friends and I had seen many of his performances – at Oxford as the Player King, Peer Gynt and Falstaff, as Hibbert in the long run of *Journey's End*, at the Old Vic as King John, Fluellen, Cassius and Hamlet. He had not the stature of Becket, who was over six feet tall, and he was 31 to the martyr's 52. But he had the understanding and the voice for Eliot's play.

The 'Canterbury Festival Players', gathered during the previous five years, were to fill the other male parts. There were two good ones. William Stevens was a roistering First Tempter and led the Knights as Fitz Urse. Philip Hollingworth was the baronial Third and the 'youngest member' of the Knights. For the Second, I was allowed one more professional and engaged Frank Napier, who proved a blessing to every Festival up to the war.

The Chapter House, despite the historic series of productions it housed, is a building for which I have no affection. Its reverberant acoustic makes speaking a misery, and its platform stage was thirty-six feet wide by only nine feet deep. At the stage front, a flight of steps led down to the centre aisle, ninety feet long, which was the only way in or out of the building. Stage lighting is rendered almost useless by the huge windows.

For the Chorus, we naturally turned to the Central School; but because of exams the Women could only come to Canterbury for two rehearsals. Miss Fogerty spent the first in coping with the nightmare acoustic (she left a vivid account of this, see Marion Cole's *Fogie*, pp. 165–6). The dress rehearsal was the only full one. It was also the only one which Eliot attended. Fortunately he seemed to agree with my treatment of the play. Since I was playing the Fourth Tempter as well as directing, I couldn't have changed it much at that stage.

He had already consented, as reluctantly as I, to cruel cuts in the script, necessitated by Miss Babington's over-tight schedule (shades of Exeter!). Mercifully this did not vitiate the critical response.

14 *Murder in the Cathedral* (T. S. Eliot), first production in the Chapter House, Canterbury, 1935. Robert Speaight as Becket with the women of Canterbury. Designed by Stella Mary Newton. Photo by permission of Fisk-Moore Studios Ltd

One hadn't listened two minutes before one felt that one was witnessing a play which had the quality of greatness.

Conrad Aiken (*Collected Criticism*, Meridian Books, New York 1958) took a bigger leap than any of the English critics, but most of them perceived that Eliot had broken through the tradition of historical drama to re-establish the oldest kind of play in the newest kind of writing.

Because we had had to prepare it piecemeal, none of us realised how epoch-making was the work we staged on 15 June 1935, and after eight performances the run of *Murder in the Cathedral* was over. No masterpiece, I suppose, was ever born more privately. To the theatre as it then was, the play was a non-event. No manager came, or even sent a scout. The notices meant nothing because the

Festival and its play were 'religious'. The only English theatre-man interested was Ashley Dukes, owner of the tiny Mercury in Notting Hill Gate.

Ashley was the embodiment of civilised man: fluent in the main European languages, a writer of elegant prose and shapely plays, a connoisseur of wine – the Garrick Club cellar was for years under his management – of food and of all the arts, including ballet to which, in the person of Marie Rambert, he was married. He was the English editor of *Theatre Arts* and a close friend of Edith Isaacs. No one less like the commercial theatre manager could well be imagined; but he had a shrewd business sense, and kept the shoestring budget of the Mercury balanced.

Out of the proceeds of his most successful play. *The Man with a Load of Mischief*, Ashley and 'Mim' bought the school-building of a church in Ladbroke Road. It had two large rooms of equal size. One was the ballet studio, with flat floor and barres round the walls; the other was raked for 136 seats and had a stage eleven feet deep behind the low proscenium, but with quite a large projecting 'apron'. Mim's Ballet Club played Sunday nights; and in the week, Ashley began to produce poets' plays. In the early months of 1935, he had been talking with Rupert Doone of the Group Theatre about a season of Yeats and Eliot, possibly to include the latter's new play. Ashley came to see it at Canterbury and bought the professional production rights. What that could mean we had no idea, and in fact I don't think we took it very seriously. While I taught at Miss Fogerty's Stratford summer school, however, we saw something of Tom Eliot who was staying at Chipping Campden, and it became gradually clear that Ashley did mean to do *Murder*, with me to direct it, in the autumn.

After Miss Fogerty's, I taught at another summer school in Dublin for May Carey. She was a Yorkshire woman, a good character-actress, who was married to the head of the Eire customs and had three sons. One of them, Denis, joined Bobbie Speaight (who happened to be in Dublin) and me in a reading of extracts from *Murder* on a Sunday night at the Abbey Theatre. Denis played small parts there, rehearsing at lunch-time or after his work in the offices of Wills' cigarette firm. I got back to London on 1 October, and found that Ashley planned to open *Murder* on 1 November. All Saints' Day was extremely appropriate, but also extremely close!

I set about assembling a professional cast. With so tiny a theatre, salaries would be absolutely minimal – I forget whether there was yet an Equity minimum, but I am sure that if so, all the men except Bobbie were on it at a salary of £3 a week. Guy Spaull came as First Tempter and Knight; Frank Napier moved over to Third Priest (who has the great apostrophe to the departing Knights) and was replaced as Second Tempter and Knight by Gerik Schjelderup, a tall Nordic figure: he was both actor and painter, and after his long association with *Murder* came to an end, opted for the other art. In looking for the prescribed 'youngest member' at number three, I happened upon an older actor, Norman Chidgey, who seemed so exactly right in every other way that I engaged him and persuaded the author to change the word to 'eldest' – in which form it appears in all editions after the first. For the First Priest, I brought Alfred Clark, who had once been with us in Sussex, out of retirement. His amused wisdom contrasted well with Frank's ascetic intensity and the eager immaturity of the Second Priest, Charles Petry, straight out of the Central School.

This was the first time I had directed a new production with a wholly professional cast. I had advantages in knowing some of them already, and in the fact that this play was new in kind, so that we were exploring fresh territory together. For an actor, who is preparing for an exposure to the public which leaves him feeling just as naked whether (as now) he takes his clothes off or keeps them on, this excursion is always frightening. I tried to be a good guide, and will now try to describe some of the features of the journey.

The Tempters and Knights, played by the same actors, posed the knottiest problems. Is the Tempter in Thomas' mind? a reflection of himself at some stage in his development? This isn't true – or at least isn't the whole truth – of the first three, for each speaks to Thomas as a person other than himself. The First is a boon-companion of his youth, the Second a 'collaborating' politician, the Third an unexpected visitor from the country. Yet Thomas' mind calls them up; and the actor must keep his interpretation within that compass. We found that each part needed playing for type, not for historical period. Stella Mary Pearce helped each actor to find his Tempter's immediacy by incorporating in each costume a twentieth-century indication: a top hat for the 'man about town', medals for the diplomat, 'plus-fours' for the country squire. These, and the spiky verse, with

15 *Murder in the Cathedral:* design for Tempters: the ground is a clear yellow. Reproduced by permission of Stella Mary Newton

the 'dark generality' in which all three of these characters 'wrap their meaning', suggest to the actor the style for his performance.

As always with Eliot who, as I early discovered, heard rather than saw his plays when writing them, the visual variety which an audience needs had to be evolved with the actors. Its form was different, therefore, with each cast and particularly with each Becket. Robert Speaight, whose gifts of voice excelled those of movement, liked to play these scenes sitting in the Archbishop's chair and letting the Tempters circle around him. This arrangement reinforced the impression that they were in his mind, and that, as Eliot says in a letter to me (5 March 1935), 'what is offered is a memory of temptation: everything offered is what Thomas has ALREADY thought about'.

Later Beckets were more inclined to move. But one question had in either case to be answered: does Becket at any point meet the eyes of each Tempter? Nearly all the actors who played them wanted him to. We tried it: but Becket's experience is better unified if the nearest he ever comes is to looking at an object the Tempter holds – the scroll of office in the Second Tempter's hand, for instance.

With the Fourth Tempter it is different. He has no roots in the world outside Thomas' mind, as the others have; he is 'only here, Thomas, to tell you what you know', to bring the deeper levels of Thomas' present desire up into consciousness. This deeper disturbance motivates movement, and eventually at Thomas' 'No' a confrontation. Speaight and I played it so that, as Becket turned away in horror from the vision of vengeful glory he was forced to look into the eyes of that other self who had lured him to it: 'Who are you, tempting with my own desires?'

The Knights, up to the murder, are straightforward, impersonal toughs: although their names are in all the history books Eliot lists them only as First, Second, Third Knight. But suddenly after the murder they abandon their gangster grouping (with their doggerel verse and the helmets behind whose nose-pieces they have hidden their personalities), and emerge as individuals putting forward, in colloquial prose, their various points of view. We worked out more and more closely the correspondence of each one's approach to that of the Tempter he had played:

> THIRD TEMPTER:
> It is our country. We care for the country.

16 *Murder in the Cathedral:* design for Chorus: two greens, with
appliqué of deep red and blue. Reproduced by permission of
Stella Mary Newton

THIRD KNIGHT:
We are four plain Englishmen who put our country first.

SECOND TEMPTER:
To set down the great, protect the poor,
Beneath the throne of God can man do more?

SECOND KNIGHT:
Had Becket concurred with the King's wishes, we should have
had an almost ideal state.

This fed each of the actor's parts from the other, and restrained the
constant and natural tendency to play the 'Knights' Meeting' for
laughs.

The Priests, like an earlier and larger group of disciples, are
depressingly craven when the test comes and the actors have to
give way to this panic. But in their earlier scenes each has the
chance to establish an individual personality. Though they too are
numbered One, Two, Three, they are very different people. One is
the cautious, worldly-wise ecclesiastic who, seeing Thomas as
'always isolated . . . always insecure', fears for him – and likes roast
pork. Two is the young housekeeper, aggressively loyal, male-
oriented. Three is the seer – the first character to speak of the
wheel, which for Thomas (as for Eliot) has the still centre about
which all revolves. Even more disillusioned than One about 'the art
of temporal government', he is in the end the prophet of the
murderers' doom. With the cocky, know-all Messenger, the actors
have scope for a quartet of good cameos.

A month after the opening, the young priest, Charles Petry,
collapsed on stage. In this emergency I thought of Denis Carey. It
was a wild idea to yank a man out of a safe job and bring him
across the Irish Sea to earn a pittance in a small part in a 'fringe'
theatre. But Denis had spoken to me of his great desire to become a
professional actor: he would take the risk of giving up his job if he
could start with a prospect of several months' work. *Murder* was a
success and he knew the play. Well, I would offer him the part. I
rang up Dublin (then an adventure in itself) that night. The next
night he was on the boat, and after a day's rehearsal he went into
the play, with which he was to be almost continuously connected
for seven years.

Murder reached its hundredth performance at the Mercury on 25
February 1936, and seemed set for an indefinite run. But Ashley
Dukes was determined to show it in the university cities, and took it

off on 16 May in order to visit Oxford (the old Playhouse), Cambridge (the Arts) and Dublin (the Gate). Meanwhile, plans were far advanced for the next Canterbury Festival. Miss Babington had asked me to suggest an author, and my first choice was Charles Williams. When I took him to Canterbury, she said 'Mr Williams, I have one request to make. So far, every Festival hero has been carried out dead from the Chapter House: could you choose one who needn't be?' Charles did not hesitate for a moment: 'Cranmer: he ran to his death.'

Thomas Cranmer of Canterbury was the result, and to me it is almost as precious as *Murder*. It has been little appreciated, and has never been performed again in Britain except by a few amateur groups. In America, I did a very successful student production (1960) but an attempt to get it staged professionally came to nothing. It is a work so profoundly and adventurously Christian that its chances have progressively declined in recent years. I suppose anything that followed *Murder* would have suffered a severe handicap: but I should like to try to redress this balance by writing about *Cranmer* in some detail.

The author himself deserves a critical biography to enlarge upon Alice Mary Hadfield's excellent *Introduction to Charles Williams* (Robert Hale 1959). My first memory of him is an evening lecture on Milton given in a bare schoolroom I don't know where or when, at which a very spare, short-sighted man read with a Cockney accent *Of Man's First Disobedience* and set the room aflame. I have never met any human being in whom the divisions between body and spirit, natural and supernatural, temporal and eternal were so non-existent, nor any writer who so consistently took their non-existence for granted.

Cranmer was to be his subject, a weak man in contrast to the strength of Becket, but a man on whom worked just as powerfully what Speaight has called 'the initiatives of grace'. It was those initiatives which Charles Williams was dramatising, and indeed embodying in a figure called the Skeleton. The play was to be at once a biography, starting with Cranmer as a contented don at Cambridge and ending with his race to the stake, and a contest with this spiritual antagonist to reach 'honesty, the point where only the blessed live'. It was to be a political unfolding of the essential issues of the Reformation, and a personal unfrocking of Cranmer's body and mind to reveal him to himself.

Williams delighted in ambiguity, because it expressed truth. Not only are human motives never simple, never single, but the divine plan, being creative, is ever changing, and uses impartially what we call 'good' and what we call 'evil'. 'All luck is good' he loved to aver, because God turns it all to his purposes. He was absolutely committed to the Positive Way, and as absolutely realistic in his estimate of its cost. He was also realistic as a workman, in the hard though beloved daily grind of the Oxford University Press, in the immense load of reading, writing and criticism which he carried – besides those unassuming lectureships – to make a quite humble living for self, wife and son, as well as to satisfy the soaring of his spirit.

The form of the play was to be that which the Chichester conference had declared to be best suited for Church use, the masque. For the Chapter House, with its shallow platform that seemed to unroll a play like tapestry, this was an inspired choice. But it was strangely misunderstood. Perhaps it is impossible for the English to see so upholstered a period as the Tudor ironed out flat. Laurence Irving designed for the Skeleton a costume which said everything about him; but he commissioned his assistant to create Holbeinesque portraits of Henry VIII, the Lords, Cranmer, Mary and the rest. Williams was contradicted every moment you looked at them. What he had seen was the essences: the Priest, the Preacher, the Bishop, the Commons, the Lords and *The Prince*, of which Henry, the 'protected' boy Edward VI, and Mary were all embodiments, with the Crown remaining a permanent symbol, worn by Henry and Mary and hanging above the throne of the absent Edward with the Lords as 'supporters'. So the monarchs should have worn, not Holbein's walking-dress, but coronation robes: and in these terms the whole should have been conceived.

Williams achieved a kaleidoscopic compression of history: his problem, and parts of its solution, remind me of Christopher Fry's *Curtmantle* which attempted the same for the life of Henry II. At Canterbury, the play, like *Murder*, had to be shortened; it is designed in two parts with the break just before Mary's accession, but had to be reduced to one, with the omission of Anne Boleyn as a character and the loss of the magnificent Cranmer–Skeleton scene that ends Part I. To help the audience to keep abreast of the flying years I had a boy in one corner turning over the leaves of a calendar of dates and events. But one did not need to identify all the historical detail to be gripped by the play's power. At the dress rehearsal, in fear of Miss Babington's one-and-a-half-hour stop-watch, I asked one of the invited audience to time it for me. Returning from my final run out I asked 'How long?' 'Two hours and twenty minutes.' I can still remember the chill . . . 'No, I'm sorry, I'd lost all sense of time: *one* hour and twenty minutes.'

Within the formalised historical masque, two figures take on fully human character. Henry VIII is more sympathetically shown than he probably deserves: but he is being seen through the eyes of Cranmer who becomes his friend:

> HENRY
> I have always lost the thing I sought to find,
> You are the nearest thing I ever found
> To the thing that I looked for; you are an honest man.

Cranmer is looking for his own honesty throughout the play. He has been seen by most historians as a trimmer, a man projected into power against his will and doing his best to keep afloat in a strange, stormy sea. Williams' portrait is again a sympathetic one, not excusing Cranmer's weakness but showing both his compassion and his attempt to stand for the basic Protestant principle: it is Cranmer who instals the open Bible in the churches and who writes the Book of Common Prayer. His enemies, who nearly destroy him more than once, are the ruthless Lords, the *nouveaux riches* of Tudor aristocracy, who bid Henry despoil the monasteries: 'It were good the gentry of England had their goods' and when Cranmer cries 'My lords, the poor', answer:

> Leave the poor to us, Archbishop;
> We will see to the security of Crown and Gospel.

Two of the finest passages in the play are dreams. Henry, dying, has a dream of lost identity; Cranmer, as the Catholic Mary approaches the throne, has another:

> When the Queen came riding yesterday into the town
> She had no head, over her shoulders the Crown
> threw a golden light; her hands emerged on the rein;
> at her horse's pacing my limbs jerked in pain,
> as the Queen rising, riding came steadily in.
> Purge, O God, a sinful man of his sin.

Cranmer is degraded; he recants like Saint Joan, and like her, recants his recantation:

Therefore I draw to the thing that troubles me
more than all else I ever did – the writings
I let abroad against my heart's belief
to keep my life . . . if that might be . . . that I signed
with this hand, after I was degraded: this hand,
which wrote the contrary of God's will in me,
since it offended most, shall suffer first;
it shall burn ere I burn, now I go to the fire . . .

But this is not quite the end. Before he runs to plunge that hand into the fire the Skeleton bids him:

Friend, let us say one thing more before the world –
I for you, you for me: let us say all:
if the Pope had bid you live, you would have served him.

CRANMER
If the Pope had bid me live, I should have served him.

SKELETON
Speed!

CRANMER
       Speed!

ALL THE PERSONS
       Speed! [*they all hurry out*]

The Skeleton has made Cranmer 'say all', as Laurence Irving's costume, I suggested above, 'said everything' about the Skeleton. The body-tights are black, with the white bones imprinted on them, and the face has a half-death-mask. Round the throat is a high collar of scarlet, which is repeated on the actor's mouth. A huge black cloak is lined throughout with the green of spring, which appears again as ivy-leaves round the brow. So the Skeleton is uncompromisingly death, but as clearly bears the promise of life. Only through death did Christ pass into life, and his follower has to travel the same road. As Cranmer faces despair, the Skeleton unveils this figure:

Mine is the diagram [*Figura Rerum*, his sub-title]; I twirl it to a point
the point of conformity, of Christ. You shall see Christ,
see his back first – I am his back . . .
I am Christ's back; I without face or breath,
life in death, death in life . . .
this is the body of Christ which is given for you;
feed on it in your heart by faith with thanksgiving.

He is *Figura Rerum* in another sense: 'I am the delator of all things to their truth.' He has, as Mrs Hadfield puts it, 'a horrible knack of showing how the best intentions can with only the least self-deception arrive at the worst results'. It is Cranmer, of course, who has to endure most of this treatment, but others also have to face him:

> Is your image broken, Anne? . . . I
> am the broken image, the bones of the image.

From Cranmer, the Skeleton strips off layer by layer the 'curves of deception' until the very last layer, as we have seen, bares the totally honest man at the point 'where only saints settle'. It is a process of terrible wit, parallel with, yet more subtle than that of the Accuser in the book of Job; and the audience is not exempt from it:

17 *Thomas Cranmer of Canterbury* (Charles Williams), in the Chapter House, 1936. EMB as the Skeleton. Costume by Laurence Irving. Photo by permission of Fisk-Moore Studios Ltd

The Son of Man comes as a thief in the night.
After my mode I have gathered many souls;
who shall prevent me, coming swiftly for all?

Williams took a passionate delight in words, their 'twy-flash dazzle' of meanings, associations and sounds; as a constant user and lover of the Book of Common Prayer he would fain celebrate Cranmer's literary genius. His first meeting face to face with the Skeleton takes place when he is writing the Order for Holy Communion:

CRANMER
[*writing*] It is very meet, right and our bounden duty, that we should at all times and in all places give thanks . . .

SKELETON
Ah, how the sweet words ring their beauty.
It is meet, right and our bounden duty,
but will you sing it with unchanged faces
when God shall change the times and the places? . . .

CRANMER
I am blind, I am afraid; what are you?

SKELETON
A moment's geometrical formation of fate;
a functioning spectrum of analysed eternity . . .

I am the only thing that outruns necessity,
I am necessary Love where necessity is not.

These quotations serve also to illustrate the nature of the verse. Its distinctive features are the use of rhyme, internal as well as at the line-ends, of alliteration, and of a dance of unaccented syllables which give to much of it a light, almost quivering movement. It is extremely good to speak and effective to hear. Williams evolved it for this play and it served him well in the nine years remaining to him.

Robert Speaight 'undervalued the play [he confesses] at the time', Cranmer was for him as actor 'the wrong kind of contrast to Becket'; but he gave him dignity and humanity and spoke his writing with proper magnificence. Philip Hollingworth, outstanding among the Canterbury actors, suited this mild version of King Henry. Frank Napier consented to sustain the Lords by being one of them. As it had for *Murder*, Canterbury provided a small choir to sing liturgical music in a gallery built above the west doors of the Chapter House.

I specify the original doors because this year we had the blessing of a new one. During the winter of 1935–6, the King's School had done a play in the Chapter House for which the headmaster/director, Canon Shirley, had found that he needed a door into the passage north of the building. He persuaded the chapter to cut through the medieval wall to supply his need. This is, of course, how things were really done before conservation. You needed a door, so you cut one through no matter how agèd a wall. We, who could never have hoped to achieve this ourselves, were duly grateful for the uncovenanted canonical mercy.

I was more deeply grateful for another. The Skeleton, as a part, gave me a satisfaction more complete than any other in my acting career. My acting talent was strictly limited; in naturalistic plays I was downright bad, but parts like the Fourth Tempter (and later, by extension, Becket himself) or Raphael in *Tobias and the Angel* suited me; and the Skeleton made the maximum demand on my peculiar capabilities, as well as a humbling demand on my understanding. Two days after we opened, this sonnet reached me:

Canterbury
22 June 1936

Must you show me the Skeleton then, not only in art
by one part played and other parts designed,
but by the bony fingers probing the heart,
chilling and determining the pretentious mind?
Must you show me, I say, the way I hate to go,
yet lately drew in a chart, of such neat lines?
'Things spoken seem unfamiliar' – o but no,
familiar enough this, though my will inclines
little to the bitter warmth of that true cold.
Nor a week ago could I think, Martin, to behold
such neatness in your exact mathematical sight;
not merely cancelling your rightness (that, though much,
were little in truth), but with a rarer touch
forbidding the better rightness to think itself right.

c.w.

Henzie and I had asked Miss Babington to find us 'billets', since she had persuaded a number of Canterbury residents to offer hospitality to actors and musicians for the Festival. We went early in May, for preliminary rehearsals, to a 'billet' which later turned into a home, its host and hostess into two of our dearest friends. John Prickett had lately become the very young headmaster of

Kent College, the Methodist public school on the hill above the
west end of the city. Nellie, his wife, had been brought up in Egypt
where her father had been in business, and they had met when
John was teaching there. We all found ourselves so happy together
that we persuaded Miss Babington tactfully to cancel our following
'billet' and let us stay at Kent College.

The notices recognised the 'distinguished' quality of *Cranmer*,
and gave both Robert Speaight and myself credit for 'admirable'
performances. *The Daily Telegraph* noted that 'in some odd way the
very understatement of the play as a whole gives it a subdued
tensity which grips throughout'. *The Times* made a very interesting
analysis of Cranmer's character from the famous portrait, and
suggested that the play 'emphasises just those conflicting points of
character which Flicke set down in paint, and, having emphasised them, applies as touchstone a bold conception of grace that
enables this strangely mingled nature to achieve in the end a
strength made perfect through the admission of utter weakness'.
This climax was said to be 'exceedingly moving'.

The archbishop, Cosmo Lang, came to the matinée on Youth
Day, and sat enthroned in the front row of an audience from the
local schools. At the end, he marched up the steps onto the stage
and, commiserating with the young people who could not have
understood much of such a difficult play, gave a short impromptu
lecture. Next morning, Miss Babington was inundated, to her great
glee, with telephone calls from the schools, all registering the
indignant protests of the children. 'We understood the play perfectly,' they said.

Charles Williams developed his dramatic talent up to and during
the war. I grieved at his early death in 1945 not only for the loss of a
unique spirit and a beloved friend, but specifically because he was
not here to be one of the poets whose new plays I was to produce at
the Mercury, where for the first time he would have been unfet-
tered by having to write for special occasions.

The Mercury, where *Murder* resumed its run in the autumn, was
on what is nowadays called 'the Fringe'. Theatre folk were full of
rebellion against the control of the West End by the bricks-and-
mortar men, and with reason; but the great actors break through
these brick walls. This was the decade of John Gielgud. On our
arrival in 1930 we had seen his young *Hamlet* transferred from the
Old Vic to the Queen's. He showed more facets of the character

than had ever been revealed to us before. The nobility of this Prince, freed from the stately delivery of the older generation, was matched by his mental and nervous energy, the disgust and depression by his barbed, ironic humour. It was a performance in flashes of vari-coloured fire, which flickered especially, in contrast both comic and pathetic, on Martita Hunt's brilliantly stupid Queen. One does not forget those two performances even in the memory of Gielgud's two later Hamlets in the thirties, the long-running one at the New, and the closing performances of Irving's Lyceum where Ellen Terry's great-nephew must constantly have recalled her Ophelia. There were many other treasures of the period, from his Noah in Obey's play directed by Michel Saint-Denis who had created it with the Quinze, through Richard the Second in both Shakespeare's and Gordon Daviot's version (*Richard of Bordeaux*) to John Worthing in *The Importance . . .*, and by the middle of the decade Gielgud the director was rivalling Gielgud the actor. The New *Hamlet* and *The Importance* were directed by him, as was the experimental *Romeo and Juliet* in which he alternated as Romeo and Mercutio with Laurence Olivier, three years younger and moving up to match him.

In early October, a West End manager did at last come to the Mercury. J. P. Mitchelhill owned a single theatre, the Duchess. He managed it himself and had a very good record of success, notably with plays by J. B. Priestley. He invited us to move to the Duchess on 30 October, two days before the first anniversary of our Mercury opening. After five months at the Duchess, we did two long tours in 1937. Between them, we played a summer season at the Old Vic. Lilian Baylis welcomed a play which represented so much that she stood for both in drama and in religion. She said to me personally, 'My dear boy, I am glad to have got you here at last.' I am glad too, for she died later that year.

After that, we played a week at the Tewkesbury Festival, before the west front of that magnificent Norman Abbey. Here I used in reverse the ending of the original production. From the Canterbury Chapter House, as many who saw it still remember, Becket's body was borne out into the cloister. The Priests and Chorus carried candles and sang the litany which calls the roll of the Saints to which Thomas' name has just been added. The procession continued round the cloister as the audience dispersed. At Tewkesbury, the Abbey nave was dark as the procession entered from the light outside, and the points of candlelight became smaller and smaller as the archbishop was carried towards the high altar.

1938 began with a visit to the States. It was ill-fated. Owing to an agent's mistake, the play had already been seen in New York, and despite appreciative notices the English production did not draw enough of the Broadway public. Henzie and I made the most of this chance to see our friends again: the Stouts were living in New York now, and we enjoyed the music that Edwin Bry (son of the man who first took Henzie to the Queen's Hall) and his wife Jeannette made in their home with players from the Philharmonic Symphony Orchestra.

Henzie had joined the *Murder* Chorus. For the first time, I had looked outside the ranks of the 'dulcet-tongued damsels from South Kensington' (as Bobbie Speaight called them) whom Miss Fogerty and Miss Thurburn had supplied. Their interpretation had remained highly sensitive to the poet's words, carefully watched over by these two great teachers. They provided replacements whenever a girl got the chance of exchanging our pittance for something better, and the list of chorus-members in two-and-a-half years came to be a long one. Many hundreds of audiences had received from them a memorable experience. But it was necessarily limited: they could not be expected to *act* the poor women of Canterbury; and I wanted to extend it by introducing some older players.

Miss Fogerty found this difficult to accept and had treated Henzie disparagingly at some London rehearsals. Characteristically realising how wrong this was, she sent a letter of apology and encouragement to the boat, which touched Henzie deeply. Pamela Keily was my other new recruit.

After the end of our three-week run, we three decided to change the return halves of our tickets to the Italian line, sail to Naples and travel home through Italy. It was a chance not to be missed, especially as the fascist threat was becoming rapidly stronger. We had found Orson Welles' fascist version of *Julius Caesar* frighteningly relevant as Hitler took over Austria. When we sailed into Naples harbour, we passed rows of submarines, though each had an innocent-looking line of washing hung out along its superstructure. On our first stroll we came into a large piazza, one side occupied by a church whose deep portico had a double row of columns. Workmen were introducing between them a row of dummy ones, building only the front halves. In my bad Italian, I asked what they were for. Hitler was about to pay a return visit to Mussolini, and would speak here – with his bodyguard thus concealed.

In Rome we attended the Palm Sunday ceremony in St Peter's ('God's drawing-room', Henzie called it), and went on to Assisi. I had planned the trip so that we could spend Holy Week and Easter there. On Wednesday we walked out to San Damiano, the tiny church and convent which Francis restored and where Clare and her first sisterhood lived. There we heard *Tenebrae*, a rite which has been discontinued, to the Church's loss: for it is the one moment of the year when the soul is led through the darkness that must precede the dawn. It reminds me of one of the Skeleton's lines to Cranmer:

> When you have lost him at last you shall come into God.

The only light is a triangular stand with fifteen candles. Fifteen psalms are said, with lessons between them. After each, a candle is put out, until only the top one is left; at the end of the last psalm (fifty-one) this is hidden behind the altar. In the darkness broken only by the minute glow, you leave the church.

On Good Friday at midday, the Veneration of the Cross in San Francesco; a great crowd kneeling to kiss the feet of the Crucified while the Reproaches were sung:

> O my people, what have I done unto thee: wherein have
> I wearied thee? Testify against me.

At night, the people's own celebration. Towards dusk, a stream of carts, cars, bicycles and families on foot poured into the Piazza San Francesco. Thousands of little glass bowls with wicks floating in oil appeared on every window-sill, balcony and wall-top along the main street leading up the hill. A brass band and troops of scouts, monks and students gathered; and then came processional crosses, choirs and servers from a dozen churches. At the rear of each little procession was a man, barefoot, in a hessian robe and loose mask with eye-holes, carrying a great cross of rough wood. Finally, the doors of San Francesco were opened, and the walk up to the cathedral, a mile away, began. After the band and the secular cohorts came the parishes with the recurring figure of the barefoot crossbearer in sackcloth; at the end came two litters, one bearing the crucified Figure whose feet we had kissed, the other a waist-length upright figure of the Virgin Mother, with seven swords quivering in her breast.

All the city followed, save the old and the very young whom we could see in the windows by the light of the flickering nightlights. Except for the band in the far distance, there was no sound but the shuffling of feet. At the cathedral, a dense mass of people: we could not get in, so we walked back through streets from which the crowd had melted silently away, keeping the same silence.

After Easter, Pamela left for home. Henzie and I took a train to Arezzo to see the Piero della Francesca frescoes. Walking from the station we found hanging from every balcony and every window a rug, a curtain, sometimes a flag. 'Why?' we asked. 'Hitler arrives in Italy today.' 'Do you welcome him?' 'It is commanded.' We did not cross Hitler's route, since we made a detour to Ravenna, but we were aware of his lowering presence as we made our way home.

One does not stay still and wait for a storm-cloud to break. Henzie played the Tewkesbury Festival of James Bridie's plays, as Anna in *Tobias and the Angel* and as Eshtemoa, a brilliantly written society hostess, in *Jonah and the Whale*. As Christopher was going away to school she felt free to look for work on the London stage, and got a part in *Elizabeth of Austria*, a play by Elizabeth Sprigge and her sister, at the Garrick. I got a part, which I played badly, in a bad play at the Arts Theatre Club. Over these unremarkable personal happenings, the Czech crisis loomed. My play opened on Sunday 25 September, ten days after Chamberlain's first flight to Berlin. On the 29th, I came out of the theatre after the show to find Leicester Square in a turmoil. The Munich agreement had been made. Relief seemed uppermost – even a few fireworks were being let off; but mingled with it was shame.

6

The Pilgrim Players: I

Henzie wrote and published 'Pilgrim Story' in 1945.
This chapter and the next are condensed from it.

The wheels begin to turn: 1939

Since Munich, and 'Peace in our time', the armament factories throve, no doubt, but the youth of England were not yet on fire. Silken dalliance was being kept well out of the wardrobe until the last possible moment. We were fitted for our gas masks, and put them away 'in a dry cool place to preserve the rubber'. Once or twice we rehearsed our parts, as the pigs we should all have to look if gas came; but that was all the precaution we took. But a gradual paralysis was creeping over the theatre, not stopping its routine, but making people less and less inclined to do anything new. And yet, anything that needed to be done must be done quickly, while there was time. T. S. Eliot, feeling this, urged my husband forward with the production of his new play, *The Family Reunion*, at the Westminster. The first night on 21 March was a big event of the theatrical year: whatever the author of *Murder in the Cathedral* wrote would be important, and Michael Redgrave was playing the lead. The play is difficult, and what it had to say could hardly penetrate people's minds, which were occupied by the news of six days before. Hitler had taken Czechoslovakia. The die was surely cast? As I walked through the streets to the theatre, which held for me the delight of playing a fine part in the best of company, I was continually appalled at what my imagination saw. A broken ruin replaced those ordered buildings. The clear sky of spring was darkened with enemy planes. Fear swamped me: fear more black and terrible than any I knew in the tests of war.

The play was only a *succès d'estime* and came off after five weeks.

Martin produced two plays at the Tewkesbury Festival in July. The Abbey tower had been for four years under repair; now it was finished, and to celebrate the achievement a special play called *The Tower* was written by Christopher Fry. It brought in various local groups as well as a professional cast. The play was given on fine days outside the west front, where a miniature tower was built to house me as Our Lady. On wet days we played inside the Abbey, and the Heavenly Seat was placed on the ledge of the great west window. I had to climb a long, swaying ladder before the audience were admitted. One afternoon, two ladies were the first arrivals, and noticed an unfamiliar figure sitting there. 'Canon Gough is really very *high*,' said one, 'the things he's put in the abbey! Look there now, a coloured statue of the Virgin.' But a 12-year-old prep school boy indignantly interrupted: 'That's not a statue; that's my Mummy.'

We went next to Malvern, where our two boys, Denis and Christopher, joined us from school. We called on Allardyce Nicoll and his wife at their cottage overlooking the Malvern Hills from the Herefordshire side. We talked, of course, of the theatre both here and in America, where Allardyce was head of the drama department at Yale; and one sentence stuck. Mrs Nicoll, talking to Martin of the religious plays which were his particular interest, said in her sudden, dynamic way: 'Take them round the country in a wagon!' We all laughed, for it seemed so remote from immediate possibility.

But a month later, we found ourselves in Malvern once more. War had just been declared and we were taking the boys back to their school. Like all country schools, it had opened early to receive children who lived in dangerous areas – for everyone expected immediate and colossal raids on the big cities. A kind friend gave us a bed – kind indeed, for Martin developed jaundice.

It took him a week to recover: but the jaundice did not seem to have its usual effect on this patient. He lay in bed and read the papers and thought a good deal. The war news was concerned only with far-off Poland, where events moved swiftly to their inevitable climax. But more of the space in the papers was occupied by changes in the lives of our own people. Petrol rationing was to start on 16 September. Buses and trains were drastically cut. Train-load after train-load of children had been taken with their teachers to the remote country villages. News began to come in of the way in which this extraordinary invasion was being dealt with, and of its effect both on the strangers (now labelled 'evacuees') and on the country folk. Enemy planes on reconnaissance had been seen over the east coast, and a gas-proof safety kennel had been produced for dogs and cats.

But more startling than all this to a theatre man was the announcement: 'All places of entertainment will be closed during the initial stages of hostilities.' In fact, they only remained closed for just over a week, but they were very unlikely to re-open to normal business. So many of their patrons were scattered throughout the country, far away from any theatre. The theatres closed in Shakespeare's day when the plague ravaged London; and the actors, whom after all the law labelled vagabonds, took to the roads. Perhaps an echo travelled three miles along the hills: 'Take the plays around in a wagon!'

The Pricketts rang up from Canterbury and asked us to make our home with them. We could be useful in the school: and perhaps we should find other work to do as well.

With returning health ideas began to crystallise in Martin's mind. Thousands of people were going to be deprived of their recreation, just when they most needed it. A small company should be formed to take the theatre to them. He had always felt that the link between the contemporary theatre and its audience was too tenuous. Now, in time of common trouble, actors and audience together might discover something new. In Shakespeare's day the theatre was a place where actors and audience exchanged experiences. The platform stood in the middle, the audience sat or stood around it. The plague sent Shakespeare to inn-yards, banqueting-halls, the village green . . . should we go there, taking conditions in Britain as we found them? Not a job for which actors could be hired; but an experiment which a group of actors must work out together.

Ideas kept on forming. Food rationing had begun. Food: bread. 'Man cannot live by bread alone, but by every word that proceedeth out of the mouth of God.' We would do religious plays. Let the Oxford Dictionary define religion: 'Human recognition of a superhuman controlling power, and especially of a personal God entitled to obedience.' We would do plays showing the effect of such recognition on conduct and mental attitude. They could and should include comedy and farce, as well as suitable plays from the old mysteries and their modern counterparts and liturgical plays to be done in church. Thus every type of audience could share in the repertory.

But what about money? An aunt had just left us the sum of £50. That would see us through the initial expenses of launching a production, and perhaps leave a little over. But the venture must pay its way. How that was to be we did not see as yet: but there was enough light for the next step. Yes, we would joyfully accept the Pricketts' offer. We told them of our plans, to which they responded warmly. East Kent was then a reception area, full of evacuated schools from London who would surely welcome us, and Kent College could find room for rehearsal. On 14 September Martin, now fully recovered, drove us back to London. Living in a flat with no blackout wasted a lot of time: but by the 16th we had found a stray pantechnicon with a day to spare, and on the 18th we set up our home with the Pricketts.

We took on a little work for the school, some speech classes, and play-reading with the older boys: and with John produced two plays that term. But by now Martin was laying plans for the travelling company in Kent. His first call was on Miss Babington. She was secretary of the Kent Nursing Association and in charge of personnel for the city shelters. But she was interested in the new project: and, with her, interest spelled action. She volunteered to act as organising secretary for us, placing her unrivalled knowledge of Kent, and the goodwill of the Friends, at our disposal. Soon she was speeding through the city on our behalf, mounted upon her famous bicycle.

So we were to begin in Canterbury, and go out from there. In the days of peace the Festival had drawn its great audiences, first from the Kentish towns and villages, then from the length and breadth of England, even from across the seas; in remoter, medieval days pilgrims from all over the country, from all over Europe, found their way through the same city gates and narrow streets, up Mercery Lane into the cathedral. In these upside-down days we would go out on pilgrimage to find our audiences, first in the near-by villages and towns, then further and much further afield. There was no need to find a new name for us. There it was waiting, ready made: THE PILGRIM PLAYERS of Canterbury.

At this point Annette Wellby came down for a night to discuss the plan. She was secretary of the Religious Drama Society, and undertook to let all members know of the new venture. As the route of pilgrimage grew longer she became advance manager. Ruth Spalding wrote at the same time, desiring to do work on similar lines. She had been travelling producer for the society before the war, and lived at Oxford. This opened the way for two Pilgrim companies; the second one was called the Oxford Pilgrim Players and started work within a few days of ours. The principles of each were the same, and they shared some of the plays in their early repertory; but the management was entirely independent.

The next task was to choose the first play: and we chose our biggest success. *Tobias and the Angel*, by James Bridie, seems to suit a larger number of different audiences than any play ever written. We had done it before, but under normal theatre conditions. Now we must do it without any setting and to audiences mostly unacquainted with the theatre. So it must be 'put over' by direct appeal to the audience. We asked the author for permission to play an emergency version; and he responded by writing a series of prologues in his wittiest vein for the Angel as compère.

In *Tobias* we had a play with a religious idea of the first rank as drama and as entertainment. Martin took the plan and the play to the archbishop, Cosmo Lang, and asked for his blessing. He became our patron, and helped us by personal announcement at his Diocesan Conference. At a tea-party before we set out he met the whole company and bade us godspeed.

Costumes were next considered, and here Miss Babington once more befriended us, by lending us dresses from the Festival wardrobe. These, with additions from the Pricketts and other friends, provided colourful, if scarcely homogeneous, costumes for the first of our many productions of *Tobias*. The cost was only a few shillings.

That was an important consideration, for we were not a little troubled by finance. But Pilgrim finance was 'without tears' in 1939. Readers of today, though they will find the figures easy enough to understand, may find them incredible; it may be hard to realise that in those days promoters felt so uncertain of their public, confused as it was by the strange darkness of roads and the menace of raids, hampered by the lack of transport and as yet unused to walking, that they hesitated to undertake the risk of a show at all. But we were certain that people needed plays, and that to get our services accepted we must reduce the risk to almost nil. So at the beginning we fixed the minimum guarantee for a performance at thirty shillings!

There was principle as well as practicality in the way we adjusted the debit side of our budget. We were all to be on war service; so all, whether they brought age and experience or youth and eagerness to the job, would take a Tommy's pay. Actually, we did a good deal worse than he. For we had thirty shillings a week, of which twenty-one shillings went in billeting fees; and out of the nine left we had to clothe ourselves as well as meet all the incidental expenses of life: shoe repairs, haircuts, cigarettes, stamps, and the precious batteries for our torches, which would work so hard night by night. And we couldn't be ill for nothing, as the Tommy could. But from the first the company was to own its assets in common, and by degrees perhaps some of these expenses could be communally met.

It was a mad idea, perhaps, though Actors' Equity was willing to give it provisional approval. A lot of actors naturally thought it too quixotic even for wartime. But quite a few were interested, and at first we thought we had a company. We needed three men and two women besides ourselves to play the 'emergency version'. But actors are apt to slip away, for perfectly good reasons, and there was one day when it seemed that we should reach our first engagement, already booked, with no company at all. At last, however, we were complete, and rehearsals began in the hall, papier-mâché was being made in the dining-room, sewing and secretarial work went on in the drawing-room, in fact Kent College was inundated with preparations for the first performance. This was given on 13 November to the boys and staff of the school and a few friends: of them a collection was asked to further the work, and Nellie gave it encouragement by the loan of a pound note, a ten-shilling note, a half-crown and a florin. Fortified by what remained after their repayment, the Pilgrim Players set out next day for their first public show.

Pilgrimage from Canterbury: 1939–40

I should like to place on record the names of the original Pilgrim Company, though only one of them remained with us through all the ardours and endurances of Pilgrim history. That was Ronald Long. In *Tobias* he played the Bandit and Raguel, the father of

Sara. Sara was played by Evelyn Neilson, who also took on the secretarial work. Stuart Burge, our Tobias, was the treasurer; he combined with the charm of his performance a humility rare in financiers and not very good for the exchequer. After the show he would collect the Pilgrims' share of the takings and enter it in a coverless little notebook with a short stub of pencil; but he was so anxious that we should not leave any local expenses unpaid that he would beseech the organiser to recollect any outstanding charges. Martin played the Angel; I played Anna, Tobias' mother. Tobit, my husband, was doubled with the Demon by Eric Crozier. He made himself a devil-mask, to hide the benign make-up of Tobit while appearing intermediately as Asmoday, and a fearful costume incorporating an umbrella transformed into wings.

The first public performance was in the village hall at Chartham, five miles from Canterbury. It was a small hall with a passage behind the stage to serve as dressing-room. A white sheet with a hole in it formed a partition between ladies and gentlemen. I safety-pinned a cleansing tissue over the hole. Soon, such niceties were no longer considered. In that same week we found ourselves dressing in the tiny 'cloakrooms' at the audience-end of a hall and having to creep through the audience on to the stage. The vicar requested the audience not to use the cloakroom, as the actors were there, but of course we had to make exceptions.

On our first circular we had offered 'performances any time, anywhere'. We were fulfilling the slogan. One of the reasons for it was the lack of shelters. True, there had been no raids yet, and though Canterbury had an alert as early as 17 October, rumour ascribed it to the dusting of 'something to do with the Sireen'. But till shelters were built the numbers allowed at any assembly were restricted in all schools and in the coast towns: so relay performances were the only way of giving everyone a chance. Consequently, 9.15 one wintry morning saw us playing in a classroom at Ramsgate, with the children banked upon the desks in order of height, and the play given on the floor in front of a screen which formed the only entrance and the only setting. At the village hut, Wychling, there were no dressing-rooms. The girls had two feet of wing space, the men a bell-tent in the field outside. An oil-stove kept them warm in the tent, but the trip to and fro, in oriental garments, was a chilly one. Oil lamps for lighting were frequent; and low prosceniums would sometimes decapitate the Angel.

Petrol was always our chief bugbear. The authorities did come to understand, after a personal visit, what we were after; but it was to them an aim of quite secondary importance, and the precious liquid was doled out to us in very small quantities. Twenty-two gallons a month between two cars doing daily shows was the usual ration. We always freewheeled downhill, of course; and members of the company, lodging in various parts of the city, had long walks home. When kind organisers asked us to a meal a mile away from the hall where the show was, hunger had to fight it out with petrol economy. Driving in the black-out was very hard at first: 15 m.p.h. was good going at night. As December wore on, we had to make early starts to get the drive done one way in the daylight and spot a few landmarks to guide us home.

Christmas was coming, and for our second production Martin devised *The Merry Play of Christmas*, an adaptation from the York, Coventry and Wakefield Mysteries. It embodied the whole of the *Second Shepherds' Play*, but the farcical sheep-stealing scenes could be omitted in church. We played it in many of the village churches in Kent. The church was often the only building not taken over for military or civil defence service, and people were glad to have the play to help them to keep Christmas in the strange uncertainty which filled everyone's heart at that time.

For us it was a happy Christmas, in spite of the war. Our boys were already at home at Kent College, and Christmas was no different from peacetime: tree and presents were there, and the celebrations in a larger community were all the gayer. We gave several performances in the cathedral crypt, using the Chapel of Our Lady Undercroft, where the Black Prince offered his petitions before setting out for war. To make a suitable backcloth, I gave Ronnie Long a pair of old double sheets, which he dyed to match the stone walls and then emblazoned them with suns and stars. The first snow fell during those days: and the cathedral had an unearthly beauty in the snow-reflected moonlight.

But the beauty of snow is dearly bought in discomfort by those who have to go out in it! We had to coddle the cars like babies to keep their radiators from bursting. On 16 January the severest snowstorm of the winter fell. We were due to play *Tobias* at Elvington, a mining village on the heights above Dover. The actors were put on the train. Martin, driving our little car with the costumes and properties, lost his way in the blizzard and finally stuck in a snowdrift. He got out by going into reverse and then driving off the road into the neighbouring ploughed field, the surface of which gave the wheels a grip. But at the end of that he had to go back on to the road and stuck again. With a spade borrowed from a near-by cottage, the car was dug out and finally got to Elvington. Any time, any place, any weather! During the next few days several shows were cancelled (a rare event in our history) as the halls were snowed up and inaccessible.

The following week we played our first prison. Maidstone Gaol is a building dramatically grim, a fortress with double iron gates. One is admitted into the first, it is locked behind one, and only then is the second opened, with the clanging of a bunch of heavy keys. We played *Tobias* on an improvised stage in the chapel, at the opposite end to the altar. The Governor kindly warned us of some unusual circumstances. The previous week an 'old lag' had died. His name was Tobias, and he was always in trouble. So when the chaplain had inadvertently announced the play as *Tobias with the Angels* there had been signs that some extra laughs might be expected. A riotous afternoon culminated at the moment when Tobias' father-in-law, giving him up for dead, crosses the stage with a spade to dig his grave. Those who had recently taken part in this 'fatigue' were loudly sympathetic. At least a quarter of our audience were educated men, who appreciated the finer shades of the dramatist's wit, as well as the references to the government, an unfailing source of mirth in prison. The show, of course, brought us no fee; but we agreed that none had been more worthwhile, as we stood outside the gates, contemplating the snowy hill that led to Faversham, where the evening show was.

We were now at the end of January and in rehearsal for our next play, D. H. Lawrence's *David*. I was not in this. Ronald Long, who had made some good properties for us, offered himself as designer of costumes. The same ladies of Canterbury, who in peacetime made the Festival clothes, kindly transferred their energies to our wardrobe, and a striking décor was produced. The most difficult property was the bleeding head of Goliath, which Ronnie himself made of papier-mâché with close curls of copper wire. He painted a tragically noble countenance, with a gory neck beneath. 'Golly' was our pride, and I was somewhat taken aback when a lady in the audience turned to me and said, 'Not very nice, is it?'

This was in London. We had by this time received many

enquiries from people all over the country, and thought that it would be a good thing to let those who ran the large national organisations for social and educational work see what we were doing. So we had accepted an invitation from Geoffrey Whitworth to play in the British Drama League's lecture-room. London in the blackout was most baffling; it was so much darker than the country. If one lost one's bearings, say at Piccadilly Circus, it was impossible to search for familiar buildings with a torch; the harsh cry 'Put that torch down' greeted any attempt to scan a near-by signboard. Till the edges of the kerbs were painted white, one fell off and jolted one's spine at every few steps. London had become a strange city, at least by night.

18   *The Way of the Cross* (Henri Ghéon), 1940, as produced by the Pilgrim Players. Photograph taken in banqueting-hall at Dartington, with Pamela Keily as Reader, EMB as First Man, HB as First Woman (recalling Mary holding the dead body of Jesus in her arms), Brian Carey as Second Man (John) and Elna Graham as Second Woman (Magdalen); costumes by Stella Mary Newton. Photo by Stuart Black, reproduced by permission of I. C. Macpherson

But Pilgrim life was becoming more familiar; it was taking form as the tiny community got itself organised. The company meetings, which up to now had been held only when needed to cope with an immediate problem, became more regular and systematic. We all felt that this was necessary to cement our fellowship and deal fairly with the division both of the work and of its rewards. So we aimed at a weekly gathering, with a secretary taking minutes and a report from the treasurer. The first recorded minutes are dated 11 February 1940, and open with a statement of the principles on which the company is run:

The capital is administered co-operatively by the company. The artistic control and control of engagements are in the hands of the Director.

Two other items which foreshadow developments are these:

A grant of £150 per annum had been made by CEMA [the newly formed Council for the Encouragement of Music and the Arts, which became the Arts Council], mainly for the purpose of increasing salaries. The possibility of giving the company a holiday on pay was discussed.

A few days later we left London for a south-country tour. Our first billet was a mill. No ordinary mill, for here was ground the finest wholewheat flour, on the highest principles of vegetarianism. The bread certainly was delicious. But we found raw salads and baked potatoes left some gaps in the diet of busy people. For we were busy in those days. Two plays, and quite exacting ones, in our repertory, and a third being rehearsed; the diary shows ten and eleven performances per week, which means setting and striking stage eight or nine times, and driving hundreds of miles as well as playing and rehearsing. In the week of 3 March twelve shows are recorded, including the first performance of Henri Ghéon's *The Way of the Cross*.

This was our Passion Play, and remained in our repertory. It is a dramatisation of the Sorrowful Way of Jesus from Pilate's Judgement Hall to Calvary, of the Crucifixion and the Resurrection. A narrator announces the stages of the Ascent; two men and two women play out the scenes. As a critic described it:

They are spectators who are, as it were, outside time and space, who suddenly change into a tragic embodiment of the things they see ... A gaunt, concerted stare calls up the pure reality of some decisive incident in that Procession; a foot thumped down on those wooden boards suggests the weight of the Tree and the agony of its Carrier.

Rehearsal is always an exhausting business. It is through a battle of the spirit that the author's creation becomes incarnate in the actor. Once the battle is won, the repetition of the creation is for the actor a matter of imaginative memory, coupled with technique; never so severe a strain as it was in rehearsal. It is now the audience who, in the sympathy evoked by the character, suffer the experience. The birth-pangs of this play, by its very nature, were unusually hard; but though through its hundreds of performances it never ceased to make demands on the actors, the giving was repaid by the response of audiences. Stella Newton created a quartet of black and grey robes which completely expressed the spirit of the production, allowing of a series of stage pictures infinitely varied within the austere framework of the play.

To continue working at this pressure was impossible, though the demand was so great, and so continually increasing, that it was hard to resist. Gradually the company built up a defence mechanism. We insisted on a Free Day in every week. At first this was subject to interference by journeys or other business; but finally even the advance secretary, who had to fend off the importunate demand for shows, recognised it as inviolable. One must have a break to write one's letters, to do one's washing, to get away from the people with whom one spent the whole of the other six days, travelling, dressing and often living together.

By Easter the company had increased to nine and acquired the members who were to be its strength for the next three years. Two Irish brothers, Denis and Brian Carey, took not only a lot of our leading parts but also responsible positions in the administration. Denis was stage manager, which meant managing not only the stage but also the loading of the baggage for transport and the allotment of work to all the stage-hands – that is, to all the actors in the company. Brian became transport officer, which involved not only driving but petrol coupons, repairs, and the seating of the company, who took his orders as to where they travelled for each journey, thus ensuring that each had a turn in front. By now we had two cars and a trailer for each; the job of loading these was a highly expert one calling for all the ingenuity of the Carey brothers. But with their green tarpaulin covers the trailers added a note of gaiety to the convoy.

Norman Tyrrell was younger in stage experience but was to

become an invaluable Pilgrim. He had a natural talent for composition, and became the trainer of the little choir which we formed
among ourselves; for we were fortunate in having plenty of good
voices. Pamela Alan divided with Elna Graham the juvenile parts.
The two girls were both dark, but in other ways made an excellent
contrast to each other. The third girl was Pamela Keily, who had
been in *Murder in the Cathedral* and *The Family Reunion*; she became
secretary and treasurer.

The last of these new Pilgrims came during the school holidays,
and this made it possible for me to spend them with the boys at
Kent College. They were the last holidays we should spend
together for over three years; but mercifully none of us knew that.
Most of the days were uneventful, but the last was a gala day. I
came up to Town with the boys early in the morning. From
Victoria, we went to a Lyons Corner House and had elaborate
soda-fountain drinks. Then to the morning performance of *Pinocchio*
at the New Gallery cinema: we all gripped each other pretty hard
at the frightening moments, and enjoyed it enormously. Lunch was
in Soho, chosen from one of those illegible French menus. There
was still an hour before Christopher's train left: what should we do
with it? We went first to Westminster Cathedral; then to perform a
beloved rite, the feeding of the pigeons in Trafalgar Square. Here
time was forgotten, till I looked past a bird-covered Christopher at
the clock of St Martin-in-the-Fields and saw that we had twenty
minutes to get to the station. As we caught the train, that was all to
the good; for of all the uncomfortable minutes in life those before a
school train goes are some of the worst. Christopher went off
happily – and nearly took Denis with him, so brief was the moment
left for saying good-bye.

Denis had a whole day before him, for he was becoming a
public-school boy, and Marlborough didn't assemble till the
morrow. We bought his first sports coat 'for next holidays'; we
dined at the Café Royal and finished the evening with a call on
Sybil Thorndike, his godmother, in her dressing-room at the
Piccadilly, where she was playing *The Corn is Green*.

Back in Canterbury the war soon got nearer and louder. At
4 a.m. on 10 May I was startled out of my sleep by an explosion. A
bomb had fallen in a wood a few miles off in the first raid on the
district. In the morning that excitement was eclipsed by the news
that Holland and Belgium had been invaded and our troops were

rushing to their defence. Later in the day more excitement: Mr Chamberlain had resigned.

At this moment the Pilgrims had undertaken to produce a new play. *England's Green* dealt with the Norman invasion of Saxon England and tried to draw a parallel between it and our own day. As it proved, the parallel was almost too close.

We had an invitation from Benenden School to rehearse in their hall. The village, with the largest green in Kent, is a lovely, peaceful spot. But when we got there the very peace of it was troubling. In the placid-looking countryside, with lilac and may in bloom and the fields full of buttercups, fear and suspicion were growing. 'Fifth column' was talked of in the pub, and we were aware that as strangers we were suspected by the village. Gradually a vibration began to fill the air; it grew into a rumbling, and then into a heavy, unending boom. At nights we would walk home to our billets from rehearsal through the scented fields bathed in moonlight, heartbreakingly lovely. The nightingales sang their loudest as if in competition, but to our ears the guns were winning and speaking of doom. On 24 May Boulogne fell. The school was given orders to evacuate; we played our first dress rehearsal to the few children who were left after the main body had gone, and a second to an even tinier audience of the staff as a relaxation from their hard day's packing. The opening had long been arranged for that Sunday, in the famous barn theatre attached to Ellen Terry's cottage at Smallhythe, where each summer in peacetime her daughter, Edith Craig, invited members of the profession to give a memorial matinée. These were joyous occasions, which we always attended and sometimes played in. Now Edy, and her friends Christopher St John and Tony Atwood, were the village air-raid wardens; but they still wanted a bit of theatre. A surprisingly large audience gathered, and the play of English country life fitted the barn's atmosphere and seemed to thrive on the primitive lighting given it by Edy and Tony with two motor headlamps from the front row. Martin was watching the audience come out when he saw a woman stop suddenly and then say to her neighbour, 'What's that noise?' 'The guns, my dear,' replied the other. 'Do you know,' said the first, 'I'd quite forgotten them.'

Kent College was ordered to follow Benenden's example. So our home was to go: 'here is no continuing city'. One room was to be reserved from military occupation to house furniture, so we went over for a day to stack our possessions in the library. Next day we had two performances to give at New Romney. This is the nearest English village to Boulogne, and it was here that the Normans made their first attempt at invasion. The villagers beat off William's ships; so when he had landed further west and fought his successful battle, he returned to revenge himself. And now the Romney men were facing another foe. The vicar wrote to us saying that he couldn't give the guarantee for the two shows (it was three guineas each by now) as most of the well-to-do folk had gone and the place was full of troops; 'But,' he added, 'come if you can, because those of us who are left need you more than ever.' Of course we went – and took exactly six guineas. After the evening show the colonel of the battalion stationed in the village came to see us and said: 'This is the greatest help you can possibly give us. You must do it all over England.'

We knew that we must do what this soldier had set before us. Our Pilgrim home had gone; so our home must be wherever we hung our gas-masks. Even though the future seemed so menacing in its uncertainty, we should be wanted and useful if we followed the road. So we became the first of the vagabond companies of the theatre in wartime.

Vagabonds in England: 1940

It is one hundred and seventy miles from Benenden to Dorchester, and the road runs along or near the coast for most of the way. I knew it well, and when we made an early start on Sunday 2 June, I looked forward to a pleasantly familiar drive. But this journey seemed to pass through a nightmare version, at once terrible and pathetic, of the well-loved landscape.

Every mile or two we were stopped by a road-block. Most of them were guarded, but the guards were not in uniform; they were farm labourers or clerks, all sorts. We must have looked odd to them, the cars dusty and weather-beaten as they dragged their swaying trailers piled high with suitcases and with the outlandish things that come into a play. A spear stuck out at one side, a monstrous fish on the other. We were continually halted, the load carefully examined, our identity cards scrutinised, and our business enquired into. It was obvious that we presented a knotty problem to those who had to exercise their own judgement in the

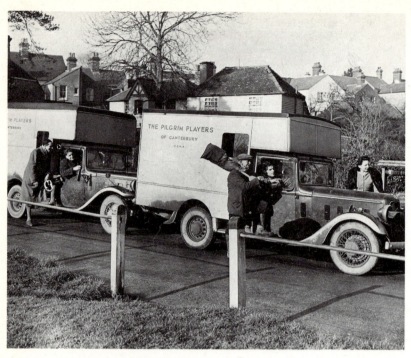

19 'You Can't Miss It!', the most familiar conclusion when one
was told the way. Brian Carey drives the leading van with
Elna Graham behind it; Eric Mitchell, driving the second,
talks to EMB. Photo by permission of Fox Photos Ltd

detection of fifth columnists. But we were allowed to pass, grateful
for the unfailing courtesy of these worried but gallant amateur
soldiers.

Driving was nervous work, for there was no warning of an
obstruction. One might come round a corner and find a barrier
right in front of the bonnet. What was more, it might be made of
anything you could or couldn't think of. A pile of wrecked cars:
wooden gates from the near-by fields; lengths of tree-trunk. Then
those crossed posts and rails that mark a piece of road under repair.
And, most fantastic of all, bathing-boxes, still in their gay striped
paint, red-and-white, green-and-white, blue-and-white, all jum-
bled one on the other to make a German holiday. How long would
these pathetic barriers delay a tank? How many seconds? The
eleventh hour had struck for England, and her coast was defended
by bathing boxes!

We stopped for lunch in Arundel Park. Under the great trees at the foot of the downs, with deer shyly watching, we unpacked our food. After lunch we had a meeting. At Easter we had been quite well off, thanks to the hard work of the early spring; but a long rehearsal period and the expenses of a new production had reduced our balance to £13. Now we were not likely to reap the reward of putting on a new play, and the position looked pretty serious. Nine into thirteen goes once, only once with not much over; and we doubted very much what sort of reception we should get at this moment in new country. Would organisers cancel their bookings? We had no reserves; and we didn't know whether the very new CEMA was much better equipped with them than we were. We might be in debt in a few days; and we had always set our faces against that. A few weeks before we had raised salaries to fourteen shillings. Well, if to revert to nine would save the situation, so be it! Back we went; and the convoy moved on.

At a late tea time we reached Wimborne, and one of the Pilgrims, who was not so dependent on the salary as others, invited the company to tea at the King's Head, a pleasant old hotel in the square. We sat in the comfortable lounge, and tea was brought by a trim waitress. The linen and china were good, the room bright with flowers, the whole scene, indoors and out, unmistakably English. Our hostess voiced thoughts that were in all our minds: 'It will never be just like this again.' Not only the little adornments, but the whole English way of life, might not ever be like this again. In the evening light we finished the journey to Dorchester, which took, all told, eleven hours.

That was the week of Dunkirk. We didn't know it by that name at the time; and it is queer to remember how little we did know, although we were right in the middle of the coast which received most of the returning army. We were aware of a desperate struggle; we saw the hundreds of exhausted men, needing food and refreshment and most of all sleep. People in the town went at queer hours to duty in canteens and hospitals; but they didn't volunteer information, and we didn't ask questions. We were strangers in the place, and could give no service except our work. We felt like children do, when the grown-ups are in trouble and not telling them. One evening we were to have given *Tobias* in the Corn Exchange, but word came that the floor was covered with sleeping men, so we played instead in a vicarage garden, where a raised terrace made a natural stage. The weather continued to be heavenly, and emphasised the contrast with the dark events we knew and did not know.

The heavy days were only lightened when we played to children. For some weeks now we had had a children's bill called *Pilgrim Pie*, composed of short plays and songs. It started with us all in our ordinary clothes, and the costumes for the first play were given out on the stage; the whole bill was presented in this informal sort of way. The children entered into the fun as if life were miraculously normal. We gave a show on the floor of a small primary school, an old building but beautifully kept, with flowers and gay pictures everywhere. It was a church school, and had that 'plus' which a living faith can give. The letter which told of results said: 'The children have insisted on acting "like the Pilgrim Players did . . .".' We all feel that your visit has been a tremendous asset.' This kind of thing showed us that we could help in the work of keeping education going; and it seemed as if *we* were to keep going, for two weeks after the picnic-meeting our balance stood at £38, and CEMA were giving us a grant of £30 a month.

Some of our evenings were spent in country places, and there we were struck by the calm of spirit which the land imposes on its workers. 'Seedtime and harvest shall not fail' even though the enemy is at the gate; the seed must be sown, the harvest gathered. So in the village, when we were welcomed as the recreation from a long day's work, the fate which impended had a certain quality of beneficence, as it has in Greek tragedy. At any rate, we gained strength from those evenings. But the journey home was often a nocturnal version of Theseus' maze. By this time there were no signposts; and we had not yet risen to the standard of map-reading required to do without them. There was seldom anyone to ask; and if there was, he often would not tell us. Our only reliable guides were of a terrifying nature. We would come round a corner and see a lantern swinging. On a dark night the glimmer would be so dim that we almost missed it, pulling up with a jerk to find ourselves looking into the muzzle of a gun. The soldiers would look us over thoroughly, their fixed bayonets catching the gleams of our dimmed lights. Then they would let us pass, and even tell us what the next village was; they seldom knew more.

By 17 June the Pilgrims were at Gillingham in north Dorset, and we were staying with three sisters, old friends of Martin's family.

We sat in their drawing-room waiting for the one o'clock news. A duchess of the court of Charles II, ancestress of our hostesses, looked down gaily from the wall. The room and the garden were full of flowers. We didn't talk or knit while we waited that day; we were conscious of what France had meant to our civilisation from Stuart days to our own . . . When we knew, the eldest Miss Stewart tucked her arm in mine and said, 'Well, we'd better go and have lunch. You have two shows today.'

A few days later we received a letter from our good friends in America, Edwin and Jeannette Bry. Martin read it to me. It was like trying to understand a letter in a foreign language that one almost knew; it sounded simple, but it wasn't making sense:

We are wondering what you have done with your children . . . whether you feel they are quite safe where they are . . .

Two nights before we had had a raid. It hadn't done much damage, but we weren't used to them then.

If you care to send them to us, we will take care of them, until such a time when you can have them back again. This exactly means that if you care to send them to us we will take care of them as if they were our own and do what we can for them . . .

The steady reading went on:

I think people have at last awakened in this country, and realise that the danger which threatens France and England is not only their danger but ours also . . . You may rest assured that all our sympathies are with you, and also the hope that the calamity which threatens France and Britain may by some miracle be averted.

Finally the letter came to an end. Martin and I looked at each other. I no longer remember what we said. Two feelings were at war within me: safety for the children with deep gratitude for the writers, and dread of this unnatural separation which had no period set to it. Knowing what the decision must be, I said to Martin that I would not make it; but because I was sorry I was a coward, I promised to subscribe to whatever he felt was right. He sent the cable.

At a company meeting we told the Pilgrims. Martin also offered to release people before the war developed on a large scale in this country; it might be very hard to book dates, and would certainly be impossible to move about if the land war came to England. But everyone decided to stick together as long as they could; and Denis

Carey took charge so that Martin and I could have leave to get the boys off to America.

Because Christopher was American-born, we were able to get both boys aboard the *Washington*, the last American boat to leave Europe. Sailing date, of course, undisclosed. There followed a week in which it seemed as if the accelerator would never be released. '"Now, now," cried the Queen, "faster, faster." And they went so fast that at last they seemed to skim through the air, hardly touching the ground with their feet; till suddenly, just as Alice was getting quite exhausted, they stopped and she found herself sitting on the ground, breathless and giddy.'

We rejoined the Pilgrims in Devon, playing mostly on the south coast. Here the fact that our island was to be a fortress became every day clearer: barbed wire, concrete anti-tank 'teeth' and stakes filled the beaches, except where a small gap allowed us an occasional bathe, almost by ourselves on the once crowded shore; mine-traps on every bridge and at the entrance to every village, pillboxes at the cross roads. Already the bathing-box era was past, and the Home Guard well under way with its job. We sought the advice of CEMA on our policy; up to what point ought we to carry on? We were living in a tiny village in very cramped quarters, and the answer came to a meeting held in the only large enough space, the hayloft. Mary Glasgow, the secretary of CEMA, wrote encouragingly; her quick imagination had clearly seen our circumstances. Our work was of constructive use and we should carry it on till we were stopped; the Council would find emergency funds for us if we were immobilised by invasion.

In July we decided to revive *Murder in the Cathedral*. At that moment, nothing less than a masterpiece would do. Eliot, like Bridie, allowed us to do an 'emergency version' for nine players. On the 17th we played *England's Green* in the Chapter House of Exeter Cathedral, and were invited to come back for the opening of our *Murder* when it was ready. That night we arrived at Dartington Hall. The plan was that we should stay a week, playing in the barn theatre there and in villages round. We did stay six weeks, rehearsing *Murder* and playing a wide radius. That is typical of the hospitality of the place, and of the Elmhirsts to whom it belonged. Three nights after our arrival the wireless gave out that the *Washington* had docked in New York. Mrs Elmhirst rejoiced with me both as a mother and as an American.

German planes passed over nightly, bound, so we gathered, for the ports. One night just after eleven o'clock the siren went, for the first time at Dartington. I met Mrs Elmhirst on her way to get the evacuated children, of whom she had many, out of bed and into the stone passage on the ground floor. I collected a little girl from the East End called Marina, and sat on a cushion with her curled up in my lap. It was comforting to be a mother for those two hours; and next morning Marina said she hoped there would be another raid tonight.

Rehearsals were a great joy, for they took place in the banqueting-hall, part of the original house which had been restored by the Elmhirsts when they bought it. A huge stone fireplace backed the dais which we used as stage. The big gothic windows let us enjoy the sunlight while the high roof made the place cool, and poetry seemed to grow naturally as we rehearsed Eliot's words there. In spare moments we would go and sit on the smooth lawn overlook-

20 Pilgrim Players' audience at a school performance. Photo by permission of Fox Photos Ltd

ing the fourteenth-century tilt-yard, now converted into an open-air theatre; twelve yew-trees, called The Twelve Apostles, flank it; and there we could hear no aeroplanes, just birds, and children's voices in the distance. Here I wrote the first few letters of a weekly correspondence with the children and their foster-parents, which we maintained all through the war, and on which the rest of this account is based.

When we had produced *Murder* in Exeter and played it at Dartington and near-by for a week, we moved on to our last stop in the south, at Horrabridge to the west of Dartmoor. After our first show in the village hall, we came out into a lovely summer night. The sky was full of stars and searchlights, their beams seeking restlessly, insistently. Soon we heard the throbbing of planes. We didn't ask 'ours or theirs?' – that question didn't arise for a long time yet. We heard plenty of noise – bombs or guns, I could never tell, but the guns were not yet so many that they would account for much of it. The all-clear went at 4 a.m. It had, everyone agreed, been 'Plymouth again'.

It *was* Plymouth again. Next day we were due to give a matinée of *Tobias* at Devonport High School. Martin rang up at 9.30 to ask if we should go. The reply was that the audience might be small, as the children would have spent seven hours in the shelters, but that they would be glad to see us. As we drove in, another raid passed over us. Later in the morning Ronnie Long and I went downtown from the school to do some shopping. By this time Ronnie had taken over all the costuming of the shows, both designing and making. *Tobias* was gradually being re-dressed, and we went to buy materials for it. As we started back on the tram the siren went; the tram stopped at the mouth of a shelter and we were all ordered in. An old woman turned to us as she stumped into the entrance, 'here goes the Ancient Briton into her cave.' We got back to find the company having lunch in the school basement, and the headmistress more depressed than ever about the prospects of an audience. But she was wrong. When we got on to the stage we found a packed house in front, and never did we have a better audience than those children.

7

The Pilgrim Players: II

An actor is not by nature inclined to communal life, and the ways in which he has to find employment encourage him to be an individualist and to look out first for himself. But if we were to do the particular job we had taken on we must all share alike in its demands and its rewards. That was why, in spite of its obvious unfairness in some ways, we stuck for three-and-a-half years to the principle of equal pay for all; intention counted before experience or talent.

We also stuck to the principle that the whole job was everybody's job. As we got better at running our life, we organised it departmentally. Transport, Stage Management, Wardrobe, Lights, each had its specialist, but everyone shared in the manual labour; and no Pilgrim, if asked to give a hand with setting stage or jacking up the van, would dream of saying it wasn't his job.

Everyone believed in the work, but they came to this belief from divergent motives. There were Christians who wanted to offer Christian ideas through their art. There were agnostics who disapproved of the outspokenly Christian plays, but felt that the theatre had a duty to the people. (Some of them were inclined to insist that 'the people' meant the working man, and to deprecate the matinée audience of bewildered maiden ladies on the threatened south coast.) There were pacifists, who found a way of service compatible with their conscience – and the tribunals agreed with them. And there were keen young women, and young men awaiting, or unfit for, military service, to whom this was the best theatrical experience available.

We naturally took a particular interest in the people we served. Every company discusses during the show whether 'they' (in front)

are 'good' or 'bad', responsive or dull, intelligent or silly. But as
Pilgrims we were not only concerned with 'them' as audience. We
lived in their houses and found that they wanted to know us
personally. We wanted to know what they needed; how far the play
we had brought was meeting their need; what they thought we
should do next; whether Pilgrim methods of production made them
feel involved in the play; what were the special requirements of
children, or young people, or villages, or churches. We wanted the
Pilgrims, in fact, to be 'their' theatre.

All this naturally made us proud of the Pilgrim name and
concerned for its honour. We continually fought two battles for it.
One was against the people who thought that, because we played
in places which none but amateurs had ever used, we must be

21   Pilgrim Players' audience early in 1943 in Hythe Church.
Photo by permission of Fox Photos Ltd

amateurs. The professional status needed guarding for the work's sake. We had to insist that the labourer is worthy of his hire, and that we lived by our work, in however lowly a fashion. We did not want an audience, whether in church or hall, to support a charity but to enjoy a work of art. We had to bring people, who had never thought of a play as food for the spirit, to realise consciously that they must have it, and that, like any other food, it must be paid for.

Our other battle was to maintain our standard and gradually to raise it, in face of great odds. Lewis Casson once said, when he visited us on tour, 'Your danger is that for you the acting is a rest.' The average show meant a drive of from ten to thirty miles in uncomfortable transport, often with a breakdown on the way, since the cars were carrying heavy loads. On arrival at the hall a lot of heavy stuff must be got in. The stage might be some distance from the nearest roadway, approached through an awkwardly blacked-out door and perhaps up flights of stairs. Often there was a piano on the stage, though we asked every organiser to dispose of the piano in advance: we became expert piano removers. Many stages had pitfalls: before the show the stage manager would come round with warnings: 'You can't get round the back, so everyone entering from the far side must be there before the scene begins. There is a hole in the downstage-left corner. The floor is uneven so don't jump or you'll upset the screens. There is no wing-space, so don't fall off when you make your exit,' and so on. After the show everything had to be packed up again, carried out and loaded in trailer or van; and at last we set out into the black night with someone reading a map by torchlight beside the driver of the leading vehicle.

The weekly meeting was for talking over these problems. Procedure soon became strictly parliamentary. Members addressed 'Mr Chairman'; fellow-members were 'Mr Tyrrell' or 'Miss Graham'. Motions were couched in proper form and agenda were posted up forty-eight hours before the meeting. Unnecessary as such elaboration may sound in a parliament of nine or ten members, it had its value. A member who transgressed against its spirit would feel here the community's displeasure; a member who had given anything good, or had anything good to offer, would have his reward or his chance. The standard, the good name, and the welfare of the company were in its own keeping.

At first the director was chairman. After a time we tried having a different chairman each month, elected (in practice on a rota of alternate men and women) by the meeting. The director, having artistic control and a good deal of executive responsibility to answer for, was not eligible. This made business easier to conduct, though not shorter: an inexperienced chairman would allow discussion to proceed unchecked. Most members relieved the tedium by darning or knitting; and it was a hardship to become chairman or record secretary, so losing one's darning-time for a month or more.

A financial statement was made by the treasurer at each meeting. Accounts had become more elaborate than in Stuart Burge's time; auditors and CEMA must be satisfied. It was hard to assess accurately what our weekly takings had been, as money for some shows didn't come in for a month or two after they were played. But from the time we turned northwards in September 1940 a steady rise in the box-office 'take' was evident. Where the south coast, threatened with invasion, had yielded us only £30 to £40 a week, the north, further from the war, produced half as much again. CEMA slightly increased its grant; so a three-figure balance replaced a two-figure one. The salary which had been cut was restored; and when the private soldier's net pay rose to seventeen shillings and sixpence, we were able to follow suit.

More important, we were able to set up the funds. These represented the second stage in the maintenance of every member out of the common purse. It had always kept us in lodging and all meals, as well as giving Tommy's pay into our pockets. Now, clothing, health and holidays were to be provided for.

The clothing fund was set up first, with a grant of £25 which we hoped would meet absolute needs for six months. A committee of three was appointed to administer this. A further grant of £10 was soon made 'in view of the fact that Pilgrims stay constantly in other people's houses'.

The fund's policy was exhaustively discussed at meetings, and it was decided that 'neat, not gaudy' was to be the guiding principle; few clothes and good ones, but of medium price. When a member applied for an article the committee took great pains to price it in various shops before giving its grant. For instance, two Pilgrims needed new overcoats. After much research £7 was voted to each. To secure the coat he personally wanted, one added some more to this, but that was his own affair. Rationing, when it came, added to the committee's difficulties in one way but eased them in another.

It must get the best out of the coupons; but there were fewer applications. The fund was established after a few months' trial on a grant of £10 per member per year. The meeting decreed that all maintenance charges (repairs, cleaning etc.) be paid in full, while to the cost of new articles the applicant should contribute twenty per cent.

The health fund started very modestly by buying a first-aid box. It was taken from the car into each performance, to treat minor injuries from snags on our stages, as well as accidents on the road. Any Pilgrim suffering from ill-health was to consult the chairman of the fund before seeing a doctor; the fund would aim at paying for treatment and medicine in full, but only up to seventy-five per cent for tonics. It also paid all dentists' bills; and for two winters supplied halibut oil to all who wanted it. This was given in capsule form, at the request of the clothing fund.

On a grant of ten shillings a week such a programme would have been impossible without the generosity of doctors, who have always been friendly to actors anyway, and specially appreciated the Pilgrims' situation. Many a time, when the bill was asked for, none was forthcoming.

The holiday fund solved the Pilgrim's most urgent problem. One couldn't save for a holiday on seventeen shillings and sixpence; and as one member said, half the good of a holiday is lost if one doesn't know how one is going to pay for it. At the first recorded meeting we had discussed holidays with pay, and twice already the common purse had contributed to holiday expenses. But now a fund was set up to assure the supply of every member's fare and maintenance 'during periods of leave'. It was the most expensive of the three; it drew £3 a week from the exchequer, plus occasional special grants when expenses were heavy, for instance on holidays from Scotland. A fortnight before the beginning of a break each of us submitted our estimate of expenses, which were discussed privately and usually met in full.

While we had been developing our tiny community the much bigger development of CEMA had been going forward. Music, drama and the visual arts were being disseminated all over the country. At first CEMA left us to carry on our own life and book our own tours, but it gradually built a larger framework. It held quarterly meetings of those running companies, to which each Pilgrim company sent its director and an elected representative.

We set up a joint committee of the two companies, and secured Oliver Bell as an independent chairman.

CEMA's help to us was not primarily financial. Our overheads were so infinitesimal that we could get along safely on a very small margin. But the Council established our bona-fides with government departments. It persuaded the Ministry of Labour to leave us some essential man-power; the Ministry of War Transport to allow us petrol; HM Customs and Excise that our peculiar methods of working did not cloak illicit profits. Only with this help could we have survived the increase in every kind of rationing and control. CEMA was always careful of our independence; however unusual we seemed to the more orthodox theatre-men among its associates, the Council itself encouraged us to work out our own methods and was always patient with our blunderings. Can a government department foster artistic enterprise? That depends on who runs the department!

HENZIE CONTINUES THE STORY
Pilgrimage northwards

For some time we had been getting requests from further north. The bookings were patchy, and the Battle of Britain was now raging, so we didn't know at all how we should fare. The first week was at Southwell, where we played in the Minster. Then we moved on to Derby. The war seemed much nearer here; all the industrial cities were alert for raids, and a lot of planes went over. We lost a good deal of sleep, and there was some bombing of factories, but nothing on the city.

On 9 September we played our first performance to the army. A chaplain of our acquaintance had charge of two camps, one on either bank of the Trent, a few miles out of the city, and asked us to take *Tobias*. He warned us that the appearance of 'The Angel' in the title would probably result in a poor attendance at the start, for a straight play was unfamiliar anyway, and the taint of religion would scare men away. 'But if you don't mind some movement during the earlier scenes, I think it will turn out all right.'

The show was in a huge marquee seating about 400. It was a fine evening and the tent flaps were left open. About sixty men were in at the start, a thin-looking house; but the doorway was full of watching faces. After about ten minutes those in the doorway began to leave. It was a flop, we thought, in spite of the obvious enjoyment of the seated audience. But no: after a few minutes men began to come in and sit down; in the first interval a crowd thronged the entrance – the men in the doorway had gone to bring their friends. Next night, across the river, we started with a full house.

October began with our first visit to Sheffield. It had had no raids yet: people said the Germans couldn't find it because of its pall of fog. They succeeded later. We were invited by the YWCA, who had just completed a fine new building: despite the war, their leaders rightly judged that the need for it was urgent. Phyllis Lowe, the secretary, booked us for three performances in their excellently equipped hall, as the lighter side of the opening week. The dedication was on the first afternoon, with *Tobias* in the evening. Elna, who was the Sara, had felt poorly all day, but gallantly assured us that she would be all right on the night. The play duly opened to a packed house, and I went on as Anna, Tobias' old mother. Act II began with Elna's entrance; she looked disturbingly ethereal under her make-up, and after ten minutes made her first exit to be violently sick. I had played her part six years before. If one doesn't think, it is possible to let a part come back from the storehouse of the brain. I quickly changed costume and make-up: Brian as Tobias helped me through; we managed it successfully, with Pamela Keily taking over Anna (which she had played many times) in the last act. The opening night was saved from disaster; the patient quickly recovered, and the emergency understudy received from the chairman yellow roses and a magnificent basket of fruit, much enjoyed by all.

Fruit! The eating sort was soon to vanish from our tables; but the fruits of that visit are still being delivered. It was the first of several; and out of them arose an insistent desire in the young people of Sheffield to create their own drama on Pilgrim lines. The Association of Christian Communities took it up; and late in 1942 the Religious Drama Society gave a grant to finance an exploratory visit. Pamela Keily left the company and successfully settled in the discovered territory. In three days she saw the need for a full-time adviser; in a month the Association had found her first year's salary; and in a year the Education Authority was giving a grant to aid her work, which afterwards spread to other northern dioceses and still goes on.

Sometimes people who liked comparisons asked us where in England we found the best audiences; and if we had to pick a county, Durham was the one. On a Sunday afternoon we went to a large village to play *The Way of the Cross* in the Miners' Welfare Hall, a big one and packed by the joint efforts of Anglican and Methodist clergy. A red plush front curtain; grey cotton ones surrounding the stage; an eager, excited audience talking at the top of its voice; all this was very unlike the atmosphere of a church where the play was usually given. But we soon became aware of a tremendous emotional response. The imagination of this audience was following every phase of the starkly told story. At the end nearly £10 had been collected in pennies and threepenny-bits. The organiser told us later that not five per cent of those people had ever seen a play by live actors before; and that next Christmas they set out to make their own play on the lines of ours.

Theatres

During 1940 we played only a few single matinées in theatres – Brighton, Eastbourne, Folkestone – plus some longer visits to Little Theatres: the Questors at Ealing, the Civic at Bradford, the People's at Newcastle. But at the beginning of 1941 came a letter from the Arts Theatre, Cambridge. Maynard Keynes was becoming chairman of CEMA, and was also chairman (and indeed had been largely the creator) of the Arts Theatre. He and Norman Higgins, its manager, invited us to play a week in March. On the Monday afternoon we were setting up the undecorated platform and ramp which, against the cyclorama, were the ark in Obey's *Noah*. (It took Martin and me back to the night of 25 January 1938 when by a blissful chance we witnessed in Boston the first night of Thornton Wilder's *Our Town*.) The chairman strolled onto the stage, to see that we were getting on all right. Were we not! Playing on that large yet intimate stage, to audiences of quick perception, was an incredible contrast to most of what had gone before (and what was to follow). To the experienced, it was sweet beyond telling; to the junior members, a revelation. Ivor Brown came to a performance for *The Observer* and wrote that 'one is naturally shy of giving particular praise where the temper of general teamwork is exemplary'.

The invitation was renewed each year. On the programme appeared this announcement:

The Directors have placed the theatre at the disposal of the Pilgrim Players, without charge, to provide capital to continue their work free from pressing financial worry. The two plays chosen for this week from the Pilgrim Players' repertory will be presented with the extremely modest staging enforced by their slogan – 'Performances at any time, anywhere'. For example, similar performances next week will be given in London air-raid shelters.

London: blitz and shelters

On our first day we had a matinée of *The Way of the Cross* in St Martin-in-the-Fields, and an evening *Tobias* at the Central YWCA, off Tottenham Court Road. This was in March 1941, the first of many shows we played there, on the flat floor of the club room because the hall was out of commission, with tall green screens as a background and a semi-circle of club leaders and residents as audience. At once we felt that we were giving enjoyment desperately needed, and everyone in the room was happy. At the end of the first act a blitz began, and Martin sent round a message to ask whether the show should go on, as he knew that many of the audience lived some way off. The secretary came, with a puzzled face, and said, 'Of course; we are all loving it.' We didn't notice the bangs much while we were playing. Afterwards, feeling rather naked about the head, we made our way through the noisy night into the tube station, and saw the shelterers for the first time. Though I had seen pictures of them, I found that wasn't the same thing at all. I was terribly moved at the spectacle of these patient people, sleeping or trying to sleep, as the trains roared past. It was so orderly and quiet. We picked our way among the sleepers to avoid disturbing them and got to our lodging at last, with the explosions still going on. Next day Martin received a letter from the YWCA secretary apologising for having been so puzzled by his message during the show:

We were all so interested in the story of Tobias that we were astonished to be told by this morning's papers that we had had this year's heaviest blitz during the performance.

We played twice most days, and after the first had mostly quiet ones. Our start in the shelters was made at Lloyd's in Leadenhall

Street. The whole basement of the great building was fitted with bunks and held over two hundred sleepers; it was comfortable as the heating-plant was there. The show was on the ground floor, in the storeroom which was the Shelterers' Club. I think that all who played that performance of *Murder in the Cathedral* will always remember it; and most of the audience will too. They sat on the canteen benches and tables. Before dressing as Becket, Martin gave a short talk about the play, and then we went through it without a break. For the first ten or fifteen minutes the form and language of it seemed strange to them; then they got caught up by it, and it was one of the most 'shared' performances I have ever known.

Not many shelters could have supplied such an audience. The people were no different from those in any other shelter – most of them came nightly from Hackney, finding the journey worthwhile to be in a strong and warm building. But the management was the Friends' Ambulance Unit (FAU). This unit, made up of conscientious objectors, both Quaker and others, took the lead in introducing better conditions into the shelters in the black days of 1940. Bunks, canteens and other material amenities originated with them; they provided good recreation and established self-government. At Lloyd's we had been invited by the Entertainments Committee. John Gough, son of our Vicar of Tewkesbury, was the FAU man looking after this shelter, but he was not on the committee; he had only told them about the play and left them to decide about having it. After it was over we were thanked by the chairman, a stevedore, in a very formal manner which ill concealed a good deal of emotion.

We played a matinée at the Jewish Presbyterian Mission in Bethnal Green. The building was almost the only one left whole in the mile-long street. Our audience was composed of motherly women, who chattered throughout the performance, discussing the characters as they would have done at a silent film. While I was playing Anna, I heard a sympathetic voice exclaim, 'Oh, she's crying, poor dear!' That evening we were in Bermondsey, south of the river, in a shelter run by clergy of various denominations. It was a semi-basement room, packed with three-tiered bunks. As the parson told us, 'They would really be safer at home; but their little houses feel so flimsy and they get so lonely in raids; they really come here to be together and to feel someone is looking after them.' Most of the audience had to lie on the top tier to see the stage, a platform sixteen feet by six with no equipment. We dressed in a room at the side of the auditorium and made all our entrances and exits between bunks through a narrow passage-way, in which some of the older folk, who couldn't climb to the top, sat to see whatever they could. We were outdoing Shakespeare in the matter of close contact with an audience.

In the winter we expected big raids again, and planned a month's season in London. We prepared a special show, *Christmas Pie*, songs and short plays, with Martin as compère, to suit the atmosphere of a big family, which we had found in the shelters we first went to. But no blitz came; and the shows were given in what one might call post-blitz conditions: halls and churches half-wrecked and usually unheated, and the younger people very much out of hand now that the community life of the shelter period was melting away. We tried to help clergy and social workers with the uphill task of fighting the growth of hooliganism.

One Saturday night we played for the Franciscans in Peckham. We had a big crowd in their hall, but at the back was a group of lads of 14 to 16 who obviously thought it might be fun to wreck the show. The first part was light, and they were sufficiently amused to let us go ahead. The last item, however, was a scene from Dorothy Sayers' *The Man Born to be King*, in which the Kings come to visit the Christ-Child in the shepherds' cottage. This meant twenty minutes of quiet listening; and Martin appealed to the boys to give the rest of the audience a chance. They behaved well, and the play finished in complete stillness. The programme was rounded off with two verses of 'God rest you merry', which Martin announced by 'Will you join us in a song we all know?' At this, one of the young men couldn't keep quiet any longer and called 'Roll out the barrel!' So they started that and we started 'God rest you merry'! Everyone on both sides of the footlights was wondering how it would end. The verse of each song finished together, and there was a moment's pause. Then Martin struck up verse two; and the others, taken aback, I suppose, by that little silence, left us and the rest of the audience to finish our carol.

Scotland

1942, from March to December, we spent in Scotland. We had been invited to the St Andrews summer school in 1941 as a 'try-out', to play our repertory, take some part in teaching, and rehearse Obey's *Noah*. The seeds then sown had borne many fruits. One of the most important was the welcome extended to us by the Church of Scotland.

That we should play *The Way of the Cross* and *Murder in the Cathedral* in St Mary's, the Episcopal Cathedral at Edinburgh, was natural. Apart from all the work we had done in the Church of England, there was a personal link, for Colin Dunlop was then its Provost. He had been chaplain to the Bishop of Chichester when Martin had worked for him. So on Palm Sunday twelve hundred people filled the nave of St Mary's to see *Murder*, and it was repeated there in the summer.

But for the Church of Scotland to take us up was quite another thing. The Presbyterians of last century would have banned us as of the de'il; and drama was still a new thing to most of the people of Scotland. The leaders of the Church had already seen, however, that it is a thing they need; and of many invitations the most significant was from Dr Warr, to play *The Way of the Cross* in the ancient Cathedral of St Giles.

Dr Warr was chairman of the Church of Scotland Huts Committee. This did most of the work which the YMCA did in England, but the male staff consisted of ministers, mostly lent by their parishes for six months at a time. The minister worked in the canteen, which brought him into contact with the men. Dr Warr told us of the isolated army and RAF units on the Orkney Islands. They were posted in the countryside in small detachments, to guard the navy from air attack. The navy itself got good entertainment, but the ack-ack men had almost none. He pleaded that we should try to go there.

Before we arrived in Scotland the Army Education authorities had already decided we could be useful to them. We were told to report at a certain spot whence a sergeant guided us to the camp, situated in a dense wood. As I stood among the pines they became bars through which I saw first the yellow sands, then the line of sea and above that the blue sky, luminous with the last rays of the setting sun. But the men who had lived among them for two years took these natural beauties for granted: what they wanted was the show – they had only had a bare half-dozen in that long time.

We played *Tobias* in a Nissen hut, which had been fitted with a foot-high stage. The unit had made a row of footlights and built us a dressing-room. It was the men's pride and joy; but it was only 8 feet by 6 feet, so we dressed in relays, the others remaining outside till it got too cold, and then going over to the sergeants' mess, picking their way carefully for fear of mines. The audience of seventy packed the hut, and they were good enough to refrain from smoking lest we should be choked, as there was no ventilation. A long interval was provided to allow of a whiff outside.

Inchkeith was a fortified island in the Firth of Forth. To play there meant going in a small tug; so we packed everything for *Tobias* in suitcases. A sergeant met us on the dock, and we steamed for forty-five minutes to the island which always seemed a few yards away, taking a tortuous course to conform to the defences of the Firth. An officer met us at the little quay and we climbed the steep rock to the Church of Scotland Hut on the top. The stage was surrounded with grey army blankets, and a pair also served for front curtains. A full house. The first funny line came: deathly silence. It continued through Act I. 'Oh, well,' we thought, 'they aren't accustomed to listening to plays and perhaps a verbal joke doesn't appeal; wait till we get to the Fish and then the Girls.' But still deathly silence, though we could feel that a lot of people were wanting to react differently. We had never met this before, and it took all we had to get through the show. When the final curtain fell, long and vociferous applause burst out. The major in command made a charming speech, in which he explained that he had told the men they mustn't laugh because this was a religious play with an angel in it – but perhaps he had been wrong! Then he invited us to tea in the mess – which he hadn't planned to do.

All this time deliberations were going on about Orkney. The RAF would fly the Pilgrims there in a bomber; the Church of Scotland Huts and Army Education wanted to promote the tour. But there were very few halls on the islands. It would be much more useful to send just a couple, who could visit the ack-ack units themselves (usually under a hundred strong) and play in their Nissen huts. The Church of Scotland Huts could billet two in staff quarters. Martin and I offered to give our summer holiday to the trip.

Orkney, since it held the great naval base at Scapa Flow, was a Protected Area, and it took us weeks to get the permits needed to fly to it, to enter it and to work in it. We left Inverness in a tiny plane, the only passengers and quite submerged by mailbags. Despite the correspondence on my shoulders I could see ahead a little between the pilot and the wireless operator. By the time we landed at Kirkwall and had shown our permits to all and sundry it was two o'clock. We asked where we should get any lunch. 'Oh, they'll knock you up an omelette at the staff hut.' Sure enough, the housekeeper produced a bowl of real eggs!

We lived in the staff hut for a week while we played the Mainland, as the chief island is called. It was July, and 'there shall be no night there' is almost literally true of those northern climes in the summer. A four-hour day in midwinter, with months of ceaseless wind, is the price to be paid for this.

We travelled on the Mainland in army cars sent by each unit. The show, an *Impression of Hamlet* and Shaw's *Village Wooing*, was devised to go into one suitcase: we had one more for our own things, so that even when we 'moved house' Martin could carry all our traps. That sort of removal was done by 'drifter'. The drifters were fishing boats chartered by the Admiralty to provide a free 'bus service' between the islands. It was a delightful mode of transport, which we employed daily in our second week when playing the smaller islands, Flotta, Hoy, South Ronaldshay and Burray. The only serious problem was presented by the skippers' habit of tying up to other boats already moored at the quay, so that one might have to cross three or four boats to get to land. This wasn't easy with luggage; but we managed all right until one evening when, on reaching the quayside at last, we found it several feet above us, the boat alongside being very low in the water. A gangplank was sent seesawing down to us, but was still three feet off the deck. Two RAF men saw my plight, put a hand under each elbow and said 'spring'. I sprang, and landed in the middle of the plank which seesawed back to the quay.

Our shows in Orkney were among the most rewarding work we ever did. Entertainment was in short supply anyhow; and dramatic entertainment was confined to the occasional amateur show put on in Kirkwall. The stages in the small camps, to which we mostly went, were platforms with a ten-foot proscenium and often no curtains, set at one end of the dining-hut; no ordinary play could be put on them. So we were a complete change; and to those units, like the ack-ack batteries, whose personnel was of high intelligence, a welcome one. Of our twenty shows we reckoned at the end that seventeen had been successful; and the confidential report from each unit which the Army Education Officer got for us confirmed this diagnosis exactly. Eric Linklater's wife, Marjorie, living in a wild spot with her three children, her husband away on war service, wrote this notice:

HAMLET IN ORKNEY

I have lived in Orkney for six years (yes, I have, and liked it!) and I never thought I should have an opportunity of seeing a performance of 'Hamlet' in the middle of the countryside. Well, now we've had it! *Hamlet* and Bernard Shaw's *Village Wooing* all in one night.

Mr. Martin Browne and his wife are the sole performers. You may wonder how two people can stage *Hamlet*. Martin Browne has adapted the play in this way. He acts the part of Hamlet and his wife plays eight of the other characters. They act the essential scenes and Martin Browne explains the rest of the play as they go along. As he himself says: 'It needs a bit of imagination on the part of the audience,' but not so much as you might think because the Brownes are first-class actors and Shakespeare does the rest.

Then, after tragedy, came comedy. Shaw's *Village Wooing* – a play in three scenes for two characters – is full of wisecracks. The audience enjoyed all of them. Henzie Browne is delicious as the simple village maiden who is out to capture the high-brow young man. And does so in the end though he is quite certain she is not his cup of tea.

James Bridie had started us on our way with *Tobias* long ago. When we came to Scotland he promised to write us a new play. He came to the 351st performance of *Tobias*, was pleased with it, and thought he had a subject. Six weeks later we received *The Dragon and the Dove*, taken from Helen Waddell's story of the Hermit Abraham, one of the Desert Fathers of the fourth century, and how he rescued his niece from a brothel by dressing up as a Roman soldier. The tale has a quality all its own, and to it the dramatist added the conceit, all his own, of making the old man adopt the airs of Colonel Blimp. We arranged to produce it in Glasgow, the author's home town, in September. Denis Carey and Sylvia Read, a new Pilgrim who joined us in Scotland, played the chief parts.

The play was in two acts, and lasted barely one-and-a-half hours. Something must go with it. The author of the main piece said he must complete the bill himself; and a few weeks later, when he gave the company a farewell lunch at the Central Hotel, he produced from his pocket the first half of *A Change for the Worse*, a half-hour morality in which the devil is defeated by finding that his machinations produce unexpectedly good effects. Martin read it aloud to the assembled company, and it added a lot to the gaiety of the party. The author promised the rights for a year for a special Pilgrim fee of two-and-fourpence. A few days later he rang up Martin and said he had finished the play and he had one bit of bad news for us. He would have to charge two-and-sixpence; the reason was that he had written two lines of real poetry, and thought he ought to have a penny a line for them.

Full circle

At the beginning of 1943, after three-and-a-quarter years of Pilgrim playing, we were back in Kent where we began. We found the coast, which we had left so naked, now mightily defended. Raids were frequent; though short, they often happened several times a day, and evidence of them could be seen everywhere. The walls of the schools were pitted with shrapnel. In this country of sirens there was a dual warning system. One just took note of the ordinary 'alert', but on the short, sharp blasts of 'planes overhead' one took action.

Shows were in great demand. This district was much denuded of population, and so even the coast towns, which before the war had been happy hunting-grounds for the commercial showman, now held no attraction for him. So the people were starved, and we were doubly welcome back to our old haunts. Shells were still coming into Dover, but we didn't get any the night we played there to a full town hall. At Broadstairs the show was run by a curate who had taken a fishing-boat to Dunkirk. On a January Sunday we went back to New Romney and our minds went back to 1940. How unimportant the tiresome raids suddenly seemed! *There had been no invasion*; for eight hundred and seventy years there had been none, and there wasn't going to be one! It was fitting to play *Murder* as a thank-offering, in the church where Becket worshipped before he embarked for France.

All this led up to the return to Canterbury. We drove in by the West Gate, as we had always done from Kent College; everything looked more or less normal. We parked the van and walked up the High Street till we got to Mercery Lane. Looking down it we could see Christ Church Gateway, still gay with the heraldic shields which were repainted just before the war. We went on for another four shops and then – Canterbury stopped. No more buildings till the suburbs. Only on our left the cathedral, now visible in all its length, stood intact. We went back up Mercery Lane and into the great building. All the glass was gone from the nave; that in the choir had long since been taken out for safety. All the treasures were wrapped in sandbags or cased in wood. Services went on as usual in the crypt. The nave had the air of a house when the family is away for a time.

We called on Miss Babington who gave us a ten-minute picture of Canterbury life since we had left it: she was welcoming and busy as ever. Then to see the dean – the 'Red Dean' before Russia became our ally, but now an esteemed authority on her affairs, in demand all over the country. Most of his house had been damaged, so he received us in his bed-sitting-room in the old tower. A whole wall of the drawing-room was gone, the grand piano stood, a hopeless wreck, inaccessible without a ladder. The dean reassured us that his precious Chinese pottery was safe with his wife and children in Wales, and told us how the cathedral had been saved from the blitz.

Last call, at the Old Palace, to tea with the archbishop and Mrs Temple. That night we took them to see *A Change for the Worse* at an ack-ack post. They chuckled all through the performance, but the famous laugh was fully released when the Bishop-Saint Eloi, at the end of the play, uttered some particularly relevant comments:

> A clergyman, it would appear,
> Must hesitate to interfere
> In matters so abstruse and austere
>   As the Economic Law.
> He must refrain from taking a hand,
> And leave to those who understand
> That esoteric saraband
>   Called sometimes 'Luck of the draw'.
> Possibly those who take that view
> Are in the right: it may be true . . .

While we revisited places and people, and re-learnt our old ground, Pilgrims were also looking forward. Big changes were coming to many of the little company who had stuck together so long. One couple had married, others wanted to do so, and other people's houses are not the best places in which to start married life. At Christmas Martin and I had made up our minds to get our boys home. This meant that several members would be leaving at once. The emergency plan had served its turn. Pilgrims would not cease, but they would function differently under CEMA.

We decided that May was the time to make a break between old-style Pilgrimage and new. After a summer spent for a change in other jobs, some of the members would rejoin Martin to establish the company on its new basis. The assets were vested in him for the purpose. Meanwhile we made one more production, of good omen, W. B. Yeats' *The Resurrection*, for about fifteen performances in Lent and Eastertide. The last of these brought us to London.

The BBC invited us to give a radio performance of *The Dragon and the Dove* on a Sunday night. When we had played it for a week in March at the Arts Theatre Club, Lewis Casson, now Drama Director of CEMA, had overhauled the production for us. For the broadcast on 23 May he took over the lead. From this pleasant occasion each Pilgrim went, for the time being, his own way.

8

New Plays by Poets

Henzie found this in a letter I wrote to her before we were married:

Poetic drama is my great love, and I daresay my forte too.
My dream is to have a Poetry Theatre with a repertory
company playing poetic plays.

From August 1943 we lived with the boys in a top-floor flat too near Broadcasting House. But despite the V1s and V2s, we, like everyone else, were looking forward to After the War. The Pilgrim tours were to go on, with our flat as headquarters and workshop, for another two years. But the dream was taking shape, and my tours gave it opportunities to develop.

George Every was a lay-brother of the Society of the Sacred Mission, one of the Anglican orders of monks. When we were in their part of the east Midlands they invited the men of the company to lodge with them, and George, himself a poet influenced by Eliot, had many talks with me about the prospects for poetic drama. He was in touch with a number of younger poets, and urged me to meet them and build up a repertory.

Norman Nicholson came to see *Murder* at Ulverston, not far from his home at Millom on the tip of Cumberland. This was a major expedition, however, for a man who had barely escaped alive from tuberculosis. We found ourselves at one in having a special love for the Elijah story. 'Nic' had already the germ of an idea for a play, transferring it to the fells. We talked as long as time allowed about the practical problems of constructing and setting the play; and then had to carry on by letters to and from that remote spot.

After a show at Bude I was approached by a short man with strikingly sad eyes beneath a massive brow. 'I am Ronald Duncan [yes, I knew about him from George Every]. Can you come to lunch tomorrow? I have something to show you.' I took a bus northwards into Devon, got off at Welcombe and walked down steeply towards the sea. Here was West Mill, a cottage where he lived with Rose Marie and their two young children. After a farmer's lunch Duncan took me into his study, a whitewashed shed with a desk, a chair – and four Gaudier-Brzeska drawings on the walls. 'I've been trying to write a masque about St Antony [the saint of the Bosch *Temptation*], and I want to put his soliloquies into the most complex verse-form, Cavalcanti's *canzone*. I've tried one. Will you look at it and see if it could possibly work on stage?' I looked at the proffered sheets. 'The only way I can tell,' I said, 'is to read it aloud.' So I read, at sight, the elaborately patterned anguish of the solitary. We both felt its power: poetry without physical action, poetry *as* action. I urged him to finish the play.

Two other poets I already knew. Anne Ridler had before her marriage been Eliot's secretary. Christopher Fry was living in East Sussex when he wrote *The Boy with a Cart* for his village and George Bell showed it in his palace garden. Fry had executed two commissions for me in 1939, *The Tower* for Tewkesbury and a pageant for the Girls' Friendly Society in the Albert Hall which we amused ourselves devising together and called *Thursday's Child*. The heroine, Marjorie, had 'far to go' after leaving school; the great arena was filled in turn by groups miming, to music by Martin Shaw, work in house, office and factory, and a 'Saturday Night Down Town' for which Christopher wrote a catchy tune as well as words. When the war began, he was working on a play about Moses and the firstborn son of Pharaoh. I asked him to join the Pilgrims, for he had been actor and director as well as writer, and we needed plays; but that was too easy an option for his conscience and he enlisted in the Pioneer Corps. We next met in the Strand during an air-raid in 1940: over a cup of tea in Lyons Corner House he told me he was digging out blocked drains. Mercifully and amazingly, he was posted in 1943 to an army food depot outside Derby – in the garden of the home of the Pilgrims' northern secretary! So he could take refuge in the house to finish *The Firstborn* and in due course consider a smaller-scale play for me.

In spite of war-weariness – or perhaps because of it – the theatre was awakening to new life. CEMA tours were now nationally organised, and all of us who went about on them were aware that we had found a huge new audience. Added to our former clientele were the munition-workers, for whom CEMA had a special responsibility. The locations of their hostels were secret, in remote parts of the country, but the workers' life was better than many had known in peacetime. As audiences they were lively: theatre was a new experience which they were receiving – from the Old Vic, for instance, or the Ballet Rambert – in a form and quality that nothing but war could have brought them.

In London from 1944 we saw the most brilliant series of productions to grace this century. Olivier and Richardson led the Old Vic company, housed at the New (now the Albery) Theatre, as Richard III and Peer Gynt, collaborated as Hotspur, Falstaff and Shallow, and each scored a legendary success, Richardson as Cyrano and Olivier as Oedipus and Mr Puff (in one evening). On a quieter note, we rejoiced at the first night of Mr Bridie's best play, *Mr. Bolfry.*

When the Control Commission was set up in Germany after VE Day, Ashley Dukes was appointed Cultural Adviser for music and drama. He offered to let me the Mercury Theatre for a season of New Plays by Poets. Here was the opportunity to put on the stage those scripts I had been nursing. Here too was a base-theatre from which Pilgrim tours could be sent out under the Arts Council (as CEMA had become). For the tours, the Council gave a small subsidy; for the theatre, somebody gave me £250, somebody else gave £40. It was evident that even if we all took nominal salaries the box office would have to fill the 136 seats for most performances to allow us to survive. Another of my shoestring ventures; the string was stretched very tight, but didn't snap for two-and-a-half years, because I had some special things 'going for me'. The Mercury, tiny as it was, had the right reputation, and my own was linked with it. So was that of Robert Speaight, my leading man, for whom I had a succession of three widely different parts. I was also able to bring a number of my Pilgrim Players, and to use the Pilgrim name, which by now had wide currency. And I recaptured Frank Napier to be both the second leading actor and the stage director.

To launch the season we held a press lunch, and I made what I might call my campaign speech:

There has been too long a divorce between the poet and the playhouse. One of the chief glories of the Elizabethan Age lay in the fact that most playwrights were poets. I consider it would be an advantage if poets could be persuaded to write for the present-day stage. I have no desire to approach established dramatists to ask them to turn out plays in verse. I invite practised poets to write verse in the form of a play.

As most poets have no working knowledge of the theatre they hesitate to try their hand at playwriting. By way of encouragement I ask them to regard the Mercury as a workshop for poets. It is a miniature theatre where they can observe how actors work and where they can learn how stage dialogue should be written, so that the audience can grasp the significance of the lines immediately. During a performance the audience cannot ask the actor to go back over obscure lines. Their meaning is irretrievably lost. That is the major and perhaps the most difficult lesson a poet has to learn when he adopts the drama as a means of expression.

The poet has an enormous advantage as a dramatist. He can treat his characters imaginatively, seeing them against the large canvas of human life as a whole, or even in relation to the universe. Such a conception is denied to a theatre where only naturalistic drama is presented.

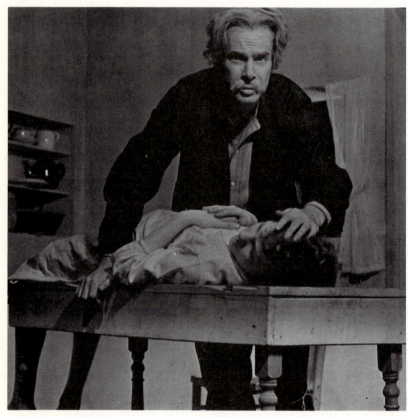

22   *The Old Man of the Mountains* (Norman Nicholson). Robert Speaight as Elijah, Mercury Theatre, 1945

A verse play introduces the added magic of word-music ... Words themselves have a musical quality which has a value for the audience irrespective of meaning. It is possible to be enthralled by a verse play in a foreign language, because, being in verse, the play has rhythm, which is a joy in itself.

Not all the poets, of course, used verse all the time. Eliot and Fry were both determined to develop a verse-form which they could use throughout a play. All the others alternated between verse and prose. In the Mercury workshop, I wanted each poet to find his own dramatic as well as poetic style. This meant experiment, so we must anticipate a failure-rate at least as high as that of the commercial theatre. Each play would have its own problems, and I would try to help the author with them. Since he would usually not have had much (or, like Nic, any) of his work staged before, the only way for him to learn might be to produce a script in a condition one knew to be unsatisfactory and let the author see what happened.

The Old Man of the Mountains gave Nic just this experience. We opened with it on 13 September. It might be described (in Bridie's phrase about *Tobias*) as 'a plain-sailing tale' of the conflict between Ahab and Elijah transferred to the Lakeland fells and re-interpreted in what we should now call environmental terms, Ahab being the landlord–developer and Elijah the hill-farmer.

> You'll answer to the Lord: you have defied His laws
> And defiled His creation to a muck-heap of money . . .
> I know your *business*. I know that you would make
> The beasts the Lord God gave, into the machines
> And the belts of a farming factory.

This verse has a fine lilt and vigour, using the vowels and inflections of the lakeland. But dialect is inhibiting to many actors, who cannot characterise freely if they are trying to master unfamiliar sounds. We enlisted the help of Margaret Cropper, a Westmorland woman, and worked hard with her, but the actors were not at ease with it, though Bobbie gave a truly prophetic gusto to Elijah's wiry, fiery verse, as in the description of the 'still, small voice':

> so quiet
> was the voice that ears could never hear it. So quiet,
> the sound of a mouse nibbling the dry straw
> would be as a gale in the larches compared to that;
> the sound of a throstle cracking a snail on a stone

would be as the blasting of a quarry compared to that –
yet it entered in my bones and ran along them
and cawed like the voice of the raven across the fells.

Besides the dialect, Nic's play had a structural problem which it took this production to solve. He lifted the Elijah story from the First Book of Kings, miracles and all. It is not so difficult to accept miracles among mountains: the scale of your surroundings makes it easier to take mystery in your stride, and no one boggled at the raising from the dead of the widow's son. This, at the curtain of Act I, leaves the play entertainingly half-way between heaven and a rocky earth; and Act II develops the conflict about that earth between Elijah and Ahab. So far so good: but the biblical story now demands a drastic change of scene and a triumphantly miraculous dénouement on the grand scale. The setting of Act III is the top of Carmel Fell. In the Old Testament, the prophet brought down the fire of the Lord, and the four hundred priests of Baal were slaughtered. Nic had not yet discovered how to do without the mountain-top, and more important, had not adjusted the characters' view of the happening to accord with their reality as twentieth-century people. (Eliot, speaking of *The Family Reunion* in his lecture on *Poetry and Drama*, accuses himself of 'a failure of adjustment between the Greek story and the modern situation'.) On stage, therefore, the play at this point ceased to be convincing.

Nic took this lesson home with him; and we corresponded about an alternative last act. A year later it appeared (and has been published by Faber and Faber, in this version since 1950). In the same cottage-cum-garden set as Acts I and II, it begins with the *descent* from Carmel. Elijah battles through a scepticism that reaches despair, to achieve an open-eyed faith. In this form, we toured the play the following season, and it has had a quietly steady life on stages since then. Nic has followed it with more plays, as well as many poems, of his countryside.

During the three-and-a-half weeks of *The Old Man*'s run I rehearsed Ronald Duncan's *This Way To The Tomb*. Henzie had suggested the title, out of a fondness for the cuffed hand with pointing index finger which used to direct one to 'sights'. The soliloquy I had read remained as a high-spot of the first part, a Masque of St Antony's fasting and temptation, with three friends who follow four abstract tempters to make seven. The spiritual experience owes as much to Gandhi, with whom Ronnie spent

several months, as to the Catholicism in the framework of which it is
set; but it is his own, and struck a responsive chord in many
people's hearts at that moment, with its combination of frankness,
the craving for roots and the search for the way forward into an
unknown age. It was greatly assisted by Ronnie's friend Benjamin
Britten, in whose triumph with *Peter Grimes* at the re-opened
Sadler's Wells we had shared in June. He supplied music for an *a
cappella* choir behind the stage to the pieces from the Latin liturgy
which Ronnie had incorporated into his poem. It contained many
images which stuck in one's head:

> my mind clings to the past
> Like a velvet train dragged on wet grass . . .

> I believe Christ lies in my heart like a green leaf in an old book
> Revealed, if I could only find my heart, open it and look

and in the songs:

> Night is no more
> Than a cat which creeps
> To the saucer of light,
>   laps, then sleeps.

The second part, satirising contemporary religiosities, had a
good deal of fun in it – often undisciplined schoolboy fun and often
beside the point, but the kind of fun which relieved the long tension
of war and which Britten enhanced with blues and boogie-woogie
music for a three-piece band. Peter Pears and I auditioned actors
for his songs and got, in Gwen Nelson and Eleanor Summerfield,
two excellent actresses who joined the repertory company we were
becoming. Ronnie came often to rehearsals: Nic had not been fit
enough to manage more than his first night.

Stella Newton undertook both setting and costumes for the
season. Duncan's play, like Nicholson's, demanded a split stage,
the mountain of Antony's meditation on stage right, the cell of his
three disciples at left; and had to accommodate in front the songs
and dances of the modern 'Astral Group' and their violent attack
on Antony when he returns at the end. Stella, like myself, did her
best work under challenge: the Mercury's extreme limitations (add
a proscenium only nine feet high, with no flying-space above, to
those already described) stimulated us both to use every inch to full
effect. This depends on scale: the human actors have to be visually
in scale with their setting which, if it is actually very small for them,

means planning every position and movement so as to preserve the illusion of space.

It proved to be a good thing that this play opened second. Despite careful publicity, the idea of a Season of Plays by Poets took some time to win acceptance. It was not until the third play that W. A. Darlington could write in *The Daily Telegraph* (20 December 1945) that it 'has become more than an interesting experiment. It is an artistic event.' Meanwhile, the experiment might have expired: in fact it very nearly did. *The Old Man* was not expensive, and lost me only about half of my very small capital. *The Tomb* was expensive (by our standards) to stage and to run: its notices at the opening had been interesting and interested but not compulsive. We played to two-thirds capacity; and towards the end of its third week I saw myself having, on Saturday night, to post the notice that would end the season with the following week.

The theatre is largely governed by luck. At noon on that Saturday (3 November 1945) the *Evening Standard* came out with its weekly theatre-column by Beverly Baxter (MP, friend of Churchill and Beaverbrook) who had belatedly, 'in a sense of duty rather than anticipation', made the journey to the Mercury (note the 'journey': Notting Hill Gate is a hundred miles further from Piccadilly Circus than Piccadilly Circus is from Notting Hill Gate). But he found 'something that is gloriously exciting' and urged his readers to

Go at once to the Mercury and witness such a blending of transcendent beauty and outrageous satire as has not been seen in the London theatre for years.

Even to such a bidding, readers don't always respond. But this time they did – and at once. Athene Seyler's charming daughter Jane Ann was instantly besieged in the Mercury's box-office window; her telephone began to ring and didn't stop for a year. The 'experiment' had been saved, to become one of the growth-points of the post-war theatre. In the next two years, the Old Vic and the Mercury were the two companies which everyone who came to London wanted to see; and we had a refreshing stream of parties of young people interested in our search. 'These poetic plays are feeling towards a new dramatic form [*The Times Educational Supplement* averred] and at the same time bringing a draught of fresh air into the theatre of today.'

With so large a cast, we did not of course make money, but we
had enough in the bank to enable me to introduce the next two
plays in repertory with the successful *Tomb*. Anne Ridler's *The
Shadow Factory* was our only play in an entirely contemporary
setting. I produced it at Christmas. A nativity play is introduced
into the factory as the solvent of a conflict of ideas between the
Director (Robert Speaight in a kind of part quite new for him) and
an artist played by Alan Wheatley. Alan had joined the cast of *The
Tomb* as the singer Julian, and remained as my leading actor of
younger parts.

In *The Shadow Factory* Anne attempted to do what Eliot asked: 'to
bring poetry into the world where the audience lives and to which it
returns when it leaves the theatre'. Her verse, according with the
industrial society's speech-rhythm, has a shorter line than is used
by any other of these poets. Some of the factory-girls watch their
fellow-workers on the Director's shadow-screen:

> They look like ghosts.
> > We know that jig's
> Too heavy for ghosts. It's dreary work:
> Four o'clock in the afternoon's
> The awful time. Then's the time
> I think I'll die if I don't get out.

Bobbie as the Director, a benevolent but blinkered dictator, shared
this rhythm until, confronted by the artist's challenge which he has
accepted, he finds himself drawn to take part in the canteen
nativity play and sees afresh at the Crib:

> Child, if I let this go, can I bear to live?
> Power that the babe possessed, the man would retrieve?
> You have taken my certainty, must this too be lost? (*He kneels*)
> O, lost – for glory and the promptings of love
> Enjoin it: Child, take and teach me to give.

The device is a dangerous one, but thanks to the reality of the
characters and the clean distinction of Anne's writing, it works,
and the 'coming down from the mountain' in Act III fulfils the
same healthy function as Nic's. The Director talks at the end to the
elderly Caretaker:

> DIRECTOR
> > Blake,
> I've lost all that I had before,
> And in its place is – emptiness.
> I simply wander about in the dark.

BLAKE

Don't you let yourself get down, sir.
Why, you must take yer time. You know
You used to look *through* me as if I was invisible.
You can't learn seein' all in a moment . . .
We must make the best of a bad job
Mustn't we, sir? You go on, sir,
Stick to what you were doin' before;
A touch of despair in it'll just put it right.

The Times found that 'her characters do achieve lives of their own independent of their values as figures in a parable'. Baxter said, 'I am afraid that you will have to go again to Ladbroke Road. Something very like the drama of the future is being born there.'

The second new programme entered the repertory in April 1946. Christopher Fry had made his play just over an hour in length, for three characters. I was enchanted by *A Phoenix Too Frequent*. It has one of those immortal stories which, like the Greek legends, are re-used again and again because they embody some indestructible truth – in this case, the resurrection of life against all odds:

Oh, how the inveterate body,
Even when cut from the heart, insists on leaf,
Puts out, with a separate meaningless will,
Fronds to intercept the thankless sun.
How it does, oh how it does.

The comic treatment of a macabre story seemed to give release from the horrors that had been so close to all of us, and Christopher, in making it glow with his wit and warmth of feeling, turned it into a celebration of life still delighted in. Before it, I played Yeats' *Resurrection*, whose dramatic argument set off Christopher's comedy:

When the thoughts would die, the instincts will set sail
For life . . .

Because of the censorship, I could not (as I had done in church) have Yeats' Christ-figure cross the stage, which diminished the climax: but the quality of the play justified its inclusion even so. *Phoenix* had a happy history. It was taken over from me by Alec Clunes, who was then running the Arts Theatre (more than twice as big as mine), for late-night showing. It was very successful, and launched both Paul Scofield (who followed Alan Wheatley in the man's part) and Christopher himself upon the West End. Clunes entered into a contract with him for his next play – which proved to be *The Lady's Not For Burning*. *Phoenix* has, I believe, been played more often than any other Fry play: and I cherish Christopher's inscription of the first edition:

Martin:
        who so beautifully made this first come to life.

Once more, *This Way To The Tomb* returned to the Mercury stage in May, with Irene Worth in her first London part as Philippa Form. She had been introduced to me on her arrival from America by Gabriel Pascal, who bought the American rights (though he never took them up). We had taken the play earlier to the Arts, Cambridge, and now were discussing an exchange with the Studio des Champs-Elysées, Paris. In June, they brought a production of Lorca's last play, *La Maison de Bernarda Alba* (translated into French

23   *This Way To The Tomb* (Ronald Duncan): Stella Mary New-
      ton's costume design for Philippa Form. Mercury Theatre,
      1945. By permission of Stella Mary Newton

24　*The Family Reunion* (T. S. Eliot): Alan Wheatley as Harry
with the Eumenides in the 1947 revival at the Mercury.
Photo: Barry Hicks

since it was banned in Spain). It provoked James Agate to two
columns of superlatives and packed the Mercury through a heat-
wave, which must have made this claustrophobic tragedy overwhelming in the tiny theatre. I saw it and saluted it before we left
for Paris, where we suffered the same heat-wave in the roof-top
Studio and found Duncan's poetry too difficult for French audiences who had been six years without hearing an English play. But
we were royally entertained, and enjoyed especially the great
exhibition of tapestries, from the medieval Revelation of Angers to
the modern, much of which afterwards came to London.

We stayed on over the Fourteenth of July, to savour the delight
of a liberated and illuminated Paris and enjoy the dancing in the
street outside our little left-bank hotel till 3 a.m. Next day we made
the first of several visits to Gordon Craig, for whom I rescued that
part of his theatrical collection which was still in London. Henzie
left this account of it:

There he was, at the station entrance, to meet us. My husband and I had travelled in the little suburban train from Paris. 'Corbeil! Corbeil!' We climbed out and walked towards this beautiful man, whose face I at once recognised because I had played for, and known well, his sister Edy. They were very much alike – so much of woman in him, so much of man in her, and the uniqueness of the Terry in both of them.

There he was, a great-shouldered man, with clear blue eyes and hair flowing onto the collar of his jacket under the shelter of a huge-brimmed hat. His shirt was blue to match his eyes, and the collar of it was turned up so that the points touched his cheeks, making him look as if he were in costume. His rich voice (Edy again) greeted my husband: 'Martin Browne, my dear boy, how ripping to meet you at last!' The slang of long ago suddenly made one aware how many years it was since he had left his native country; it was endearing, like the crinkled, welcoming smile he had for me, and also a little sad.

He was accompanied by a child of 11. 'My little girl, Toutou.' We weren't sure whether this indicated a friendly young neighbour, or a granddaughter, or the daughter of a father aged 74. However, he depended on her to give the taxi-man his orders, since he had almost no French – it was better, the exile explained, not to learn much of the language. Toutou's mother was away in England, so she was our hostess for the day.

At Les Coteaux, the *Hotel-Pension* where they were living, we found that this lunch to us was a festive occasion. We were not to have it in the *salle à manger* but on a private balcony. It was an extravagant meal, with lobster and fine wine – and France was still on meagre rations: it was a delicious treat to us who came also from a country of ration-cards and shortages; and it was typical of his generous and gay quality. There was much laughter, much affectionate chivalry, a spate of reminiscence, spreading from his days as a young actor with Irving to the occupation. We glimpsed the hardships of the last few years, and the precariousness of his present position. And then he talked of a recent visit from his son Teddy, who had been received by Toutou. 'Who are you?' 'I am Gordon Craig's daughter.' 'Then you are my little sister,' and they embraced.

Toutou, from her end of the table, enquired, with her charming slight accent (she was born in Vienna): 'Parti, how many of us are there, really?' But the question was waved aside: 'My darling, we have guests; we will talk about all that another time.'

In the autumn, I revived *The Family Reunion*. I had corresponded with Eliot about it during the summer, canvassing the possibility of revision; but we agreed to let it take another chance as it stood. The chance was assisted by Stella's design: we still possessed her admirable costumes of 1939 and they were set this time in a Wishwood of her own devising, skilfully extended over the prosenium-arch. Even more important, perhaps, was the casting I achieved. Sybil was not free to fulfil her desire for Amy (she finally played her for Peter Brook in 1956), so I secured one of the finest of our senior actresses, Henrietta Watson. When Eliot says in *Poetry and Drama* (1951) 'my sympathies now have come to be all with the mother', I suspect that Miss Watson's performance had not a little to do with it. Catherine Lacey repeated her original creation of Agatha, and Alan Wheatley played Harry with a 'moody illumination' which was for Simon Harcourt-Smith (*Tribune*) 'a continuous delight'. Another was Pierre Lefèvre's chauffeur, who carried his matter-of-course acceptance of 'them ghosts' (the Eumenides) into an exactly defined place in the country-house hierarchy. In the uncles-and-aunts chorus, Henzie was in her original part of Ivy, with Eileen Thorndike (Sybil's sister) as Violet, Frank Napier as Charles and John Burch as Gerald. This worked far better than in 1939 because I understood how to slide, not jump, from the conscious to the subconscious plane.

That was part of the lesson I had learned about this masterpiece which, flawed though it may be (and it had no critic more severe than its author), is undoubtedly destined to endure. The lesson is that, however far you may venture into the various levels on which the poet sees his characters, you must keep each one firmly anchored to his or her individual humanity. So whereas in the first production (and far more startlingly in some I have seen) the transition from Uncles Charles and Gerald, Aunts Ivy and Violet, to chorus was marked by a sharp change of atmosphere, in this one the four members of the family sank imperceptibly from their individual thoughts into the expression of those reflections which are shared (though in 'real' life not put into words) by such a family group. The actors found it natural, and the coming out of it, when someone else entered or it was 'nearly time for the news', no more of a jar than it is in actual experience.

The lesson applies equally to the main characters. Harry is the most difficult: he is so deep in personal crisis that he cannot get outside himself to anyone else, even to Mary or Agatha on whom he simply leans – there is no equal exchange between them until near the end. But they should both *try* to communicate as human beings. Catherine Lacey's performance was moulded in my first, more 'stylised' production, and in that ambience was most satisfying. In the later one, I wished that its hieratic quality might be softened by more human feeling; but a creation so highly wrought is not easily altered. Henrietta Watson's natural warmth was in danger of carrying her too far in the opposite direction and winning too much sympathy for the woman who is Harry's mother. But each one of these, and the minor characters like doctor and policeman, came out as people in the round. This is Eliot's achievement, which none of the other poets' plays can equal. Michael Elliott's production of 1979 succeeded in combining it with a presentation of the Eumenides which gave equal (and terrifying) validity to 'the nether world', and one may thankfully hail it as a definitive production of what a 1979 critic called 'Eliot's greatest play'.

That winter (1946–7) was worse than those of the war. Rationing of all sorts was still in full force, food shortages greater than during hostilities, and in very bleak weather fuel cuts were numerous. The 100th performance of *The Family Reunion* was on my birthday (29 January); the electricity supply was twice cut off and we finished the show by the light of candles.

Murder came into our plans once more because George Bell and Laurence Irving wanted to revive the Canterbury Festival and the original fund had been used up. Bobbie and I offered to replenish it by giving two matinées at a Shaftesbury Avenue theatre. We got the Lyric and much of the pre-war cast. Queen Mary promised to come, and though she had a chill (who could wonder, in that weather which lasted till mid-March?) we made £950. Laurie Lee was commissioned to write the re-opening script and I directed it. *Peasant's Priest* wasn't a good first play, though it gave Bernard Miles a fine part as John Ball. That was in June, until which time we ran *Murder* again at the Mercury. Its general audience seemed inexhaustible, and it had by now become a school text. For a week we did London County Council school matinées at Collins' Music Hall in Islington, the last of the old Halls which you entered through the bar. This was a fascinating experience. After finding on Monday that the first scenes didn't quiet the house I learned to talk for ten minutes about the Becket story and Eliot's treatment of it before dressing for the Fourth Tempter, and we got a good response. Queen Mary, and later the King and Queen with the princesses, came to *Murder* at the Mercury.

Ashley, who by now had less to do in Germany, was getting impatient with my management and wanted his theatre back. At this moment I had a piece of luck, which ultimately helped him as well as myself. The page-proofs of an Irish publication came in the post one day from its author, Donagh MacDonagh. It was a play called *Happy as Larry*. He had heard about my Mercury seasons and sent it *on spec*. I was enchanted by it and bought an option at once. It was to be done, he told me, on a Sunday night at the end of July by Ria Mooney at the Gaiety, Dublin, and encouraged Henzie and me to go. Dublin was gay with endless talk under the guidance of Donagh, who proved to be a dumpling, twinkling young circuit judge; but the play, produced as a piece of flat-footed slum realism, totally lost the sparkle I had got from the printed page. What pig had I bought? Filled with depression, I took the script from my poke: it still gave off the same effervescence. Who could transfer that to the Mercury stage?

I thought of Denis Carey. He and Brian used to sing, in the Pilgrim van on the way back from shows, the kind of ballads on which MacDonagh's script was based. He had never, I knew, directed a play, but had shown much of the director's flair. If, as I expected, the play captivated him as it had me, I would ask him to do it. He made a great success of it; and after three good months at the Mercury it moved to the West End just before Christmas.

While he was rehearsing *Larry*, I was involved in the first Edinburgh Festival, under rather surprising circumstances. A year or two before, a property in Edinburgh had been left to the Church of Scotland. It included what had been a cinema; and the Home Board took the incredibly non-presbyterian decision to bring this into use as a theatre and appointed one of its lay staff, Sadie Aitken, to manage it.

Sadie was an old friend who had been a tower of strength to the Pilgrims during 1942. We had often talked about the relationship of Church to Drama: and now here she was in it up to the neck! The Gateway was not then included in the official programme of the Festival, but of course it offered a contribution, and one in accord with the theatre's special character. I suggested that the Pilgrim Players bring Eliot's two plays in repertory for two weeks.

No one who took part in that Festival of 1947 will forget how it felt to emerge from the interminable tunnel of war and austerity into that clear sunshine. The sense of freedom, the exhilaration with which people came to enjoy the arts in that beautiful city, infected us all. Even the citizens of Edinburgh, who had expressed some hostility to the idea and suspicion of us invading strangers, thawed so markedly that when the electricity authorities proposed to douse the floodlights on the castle because they were short of fuel, people in their hundreds contributed coal from their own rations.

Our success at the Gateway had its influence on the future. Sadie invited us back next year to give the first professional performances of Christopher Fry's *The Firstborn*. And Eliot, observing how his two plays were received, was attracted by the new Festival.

I had no new plays for the Mercury when *Larry* moved to the Criterion. Brief runs of Gordon Bottomley's charming comedy *Kate Kennedy* and Bridie's double bill occupied the last weeks of my tenancy. Ashley resumed control with a production of Synge's *The Playboy of the Western World* by Denis Carey. It was time. The dream was not over, but as dreams do, it was dissolving into another shape.

9

Drama League and
Cocktail Party

Before my tenure of the Mercury ended I had accepted a job of a
different kind. Geoffrey Whitworth was retiring from the directorship of the British Drama League. The Council appointed me to
succeed him. In doing so, they gave me leave to do one production
a year, though requiring me to 'maintain vigilance over the
activities of the League during that period'. They recognised that
the League, by having a working professional at its head, might
re-establish its contact with the professional theatre, which at that
time believed it to be concerned solely with amateurs.

The measure of truth in that impression was due to the
enormous growth of the amateur movement. It was not merely a
question of numbers, but of standards and aims. By 1948 there was
a Little Theatre Guild of clubs which had their own theatre,
converted or purpose-built for their own use all the year round.
The Questors of Ealing, led by Alfred Emmet, created a theatre,
based on their own experiment and experience, which entitles them
to a place in theatrical history books. Standards of performance
could be high enough to enable such towns as Skipton, Welwyn
and Felixstowe to provide attractive entertainment for their popu-
lations by offering expense grants to amateur companies from all
over the country – plus the fun, for both actors and audience, of hot
competition. Few, of course, reached this level, but the aims of
most amateur companies, even the humblest, had risen.

The link between drama and education, which Geoffrey had
helped to make as far back as 1926, had grown very much stronger.
There was now a large number of professional County Drama
Advisers, employed by committees grant-aided by the Carnegie
Trust, so that amateur companies got training and advice on their
home ground. A Standing Conference of Drama Associations was
set up, and many counties organised their own one-act play

festivals. One of my first tasks as director concerned that National Festival of Community Drama in which I had first adjudicated over twenty years before. By negotiating a 'new plan' with the Standing Conference, I brought about the incorporation of county and other local festivals into the national network, which thus included just over a thousand teams.

Drama was being regarded also, for the first time, as valuable in the education of children. Pioneers such as Peter Slade were teaching children to create drama for themselves, and teaching teachers how to use this powerful tool. Soon it found its way into school curricula. At the Ministry of Education an HMI, Adrian Alington, was given special responsibility for drama and set up a working party. On this I spent many mind-stretching hours, arguing about the right relationship between performances children see, performances they give, and drama they create. Caryll Jenner and John Allen were fellow-members, and John later succeeded Alington as HMI for Drama.

I made many trips to meet BDL members on their own ground. It was often convenient for me, or for Henzie, to combine this with adjudicating, which is a very good way of seeing what is going on. This was possible because there was in charge at headquarters the secretary who had started the League with Geoffrey, Frances Briggs. She had nurtured it in its growth from a seedling to a tree of many thousand twigs and branches, and had herself grown with it. Quiet, wise and clear-headed, she exercised a natural authority over the staff. Her personal friendship gave to the amateur organisers from all over the country who came to our meetings the confidence on which the League's effectiveness depended.

She and I were equally fortunate in the heads of the two chief departments. The League's library is the largest theatre-library in Britain, and is constantly in use by scholars from all over the world: many books and other records in it are priceless. But its appearance is not at all of the ordered academic kind; though a decent hush is preserved, the atmosphere is that of a huge bookshop struggling to keep pace with demand. For the bulk of its work consists in supplying members (who include television companies at one end of the scale and village drama groups at the other) with plays, singly or in sets, for play-readings or for production. This has its special problems, aggravated by other problems such as the decline of the Post Office. This hire service depends on people returning books in time for their next assignment, and returning them in usable condition. Actors are notorious vandals towards scripts: the temperamental strain of creating a part is often vented upon them, and the librarian may receive a bundle of tattered rags which need repair and cleaning if not replacement – and in the latter case the play may be out of print. It is a continually losing battle, which has been successfully fought for fifty years: and in the intervals of fighting it the senior staff, and most of all the librarian herself, are engaged in recommending plays, advising students, researching for scholars, and keeping order amid the apparent jumble of constantly shifting materials.

It is people that make a library, especially this peculiar library. Just as the League itself owed its life to Geoffrey and to Frances Briggs, so the library was created, under the guidance of Professor F. S. Boas, by a succession of dedicated women. When I came, Dorothy Coates had recently exchanged this exhausting job for the quieter life of Longleat: and the Library Committee had brought in someone from another field. It proved impossible for anyone without experience of this extraordinary institution to cope with it. I quickly got Mary Garnham, Dorothy Coates' number two, into the saddle. She was tiny with a soft, plaintive voice, but a lioness in heart. Her number two, Enid Foster, is now librarian. And so it goes on: long may it do so! The director's part can only be to understand, to support and to fight for what is in fact the heart of the League's work. If it ever ceased to beat, the whole theatre, professional as well as amateur, would suffer a loss literally irreparable.

Frances Mackenzie had built up a fine training department to meet the needs of the thousands of amateur directors, actors and designers who wanted to acquire theatrical skills and disciplines. Under her direction the BDL summer schools had become famous; and in 1947 she achieved her ambition to establish a ten-week full-time course for instructors in amateur drama. I gave the inaugural talk on 20 January. In my closer association with the League, we worked out together how to balance creativity (in the name of which sloppiness is often accepted) with the standards of skill and discipline which the art of the theatre requires.

With the directorship I took over from Geoffrey the editorship of *Drama*, which he started with the League:

not [he wrote] as the mouthpiece of a particular organisation, but rather as the common meeting-ground of all those who have something vital to say concerning the art of the Theatre.

This was a task I much enjoyed. Doris Hutton, who had been his personal secretary, became assistant editor and took charge of advertising and outside sales. We had to fight to preserve the breadth of Geoffrey's conception; but this and the high standard of contributions have kept the magazine in continuous publication for sixty years.

At Whitsuntide 1949 I started a new BDL project, a 'Theatre Week'. It combined the annual conference with a week of full-length plays; in the provinces these were given by amateur companies while in London the members went to professional shows. Frances Briggs was so keen on this that she offered to organise it herself. The first experiment was at Harrogate, with companies nearly all from the north. It was successful, with an attendance of about three hundred, many sent to represent societies, so that we had a strong conference. Next year the Bournemouth Little Theatre Club lent us their Palace Court Theatre, and for 1951 we were in London.

On the professional side, the League paid homage to Jacques Copeau, who died in 1949, in a programme at the British Academy with his nephew Michel Saint-Denis, John Gielgud and Peggy Ashcroft. On Shaw's death in 1953 we offered a tribute at the Town Hall of St Pancras, the borough of which he was a councillor and in which the League's headquarters stood. I collaborated in this with Bill Taylor, the borough librarian: and we also put on a series of 'evenings with' Shaw and several other dramatists. Taylor was working up the St Pancras Festival, of which these and other joint events became a part, and which was the foundation on which the present Camden Festival was built.

Geoffrey was to become chairman on his retirement. He wanted me to spend two months in double harness with him, learning the director's job. I had some misgivings about this, but they were resolved by a quite unexpected invitation. John Burrell asked me to direct the last play of the Old Vic company's season at the New Theatre. Geoffrey was generous in helping me to accept; and we managed quite successfully to sandwich my learning period with him into the rehearsals which, since the company was playing other shows, were spread over almost two months. The play opened on 31 March, and I took over from him next day.

Coriolanus was a Shakespeare play I had never worked on, though Ashley and I had discussed a production with a contemporary slant in the 30s. The metallic quality of this austere early Rome, the antithesis of that in my belovèd *Antony and Cleopatra*, at first repelled me; then I became fascinated by it, in Shakespeare's extraordinarily consistent re-creation. Granville Barker's *Preface* appeared at the right moment. It is not, I think, one of his most inspired, and my production was not, either: but in winning such descriptions as 'lucid', 'brisk, forceful and intelligent' it gained the kind of response I looked for. The Old Vic was by this time falling from the dizzy height at which it had stood at the war's end; and the notices showed a split between those who still valued it as a mostly Shakespearean repertory company of high quality and those who, because they had believed it to be already a national-theatre-in-being, were disappointed by anything less than the great Olivier–Richardson shows of 1944–6. Having in their time taken big money (from which the two stars drew only a tenth of their potential salaries), the Vic was now subject to financial stringency, and I was 'making do with a couple of pillars and a small crowd' which all too evidently did not fill the stage (Irving had one hundred and fifty). Some reviewers looked from the left wing and felt that the production accorded too well with the patrician bias which they saw in Shakespeare. Ivor Brown (in *The Observer*) seemed to me much closer to the mark when he said that 'the weakness of the play is that Coriolanus is too much of a fool to command our sympathy'; and John Clements' shining personal integrity (which made him so satisfying to work with) made it hard for him to portray a man ready to betray his own city. I was blessed with a group of fine actors in support: Harry Andrews as Aufidius, Mark Dignam and Peter Copley as the Tribunes, the young Frank Duncan, and above all Alec Guinness. He was at first rather loath to play Menenius, since he was already carrying the leading part in *The Government Inspector* and feared he might not 'find' this very different character. But when we had 'talked through' the part he became keen to do it. I vividly remember watching Menenius come alive. At first, the actor was a neutral, not blank, but open, receptive – just saying lines, doing business, questioning both to probe their validity in terms of the character. Then, signs of it

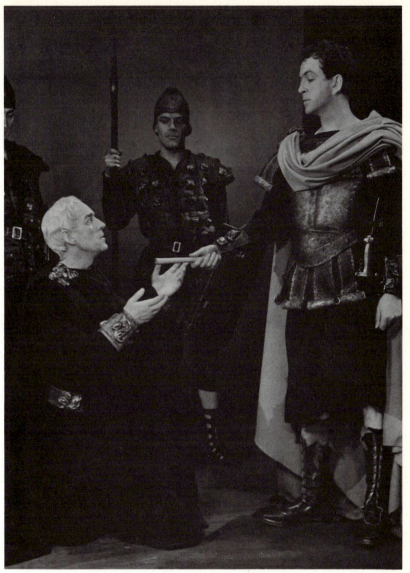

25 *Coriolanus* (Shakespeare), 1948: Old Vic Company at the New Theatre. Alec Guinness as Menenius pleads with John Clements (Coriolanus) for the city of Rome. Photo by permission of John Vickers Archives

began fleetingly to appear – two or three steps in Menenius' walk, a line or a phrase in his voice – and be deliberately neutralised again lest the gradual discovery of the character be overtaken by physical substitutes for the interior creation. Having several weeks of part-time rehearsal was ideal for this method: it enabled Alec and me to sleep on an experiment and discuss it next day, instead of being forced to finalise it too quickly. T. C. Worsley (in the *New Statesman*) otherwise disliked the show but gave this perceptive account of Alec's performance:

As Menenius he has to suggest the physical appearance of old age, the devotion of a hero worshipper and the cleverness of a compromising Liberal politician. He did all this and much more; he suggested a human person with a full life before, and outside, the events of the play, a mind rich and stocked but cynical and opportunist, a man who has learnt from a wide experience only not to expect too much from life and people.

The rest of our year, so far as the theatre was concerned, centred round Christopher Fry. *The Lady's Not For Burning* opened at the Arts on 10 March with Alec Clunes as Thomas Mendip. Henzie played Margaret, the mayor's wife. Jack Hawkins directed, and having just come out of Naval Entertainment was sceptical of Fry's apparently wayward flurry of words. He directed the play 'by numbers' – one pace to the left, count two, half a pace forward – without allowing for laughs. When we all 'fell about' on the first night, the actors had a seemingly impossible adjustment to make. But they made it, and 'Binkie' Beaumont of Tennents bought the play for John Gielgud. John was in America and never saw it in its two-and-a-half weeks at the Arts – which was sad for Henzie and others in the cast who might have been chosen for the West End production.

Christopher had also written the Canterbury play for that year, *Thor, With Angels*, which we went to see in June. In September we returned to the Gateway for the première at the Edinburgh Festival of *The Firstborn*. The play revealed its grandeurs, and also perplexingly its change of direction – for the war, as well as interrupting the author, had altered his attitude towards his mighty tale. Moses' thought is clouded by its unrewarded search for understanding both of the Power which commands him and of the tragic sacrifice (of the Pharoah's firstborn) through which the command is obeyed. The result is that on stage the secondary theme – of his sister Miriam, whose son Shendi, when rescued from the oppressed people of Israel, becomes the oppressor – proves the more exciting. Henzie was splendid as Miriam and Robert Rietty as her son. Ivan Brandt as Moses, Athene Seyler (the mistress of comedy making a rare excursion into tragedy) and Bobbie Speaight as Pharaoh had the harder tasks, but a performance was achieved which won respect and response from good audiences at Edinburgh and on a short tour. Alec Clunes produced the play in London later but without much success.

All through the seasons at the Mercury I had been in constant touch with T. S. Eliot. His firm, Faber and Faber, had published most of the plays I did. He was well aware, of course, that my highest hope was to put on the new play which he had started to write; but it came too late for the Mercury – and when it came, proved to need quite a different kind of stage.

We had corresponded about it since 1 June 1948 when he sent me the first draft of three scenes, and we spent an evening discussing it before he left for Princeton and we for Edinburgh. By the end of the year, in the midst of the congratulations on his Nobel Prize, Tom had given me enough of the script to enable me to try to get it produced, as he wished, at the 1949 Edinburgh Festival. Rudolf Bing sent me to see the manager who was to present the plays at the Lyceum Theatre, Henry Sherek.

The shock of meeting Henry was considerable. He was a very large man, whose exuberant personality seemed to shake the walls of his small office in Pall Mall. I felt very shy and young; I was the same age as he, but a child in the world of theatre to which he belonged. However, I had my passport to it in the pages of script I had brought with me. Henry read them avidly while I was in the office, and although the play was only half finished agreed on the spot to produce *The Cocktail Party* at Edinburgh.

This trio of Eliot, Sherek and Browne remained together for three plays and nine years. I reckon that, however incongruous we may have looked, the ensemble was a good one, indeed the best that could have fulfilled Tom's desire to succeed in the commercial theatre. Henry was an individual manager, taking his own risks, using his own judgement. And it was a judgement based on the most varied experience, from booking acts for variety theatres and hotels to producing many plays, including some distinguished successes in the West End. He knew his way through the jungle, its hazards and sudden mysterious changes. He had a flair for casting and a way with actors. And he had a passionate love for good writing, coupled with an acute instinct for how it would play.

I had a big adjustment to make between the 'real' theatre in which he worked and the small or specialised kinds which had occupied me till then. My best work had been evoked by the challenge of constricted stages or by buildings that dictated or suggested the style of production: and it had been done for audiences with particular expectations. The general audience, and the fully equipped theatre with its neutral stage-space waiting to be filled,I found at first intimidating. Correspondingly, my natural life-style has been in a cottage: I now live happily in the latest of several. I find it hard to believe (when I go round one of them on a National Trust membership card) that human beings were ever at ease living in mansions, and I feel out of place in a grand hotel.

Henry, I think, understood some of this and generously allowed for it; and I was fortunate, too, in that I had seven months to get acclimatised. He had accepted me with the play in January (it had to be settled early for Edinburgh's international publicity): but

26 *The Cocktail Party*, 1949, at a rehearsal at the Playhouse Theatre. T. S. Eliot (author), EMB (director), Henry Sherek (producer) talk it over. Photo by permission of Thomson Regional Newspapers Ltd

rehearsals didn't begin till 1 August. I was fully occupied till then with the BDL, while also working on the script with Tom. But I met Henry and his wife Pamela, who contributed much wisdom and understanding as well as charm, to discuss casting and presentation, frequently over lunch at the Caprice when Henry and Pamela moved into a flat in the building. Henry often embarrassed me – he insisted on calling me Saint Martin and pretended that I would be shocked at his very mild bad language, for instance. It was part of the act he felt obliged to put on to bridge the gulf he thought existed between us, but in fact it only existed at surface level. Underneath, we had a great deal in common, and the same proved to be true with Tom Eliot. Henry made plenty of jokes about the OM's godlike status in the world of letters, but that didn't prevent them from becoming friends. It may sound strange to say that it was individualism which united us, when Eliot at first saw Henry's part in the affair as just a 'financial gamble'; but he came to share my appreciation of Henry's personal commitment. To trust a man is intrinsically better than to trust a company: you know where you are, you know with whom you are – with someone who, however often you may disagree on the way, wants the same result as you do.

Henry's first bit of casting gave me much joy and a great boost: Alec Guinness said 'yes' to his invitation to play Reilly. Alec was committed to a film, which meant we could only play one week at Edinburgh and then must wait till the end of the year for him. But it meant having in the lead an actor whose mind I knew to be completely in tune with the author's, and with whom I had worked so happily the previous year.

It also gave the company a natural leader, with whom other good players would want to work; and sure enough they proved willing to join us in spite of the one-week run. Irene Worth was another with whom I had worked before. Her partnership with Alec grew so close that I felt we could play the consulting-room scene at Reilly's desk with no movement at all. It runs fourteen minutes. But only the stage manager's watch told that time: everyone else forgot time altogether.

Another special pleasure was to get Cathleen Nesbitt for Julia. Having found her joy in life infectious ever since the Oxford *Cleopatra*, I was saddened to see her looking wan as the Nurse in Robinson Jeffers' heavy translation of *Medea* in 1948, and suggested to Henry that Julia would bring her back to her proper sphere. He agreed, and it did, and was the beginning of a new life for her on the American stage and screen.

But why should I particularise, when the harmony of the ensemble was the key to its success? The actors were engaged in an adventure. Actors – even those who are masters of their craft – in a poetic play grow, like children, by exposing themselves to new experience. These actors allowed Eliot's verse-form counterpointed with feelings of his subtly drawn characters, Eliot's blend of the natural and the mysteriously more-than-natural, to work in each of them and through each on the others.

We rehearsed in London and only moved to Edinburgh on the Saturday, to open 'cold' (no tour, no previews) on the Monday. 'Getting in' to the Lyceum from Saturday midnight and dress rehearsing through Sunday in sets we had never seen before made the first night a very high jump to take. The number of laughs amazed the cast, and faced them with the problem of control. In their opening scene, for instance, Alec Guinness had to administer his dose of humiliation to Robert Flemyng as Edward without letting the audience escape their share of it by laughing at him too much. Control had to be even firmer in the consulting-room. As he forced self-knowledge upon Edward and Lavinia (Ursula Jeans), unpeeling their self-protections 'like the layers of an onion', the audience found it irresistibly funny. Good! so long as Reilly had his eye fixed on the purpose of it all, to restore the marriage, and lead them to the resolution in Lavinia's

Then we can share a taxi and be economical.

Actors as good as these know by instinct what the audience is feeling, when to allow the release of laughter and at what split second to stop it. Even so, I was on tenterhooks in the last act, when the audience went on and on laughing at Alex's absurd story about the monkeys, as the revelation of Celia's death came nearer and nearer. I need not have worried: it was not only the actor (Ernest Clark) but also the author who had control, and the blow was received in shocked silence. The most difficult part of the play to act is the quarter-of-an-hour that follows, when Reilly has to convey the meaning of the tragedy:

And if that was not a happy death, what death is happy?

and get the three remaining neophytes to accept it.

Henzie, alas, had no active share in all this. Henry, like most other managers, was firmly against the director's wife being in his cast. I knew and understood the obvious arguments against it; but it was bitter for us both that she was debarred from parts to which she had so much to bring. At the time, she was wasted in a minute part in *Harvey*, which ran a year-and-a-half. Later, she had a good one in Thornton Wilder's *The Matchmaker*, and her better luck culminated in a fine performance for Peter Brook in *The Power and the Glory*.

Henry Sherek looked for a London theatre to house *The Cocktail Party* at the year's end: but he was amazed to find that of all the landlords only Bronson Albery was interested, and he had no theatre free. Then Gilbert Miller offered his own theatre, the Henry Miller, on Broadway for January. The League allowed me time to re-direct the play over Christmas, and we re-opened at the Theatre Royal, Brighton for two weeks. On New Year's Day 1950, Henzie and I gave a party in London to celebrate our Silver Wedding coupled with the return of Denis and his bride from honeymoon. Two weeks later I flew to New York.

The Broadway Theatre has been reputed to be on the verge of death for at least forty years. The stage-crew at the Henry Miller certainly were: television had taken all but the dodderers, and my English staff were obliged by union rules to stand around and watch their slow bungling. However, we got the English sets we had brought over, and their very simple lighting, ready for the first night and the Broadway audience – which may be ruthless but is very responsive. The first-night habitués were reinforced this time by the Windsors, Ethel Barrymore, Gladys Cooper (most generous of artists), and affected, I suspect, by last summer's good word from Edinburgh. Anyway, it was a success and the talk of the season – all the more because those who were out of sympathy with the play (Brooks Atkinson of the *New York Times*, John van Druten *et al.*) joined in the arguments it provoked. I kept quiet, in the hospitable home of Rosamond Gilder: I was too exhausted anyway to join in, but it was fine to hear them all at it! I was happily able to see my old friends; we made a Decca recording of the production; and I got back to the BDL in mid-February having made some useful American links for it.

As it turned out, *The Cocktail Party* was to be my 1950 production as well as that of 1949. The American success meant a fresh cast for

London, where we opened at the New (Albery) on 3 May with Rex Harrison as Reilly, smooth and persuasive where Alec had been astringent. I enjoyed rehearsing it with a different company and discovered a lot of new things. Tom and I had worked over parts of the script during the winter, especially the ending. A detailed record of this is in *The Making of T. S. Eliot's Plays*.

The Cocktail Party changed the shape, not only of my theatrical life but of the poetic drama. Hitherto, verse had been its accepted medium, and the advantages of form and music which this gave to the poet had been reckoned to be worth any loss of freedom in relation to contemporary speech. Eliot had wanted to start at the other end, as he explains in that definitive discourse, *Poetry and Drama* (1951). This immediately followed the two productions of *The Cocktail Party*. His objective is a valid drama of contemporary life and people, at which

the audience should find, at the moment of awareness that it is hearing poetry, that it is saying to itself: '*I* could talk in poetry too!' Then we should not be transported into an artificial world: on the contrary, our own sordid, dreary daily world would be suddenly illuminated and transfigured.

But to make that possible, the rhythmic pattern of speech in the play must be a unified one. So the verse which Eliot created for his contemporary plays was designed to work at more than one level. It appeared natural in conversational scenes and yet the hearer was unconsciously affected by the undertones and overtones of what was said. So he suffered no disturbing jolt when a deeper level was revealed, since the rhythm he was hearing was still the same.

In the lecture from which I have quoted, Eliot defines this aim by analysing the first scene of *Hamlet*. That serves also to show how difficult – almost how impossible – it is for a modern audience to feel the effect of verse unconsciously. Neither the critics nor the *aficionados* will allow it to. They will persist in digging up the young plant to see if its roots are in verse, so that it wilts while they argue about it. But my cast did succeed in involving the audience so deeply in the drama that it forgot to ask, *while the play was going on*, whether it was in verse or not. Henry delighted me by saying 'no one else could have kept them on the knife-edge where Eliot has placed them'.

The Cocktail Party ran in London until 10 February 1951.

10

The York Mystery Plays

1951 was to be Festival of Britain year. The government invited the nation to celebrate its release from the gloom of war and austerity and show the skills and the wit that Britain had to offer to the future. On London's South Bank, a small, gay and inventive exhibition was to open up the area in which the Royal Festival Hall would be brought into use, and the foundation-stone of the National Theatre (in the first of its three positions) would be laid. Twenty other places throughout Britain were chosen as festival centres and offered grant-aid through the Arts Council. Each was encouraged to display its distinctive character, and to restore or bring to light its special treasures. One of the twenty was York.

The penny dropped at once. York had one special treasure in which it had shown no interest, but which I had always longed to bring to light. Its cycle of Mystery Plays is complete, forty-eight plays varying in length from twelve to thirty minutes and making up a history of the world as it was conceived in the late middle ages. A few of its plays had been produced by me and others, but it had not been seen as a cycle since 1572. To produce it after almost four centuries would provide York with an unbeatable Festival event of its very own.

And at no cost to the city! Knowing from experience how canny the city fathers are, I felt sure the offer of Arts Council finance would attract them. At once I spoke to Mary Glasgow, with whom Henzie and I had been close friends ever since CEMA days, and she put me on to Huw Wheldon, the Arts Council's officer for the Festival of Britain. He met me, with Keith Thomson, the York festival director, at the Arts Theatre Club on 29 July 1949, three days before I started rehearsing *The Cocktail Party*.

My proposal that York produce its own cycle of Mystery Plays seemed a bold one, for practically nobody knew anything about them. Following Elizabeth I's suppression of them as the most potent expression of popular Catholic sentiment, they had been first vilified and then neglected; and since they were written in the Yorkshire dialect form of Middle English, had become unintelligible to the ordinary reader. French and German scholars began to investigate them again in the nineteenth century, but in the twentieth, even Sir Edmund Chambers only collected evidence about the plays rather than studying them as theatre. In *British Drama*, as recently as 1925, so careful a scholar as Allardyce Nicoll was talking about the cycles as 'chaotic in construction', the language as 'stilted' and the writers as 'fettered by the various rimes and measures into which the dialogue is cast'. Against this, 'it is the freshness of the mystery plays which deserves our attention'. Would it be possible for me, if York invited me, to communicate this freshness to modern audiences? Wheldon and Thomson thought it well worth trying.

Length was the primary question. For nightly showing, the optimum playing-time was three hours. The forty-eight plays were originally presented by the craft guilds, each having its own 'pageant', a wheeled cart with a scene built upon it. They moved through the streets on the Feast of Corpus Christi from 4.30 a.m. till dark, playing (as the records have it, but how they got through the forty-eight remains a mystery) at a dozen 'stations' on the way. This type of production couldn't even be considered in streets choked with modern traffic. We must turn rather to the practice of southern England and the continent, and use a fixed stage with multiple settings for simultaneous action. The drawing by Hubert Cailleau of the stage for the Valenciennes Passion Play in 1547 influenced me most. It shows a row of 'mansions', small buildings for particular scenes, interspersed with gateways ('Nazareth', 'Hierusalem', 'La Porte Dorée') with a big open playing-space *platea* in front of them.

This would allow of the speed and variety of action that a modern audience expects, and give me the continuous flow that Iden had taught me to aim for in Shakespeare. But it would mean dovetailing plays, or more often parts of plays, into a single script. To do this while preserving the patterns of the verse and its authentic poetry, I needed a scholar who also had some of the gifts of a dramatist.

Thomson produced him for me – Canon J. S. Purvis, the archivist of York Minster. We met in November, each with our copy of Lucy Toulmin Smith's 1885 edition of the original text of the complete cycle. Purvis had a lively sense of humour and knew how Yorkshire folk really lived and thought. He knew and loved the plays deeply: and he knew what local actors could 'put over'. We shared a determination to preserve the shape of the cycle, its mighty sweep across the whole history of this world, seen in the light of eternity. Into that framework should be fitted all that we could manage of the detail drawn from the daily life of the ordinary people who acted it in the fourteenth century as they would in the twentieth, so that the story of God's love was their own story.

We both wished also that they might speak it in their own tongue. The dialect in the Middle English is North/East Yorkshire, which has survived only in the remoter countryside. I remembered a walk with a young friend from York when I was working there in 1923. We got lost on the moors above Pickering, and asked a farmer's wife how to get back to that town. 'Ah'll tall thee fat ta dee-a' she said. My friend recognised 'I'll tell you what to do': but if, as we hoped, we got a national or international audience at the Festival, most of them would not. Purvis decided to 'translate' into standard English (leaving as many dialect words as he dared) to be sure of 'getting over' on an open-air stage ninety feet wide.

For that was what we were going to use. Between the River Ouse and the Minster are the ruins of St Mary's Abbey. The 'Museum Gardens' in which they stand then belonged to the Yorkshire Philosophical Society; they have since passed to the city. The north wall of the Abbey nave, with the corner piers east and west of it, is still standing and preserved from further deterioration. The arcading and the clerestory windows above it are complete except for the tracery. This medieval wall has its own power to stir the imagination, and to produce the Mystery Plays before it would be to add like to like.

If stands were built for the audience, the greensward which now covers the abbey floor could be the *platea*. The clerestory windows, with a gantry running behind them, could be heaven. Into the bays beneath could be inserted 'mansions' for Pilate, the nativity stable and the High Priests. At actors' left, traditionally, must be Hell, with Limbo as prison for the souls that Christ comes to release. Across the actors' right corner should be built a higher level, reached by broad steps from the *platea*, and connected by more

steps to 'heaven'. This would serve for Eden, for Gethsemane, for
Calvary, and beneath it would be Christ's sepulchre. Alongside
this there is a small doorway through the wall, known as 'Etty's
tomb' because York's nineteenth-century painter is buried in the
churchyard just behind it. Lazarus could be raised from Etty's
tomb; and at other times it would be exceedingly useful as an
entrance since the only other ways onto the stage would be from its
two ends.

I did not use the whole width of the Abbey wall. I thought five of
the eight bays gave me quite a large enough stage: my conception
was vertical as well as horizontal, and I wanted to gather the
audience round the playing-space. Accordingly, I asked for two
spectator-stands, one parallel with the wall, and the other (eastern) one at an angle of forty-five degrees.

The British Drama League agreed on this as my 1951 production. I had there a colleague very well equipped to design the show.
Norah Lambourne was the training department's staff tutor in
décor, and spent much of her time teaching amateurs how to do the

27   The York cycle of Mystery Plays, 1951, in the ruins of St
     Mary's Abbey. Healing of a Lame Man by Jesus (Joseph
     O'Conor). Photo: A. C. K. Ware

things at which she was professionally skilled. She could thus take charge not only of design but of execution. All the work was to be done in York: the stage built by the two Heppell brothers, one of whom was a keen and valuable actor, and the costumes and props made by a large team from the amateur societies' wardrobes. Norah kept an excellent and popular authority over all the work. She was in full sympathy with my plan for the staging, and we agreed likewise on the use of medieval costume. The authors see the story as one of real life, that is, the life they are living, so their characters must wear clothes contemporary with the script. Pilate, for instance, has

> the care of this tower-builded town

and his own court of justice:

> He shall full bitterly ban that shall bide my blame.

He calls Annas and Caiaphas 'my prelates': he is the lord and they the bishops of a medieval city. We took the year 1400, by which date the cycle was in annual production, as a rough guide.

From the beginning I said, 'These are York's own plays and I invite everyone in York and its district to audition for them.' I had some eighty speaking parts to fill and a crowd to find as well. Several long days produced some promising and a few surprising results – if you can see where an actor's individuality will be just right, even his awkwardnesses may become advantages. Most of the two to three hundred people I saw had only their willingness to offer; and I had the usual problems of conflicting commitments, the usual proportion who fell by the wayside. But the message began to circulate that here was something which it might be exciting to take part in.

I knew, of course, that I could look forward to enrolling some old and trusted friends. Len Pickering had played Henry VIII in 1934. His wife Lilian had given a remarkable performance for John Hughes in Yeats' *The Words Upon the Window-Pane*. Others of John's group were John Kay of Bootham School, Alec de Little and Regg Dench our doctor, a superb character-actor whose small daughter Judi was to progress from attendant angel to Virgin Mary and thence to the top of the professional tree. The wives of the last two, Kay de Little and Olave Dench, were heads respectively of props and wardrobe. The husbands filled key roles: Len doubling Joseph

with the Beadle to Pilate (Alec de Little), Regg as Annas, with
John Kay as Caiaphas. These players set the highest of standards
and gave me invaluable support.

On one of the audition-days, the drama mistress at The Mount,
the Quaker girls' school corresponding to Bootham, brought forty
pupils. In their navy-blue uniforms, one after another read from
the scene of the birth which, uniquely in the York cycle, takes place
on stage. What an impossible thing to expect of a schoolgirl – to
hold an audience of sixteen hundred, alone on an open-air stage!
Suddenly, from one of them came a grave, strong certainty:

> Now in my soul great joy have I;
> I am all clad in comfort clear.
> Now will be born of my body
> Both God and man together here.
>   Blest might he be!

Yes, I thought, but what about the Passion? Thirty years later,
Mary must witness the agony of her son. 'Has she a mother who
could play that?' I asked. 'Her mother died three years ago, when
she was thirteen.' I gave the girl a script and asked her to study the
Passion scenes and come back in the afternoon. It was then that I
first heard a sound that still rings in my ears:

> Alas! that this blossom so bright
> All sinless is nailed to the rood.
>   *I cry.*

It was one of Purvis' few unnecessary deviations from the original;
the reiterated diphthong of grief is the Aeschylean *aiai* and was
powerful night after night, as in Athens so in the York garden, in
the clear young voice of Mary Ure.

I had determined that the two chief parts must be played by
professionals, since the energy required is such that no amateur,
however talented, could produce it night after night if he had
already done a day's work. John van Eyssen accepted Satan, and
Joseph O'Conor agreed to play Jesus on a very exacting condition.
Together with the amateur actor who played God the Father, I
asked him to appear anonymously. This was to allay the fear that
the appearance of the deity in visual form would be a blasphemy.
Joseph O'Conor made this sacrifice and faithfully kept silence
until, to my delight, the *Daily Express* published his name as a
first-night 'scoop'. Both these actors made outstanding successes.

Esmé Church had retired from direction and acting at the Old Vic to found the Northern Children's Theatre Company, which she ran as an excellent acting school, at Bradford. She agreed to the whole school taking part in the plays; so I acquired a group of vigorous and well-disciplined young actors to sustain the production at many keypoints. And Esmé herself played Mary Cleopas, with Henzie as Mary Magdalene.

I also acquired the school's movement teacher, Geraldine Stephenson, one of the star pupils of the Art of Movement Studio founded by Rudolf Laban in Manchester. Her skill is now familiar to millions of television viewers: to me it recalled the revelation of *Totenmal* in 1930, and opened the way to a use of movement, particularly in the crowd, which I should not myself have been capable of producing. By forming and informing small groups among the crowd, she created a gamut of feeling, expressed in the different degree of which each member was capable.

Rehearsals lasted throughout April and May. Henzie was fortunately free to act as associate director, and did much of the preliminary rehearsal in York, Bradford, and Harrogate where the Dramatic Society contributed a group. The individual coaching was a painstaking job, for even Purvis' script daunted a good many of the actors. The verse is all stanzaic, some of it quite elaborately patterned, and the alliteration can make the actor afraid of losing truth in the maze of verbal devices. In such a case, you spend sixty per cent of your time convincing the actor that the author knows what he's doing: that the alliterations and assonances, for instance, are the instruments by which the actor can catch the attention and push home the point. You remind him that the original audience, though closer to the actor, wasn't captive and quiet as ours would be. You show him how the firm rhythm of the verse encourages the audience to go along with the story. And this encourages him to enlarge his delivery for our large stage, on which the stone wall behind him will act as a sounding-board.

Henzie and I got the cast to learn, by listening to each other as well as to us, that the lines could truly express character and yet carry clearly. 'We heard every word,' wrote Eric Keown in *Punch*, 'though there were no microphones.'

We looked for every chance to let the Yorkshire speech-sounds come out. In the city, only a very few of the north-country vowels are in use. Country actors, mostly employed on the land and rising

very early, couldn't face our late hours of performance. We
managed to get shepherds who 'spoke broad', but most of the
dialect used was consciously studied by the actors. The effect was
none the worse for that. One of the delights of the show was
Barbara Hughes as Caiaphas' gatekeeper abusing Judas:

> Say, beetle-browed briber, why blows thou such boast? . . .
> Thou art cumbered in curstness and cares to this coast . . .

But I did not want to cumber actors with the care of *learning* a
dialect: it seemed better to let each speak in his natural way.

The Drama League was deputed by the Arts Council to publicise
the special efforts made for the Festival of Britain by amateurs
throughout the country. We published a special number of *Drama*
and mounted an exhibition at Fitzroy Square. In May we held the
first of our London Theatre Weeks, especially memorable for a visit
to the St James' Theatre, still glamorously standing under Olivier's
personal management. He was running the two Cleopatra plays in
repertory, and we saw Vivien Leigh perfectly parted in Shaw's.
That week, too, Christopher Fry's *A Sleep of Prisoners* opened at St
Thomas's, Regent Street. I had commissioned it on behalf of the
Religious Drama Society and helped Christopher through the
crises of its creation. Michael MacOwan made a 'wonderfully fine
and unified production' (my diary says) and talked eloquently
about it to the Theatre Week audience next day. The Week had
begun with a conference at which Sybil Thorndike gave what the
Americans call the 'keynote speech' and a dinner with Lewis
Casson as guest of honour. It ended with Barry Jackson unveiling a
plaque on 29 Fitzroy Square, right opposite our headquarters,
where Shaw had lived for eleven years and written several of his
earlier plays. Sir Barry told how, returning enchanted from an
evening at the ballet, Shaw danced an enquiring policeman round
the square.

After that, Henzie and I both settled down in York for the final
rehearsals on the outdoor stage. Working far into the night, always
cold, usually damp, sometimes wet, we found the weight of
exhaustion lifted from us by the fresh air, and by the increasing
hope that something magnificent was being born.

Another old ally joined me in the Museum Gardens, Percy Corry
of the Strand Electric Company, Britain's premier stage-lighting
firm. Both on the Eliot plays and in BDL training sessions I had

worked with this fine craftsman. The Mystery Plays presented just the kind of challenge he liked. In the first half of the show the lighting could only serve to focus attention on the faces; but by 9.30 it was dark and Percy gave me some memorable effects.

After the death on the cross in the lurid dimness of the earthquake, the body was taken down almost in silence and placed in the mother's arms, then lifted into the sepulchre. The door was shut. Joseph of Arimathea and Nichodemus bade farewell to Mary:

> Now done is our dear duty here
>   This tide

and to the audience:

> This Lord so good
> That shed his blood
> Amend your mood
>   And bring you in bliss for to bide

and walked silently into the darkness. Suddenly, a light streamed horizontally from the tomb. The souls in Limbo cried out in joy, the devils in horror from the fortress of Hell. Christ appeared to harrow it, bearing the red-cross flag (as on every 'Lamb and Flag' pub-sign). At the climax of his battle with Satan he called on Michael: a spotlight revealed the armed archangel on the topmost crag of the ruins.

Preparations involving so much construction-work on a central site, and hundreds of York citizens, naturally aroused great curiosity. They also sharpened the misgivings of some in authority. The dean, Eric Milner White, had always been a keen supporter; he welcomed the players to the Minster on the opening day. But the archbishop, Cyril Garbett, did not want the Passion scenes, with their physical brutality, to be shown. I went to describe how I should treat them and left him sufficiently satisfied not to object.

I was quite as much concerned about the censorship, as were Keith Thomson and the Arts Council. The censor's stated policy was that no play in which God or Jesus Christ made a visual appearance could be licensed. The lawyers assured us that this would not apply to a medieval text: but I knew very well that any competent lawyer could show Purvis' text not to be wholly medieval. For one thing, he had to write in the climax of the Trial before Pilate, where a page of the manuscript was missing. He had also, as we have seen, 'translated' throughout.

The censor was the Lord Chamberlain, and the Lord Chamberlain was the Earl of Scarborough. He was also Lord Lieutenant of the county and president of the Festival. So I thought, since I had met and liked him, why not ask him? He was very helpful. A script written before the Theatres Act, which established his jurisdiction in 1843, did not require a licence. The only circumstance in which the date of the version used could be questioned was a breach of the peace. Remembering the Protestant Truth Society, that was what I feared. Lord Scarborough suggested I consult the Chief Constable. He settled the question with a smile: 'The peace will not be breached.'

The Festival opened on Sunday 3 June with the archbishop preaching in the Minster and the first of the musical events that surrounded the Mystery Plays. For the Festival Society had risked making them the centrepiece. The first performance on a blessedly beautiful evening found us all in the grip of that uncertainty with which *The Times* reviewer begins his notice:

To have witnessed the recovery last night of a great part of the York Mysteries from four centuries of practical oblivion was to have had an experience. There was no telling beforehand what would be the effect on an audience of to-day of this cycle of medieval devotional plays that set out to rehearse the whole ecclesiastical history of the world. But from the moment God the Father, crowned and in white raiment, was revealed at a ruined window of the Abbey of St Mary, there to declare his purpose in the creation, it was evident that we were to hear a text of great interest and to see the plays revived in full imaginative splendour ...

After the wonderful prologue depicting the revolt and expulsion of Lucifer, the creation of Adam and Eve, and the Fall, the play passes direct to the story of Jesus, especially to the works of his manhood and the preliminaries to the Passion. These are presented in the text with a dramatic realism that is sometimes breathtaking and has sometimes had, it appears, to be modified out of consideration for the sensibilities of a modern audience. Even so enough remains to explain the powerful emotional effect such plays are known to have had on the men and women for whom they were written. There is blood-lust, for instance, in the crowd crying 'Crucify Him' and in the tremendous sudden jeer that greets that sight of Jesus on the cross; and even the scene of the High Priest's soldiers giving Jesus what we should now call a 'rough house' tells us how used the Middle Ages themselves were to violence. The plays, of course, have a great deal more than brutal realism. There is humour, though in this version less than might have been expected: there is dramatic surprise, as in the sudden recoil of the soldiers sent to take Jesus in Gethsemane; there is the fine if disquieting effect of Lazarus in his grave clothes lurching from

28 The York cycle of Mystery Plays, 1951: God in 'heaven', the
    clerestory window-frames. Photo: Will Acton

the darkness of the tomb; there are relics of obsolete theology, such as the
liberation of the pagans, from Adam and Eve to John the Baptist, from
Limbo; there is the glorious culmination of the play in Judgment Day,
with Christ on high pronouncing a doom that sends the damned wailing
to perdition and summons the blessed to climb the steps to heaven.
    Perhaps we cannot see these plays, so freshly direct in their language
and their approach, so astonishingly sure-footed in their drama, as their

own people saw them, since they saw with the eye of unconsidering faith. But Mr Martin Browne has left no other reason why we should not.

So by the end we could feel with the *Manchester Guardian* that the plays were 'an undoubted success' and I was happy to find it was clear that

this cycle was the Bible re-told in the tongue and dress of the guild people who acted it. The mailed soldiers who bind and buffet Jesus are no Romans but Yorkshire oafs 'marlocking'.

The verdict of the *News Chronicle* that

The revival of the York cycle is without question one of the most exciting experiences which the Festival of Britain has yet had to offer in the way of live performance

was quickly confirmed at the box office. By the end of the first week we were sold out for the run, and tickets priced at ten shillings and sixpence were being touted for £6 apiece.

The following Sunday, the two archbishops came to the evening performance together, York having invited Canterbury to stay for it. Next day I received the following letter:

> *Bishopthorpe,*
> *York*
> *11th June 1951*

Dear Mr. Browne,

I did not have time yesterday evening to say more than thank you for the performance of the Mystery Play. But I am now writing to say how very much impressed I was with it. It was produced with great beauty and reverence. The acting throughout was fine, and the elocution very clear. The whole production was quite first rate, and I admired it both for its religious teaching and for its dramatic skill. The setting was beautiful. Nothing could I think have been more fitting than the opening scenes in the twilight with the birds singing and the closing scenes in the darkness. I was also very much impressed by the silence and reverence of the audience. The success of this production has been due not only to your technical skill and ability, but also to your own faith and the reverence which naturally comes from it. As you know I had my doubts about the production of the play; these were removed last night, and I want to thank you most warmly for all that you have done. I think in some ways the presentation last night impressed me more than Oberammergau.

> Yours very sincerely,
> CYRIL EBOR

Herbert Read, a national figure who lived in and was honoured by Yorkshire, had ended his notice in the *New Statesman* by saying that 'the whole cycle should be a common possession, and the York performance an annual event'. Clearly, the pressure for its continuation was very strong. But the City Council would in future have to take the major financial responsibility. The first vote, in the autumn, went against it, since the shopkeepers reported that their sales had not noticeably increased during the Festival. But at the year's end, reports and accounts from the Castle Museum, the Minster and other such sources suggested that York had begun to appear 'on the map' for visitors, and the Festival Society was asked to put forward proposals for a second event. The Coronation caused its postponement till 1954, and this set the pattern of the future – a good one, I think, for once every three years is as often as a city of a hundred thousand people can make such a huge effort.

I was asked to an informal meeting in September 1952, with the chairman and vice-chairman of the Society and the City Treasurer. The summary quotes me as urging them to 'think in terms of making these plays a permanent event', which should not recur too frequently because 'each new production should be freshly conceived and not be a repetition of the last'. Both propositions were found agreeable, and have been the basis of subsequent development. This was largely due to Hans Hess.

Hess was the curator of the City Art Gallery, which he had reshaped and revivified in a way that seemed miraculous to those of us who remembered the old dump as it had been. He had assisted Keith Thomson in 1951, and the city fathers were shrewd enough to realise that they had an excellent artistic director already on their payroll. He was a prickly little man who made, and rather enjoyed making, enemies: I had many quarrels with him, notably about the press to which he was unreasonably allergic. But I respected him as a man of integrity and of artistic judgement which he would stand by to the utmost. The quality and vitality of the York Festival, and of successive productions which kept the Mystery Plays fully alive, are very largely due to him.

For 1954 it was agreed from the first that we revive the 1951 production, which had been shown for only two weeks and from which hundreds had been turned away. I offered everyone the chance of playing the same part again, and was lucky enough to get both O'Conor and van Eyssen to return. The music was the major improvement. In 1951 I had tried using live performers, but to make that work impossibly large forces were needed. Recorded sound was my solution. Denis Stevens made a very fine tape of medieval music with singers and brass; and its recurring themes – the fanfare for God which began and ended the show, the Cooper *Gloria* which grew in strength from the birth to the final ascent into heaven – became integral parts of the experience. For 'an experience' it was, not only for *The Times* reviewer or the many thousands in its audiences but still more for the players and helpers who were involved night after night. I can think of no more transcendent moments than those I spent in that garden.

They were interspersed, of course, with anxious ones, most of which were caused by the weather. Apart from the cold, against which audiences learned to come equipped with thermos flasks, rugs and overcoats, there was the rain, which had a way of circling

29   The York cycle of Mystery Plays, 1954: the release of Barabbas. Showing how the audience was seated, and the 'mansions' of Pilate, the High Priests and 'hell' at the back. Photo: Will Acton

in ominous clouds around York until it finally descended after sundown. The audiences were extraordinarily hardy and would sit through anything the actors could play through. But there were limits, set by the stage getting dangerously slippery and the drumming of the rain upon it drowning the actors' voices. To stop a show of this complexity in mid-career takes quite a lot of organising. I settled certain points at which it could be broken off – at the final exit of Adam and Eve, at the flight into Egypt, at the entry into Jerusalem (end of Part I), at the burial or at the Ascension (thus omitting the Last Judgement). Warnings for these had to be given ten minutes, and the 'stop' signal five minutes, in advance. To give them, and thus disperse hundreds of disappointed spectators, was my responsibility.

I did not have to exercise it on the most important day of all. The Queen and Prince Philip were coming to the plays, after a morning at Catterick Camp and an afternoon touring the Harrogate area. By the time they reached York it was already pouring rain. At show-time we all stood about the drenched stage, till we were told they had gone to an organ-recital in the Minster, and trailed despondently into the main dressing-room (the lecture-theatre of the Museum). In a few minutes the phone rang. They would visit us after the recital, in a quarter of an hour: those who were to be presented were to line up on the floor, and everyone in the show was invited to be there, the actors to be in costume. Hurried sprucing up, the wet and cold forgotten: the heart-warming interest of the Queen, the lighter touch of her husband; our gratitude to those who cared enough, after an exhausting day, to make such a gesture. But I had been given an intimation of what it might mean. When the Queen had arrived at the Mansion House I had been presented: with me, our oldest actor, a man of 82 who was one of the crowd. As he left, I heard her say, half to herself, 'It would be nice to be in the crowd.'

From 1954 onwards one play was shown on a pageant-waggon. The obvious first choice was *The Flood*. This needed two adults and half-a-dozen young people who could be drawn from secondary schools. Stewart Lack, who played Peter in the cycle, was art master successively at two of them and was my chief ally in this. We may not have rivalled the elaboration in which the Guilds competed with each other. But we gave audiences, standing round the ark, an idea of what the pageants looked like, moving through

Petergate from the Minster to King's Square, and of the vivacity that can be engendered in their confined space.

For 1957, I was invited to do a new production. Hans and the Board felt that a change in the style of staging must be made; that it ought to stand out from the Abbey walls rather than blending into them, and that instead of presenting particular points of focus like the 'mansions' it should have a neutral multi-level *platea* in the centre. Norah wrestled with these problems and evolved something which gave me the greatest possible flexibility. I did not like the look of it: we learned, I think, that to put scenery against architecture, especially architecture weathered by centuries of exposure, makes one uncomfortably aware of the flimsiness of scenic materials. Only something as rugged as the old stone itself can compete. But it did help the director.

New also was the casting. A young actor, Brian Spink, played Christ with dignity and truth though less than the necessary authority. Robert Rietty came back to me after nine years to be an Italianate Satan. Judi Dench finished her course at the Central School just in time to play Mary. I moved most of the experienced York actors into different parts and recruited quite a few new ones.

And finally, we had a new text. Purvis had made a new translation of the complete forty-eight plays, and I was encouraged to use it. The result is an example of how fine is the line one has to draw between being faithful to the original and intelligible to the audience. Looking through the letters we received each year, I see that this is the first time people complain of not hearing the words. The main reason, I am sure, is that the words were more difficult. Purvis left in more dialect and obsolete words, more strange turns of phrase, than he did in 1951. Then, he was trying to ensure that people could follow his words: now, he was bringing them closer to those of the author.

We did, of course, gain some good bits that had been previously left out: and for the players and me it was a stimulating change. I was selecting afresh from the whole cycle, and though there wasn't room to expand, I tried out alternative passages. But essentially, the great pattern remained the same: and what was new to us did not alter the impact which seemed to sharpen with each production. Robert Speaight wrote of it in the *New Statesman* on 29 June 1957

It proves, once more, its appeal to the most primitive or the most profound intelligence ... Theology and theatre have never been more memorably allied. Mr Browne's production, like Reinhardt's *Jedermann*, is likely to take rank among the classics of the modern stage. Visually, it is continually taking your breath away. The fall and transformation of Lucifer, when Hell seems to be created in an instant; the creation of Adam and Eve, when the nearly naked bodies slowly rise from the soil of the earthly Paradise; the apparition of Lazarus from the rock, with the bandages of his shroud falling about him as he comes back into the world; the Cross with the groaning Body, lifted high against the broken stone, and the *Eloi, Eloi, lama sabacthani* echoing with an appalling clarity through the night – all this was unforgettable. Vocally, too, the performance gives a deep satisfaction ...

For, as Herbert Read had written in 1951,

The York Mystery Plays are poetry of the highest order – plain, perspicuous and powerful.

11

Drama League and
Confidential Clerk

Directly after the 1951 York Mystery Plays, the League accepted an invitation from the British Council to send Henzie and me on a tour of New Zealand and Australia. We were representing the British Theatre at the golden jubilee of the Australian Commonwealth. Both countries had affiliated Drama Leagues run by strong personalities – Stan Campbell and Evelyn Tildesley. Both gave us rousing receptions and a fearsome schedule of lecture recitals and social events (which, as the Oliviers had discovered on a legendary tour three years before, were the hardest part of the work). It was exhausting but exceedingly interesting, and created both links with the League and personal friendships.

In Australia we heard the news of Geoffrey's early death. Our sadness was shared by Evelyn Tildesley, to whom he had been a father-figure, guiding her in the foundation of the BDL (Australia), just as he had been to us at several of the crucial points in our lives. We were thankful that he had seen the Queen Mother lay the foundation-stone of that National Theatre to which he had given so much of himself, and which, now it is in being, owes him a debt insufficiently recognised. To me he left the responsibility of the League, the first-fruits of his idealism.

Back in England before Christmas, I learned that I was to become CBE in the New Year's Honours. The citation specified the York Mystery Plays. But it put first 'Director, British Drama League', a recognition of the importance of the work for which Geoffrey himself had held the same honour.

In January 1952, the International Amateur Theatre Association was inaugurated at Brussels with a ceremonial jamboree. Since World War Two, Geoffrey had been developing exchange visits, particularly with France, Belgium and Holland. I had been at the BDL only a month when we entertained the Uppsala

Studentteater, playing Strindberg's *Easter* in English painstakingly learned for our benefit but painfully unintelligible. But my whole family retains as a friend the girl who stayed with us.

The Association comprised amateur federations from sixteen countries. The British ones were BDL, SCDA and the Little Theatre Guild. The Australian and New Zealand BDLs were also included. I was elected the first president. I felt shamingly inadequate, since I have no gift for languages and even my French (the Association's second language) is not at all fluent. But the members of the Executive were a lively and kindly lot whose company I enjoyed for the next few years. By 1957 we were well enough organised to take advantage of a very generous offer from the state of Monaco. It has since then housed a biennial conference and Festival. I believe it is more beneficial for groups to see each other's work than to talk about it.

Just Thorning of Denmark has been one of the pillars of the Association, and likewise one of the international leaders in religious drama. The Religious Drama Society of Great Britain (RDSGB) had gained momentum from the work of the Pilgrim Players. Until I went to the BDL I had been honorary director, and though of course I gave that up, the link between the two bodies remained close. Two secretaries, Jim Bartholomew and after his untimely death, E. N. Hogben, built up a strong Society with Carina Robins as travelling adviser. The Rockefeller Foundation gave a grant aimed particularly at international exchange, and the first of two international conferences was held at Oxford in 1955. George Bell, who had remained president of the Society, took the chair and summed up in this delightful manner:

I think we can say with gratitude that there is a new interest and contact between the Church and the theatre. They are not yet married, but they are shyly 'walking out'.

The success of *The Cocktail Party* had made Sherek eager to get, and Eliot eager to write, a new play. Tom had started it in 1951, but didn't want to show any of it to me until he had got to the end; and when a script did reach me a year later I understood why. *The Confidential Clerk* has one of those intricate plots the details of which it is almost impossible to remember, and the social implications of which need the most delicate calculation. When we finally began a series of close discussions on it, they related to what would work

best in the theatre and how to keep each character fully alive
whenever he was on stage. The permutations of the plot and
relationships had already been thrashed out, as the series of drafts I
published (in *The Making of T. S. Eliot's Plays*) shows, by TSE and
John Hayward.

These two men had been sharing a flat on Cheyne Walk,
Chelsea, since 1946. Hayward was almost twenty years younger
than Eliot. He had suffered since childhood from a form of
muscular dystrophy which had by this time confined him to a
wheelchair. But he did not allow this to inhibit him from satisfying
his brilliant and witty intellect by means of a voracious appetite for
work, and becoming the foremost bibliographer of his time. His
beautiful room overlooking the river, where I was entertained to
tea or would call for a few moments' chat when I went to work with
Tom, was a centre of literary as well as bibliographical life.

Though each man had his own full load of work, the shared
meals provided by their housekeeper, and the interlocking of their
interests at so many points, resulted in John Hayward's having a
considerable influence on the post-war plays. As Dame Helen
Gardner has shown in her admirable *The Composition of 'Four
Quartets'*, he had contributed much to Tom's last major poem by his
exact and penetrating criticism during its creation. Eliot's note of
acknowledgement prefacing the first edition of *The Cocktail Party*
serves to define the spheres in which he found each of us useful
during the play's writing:

I wish to acknowledge my indebtedness to two critics. To Mr. E. Martin
Browne, who was responsible for the first production of the play at the
Edinburgh Festival, 1949: for his criticism of the structure, from the first
version to the last; for suggestions most of which have been accepted, and
which, when accepted, have all been fully justified on the stage. And to
Mr John Hayward, for continuous criticism and correction of vocabulary,
idiom and manners. My debt to both of these censors could be understood
only by comparison of the successive drafts of this play with the final text.

John Hayward was not only skilled in respect of vocabulary but
also acute in his observation of idiom and manners. He had a great
delight in the social life, in which he managed to take an amazingly
full part. The needle of his wit would often be tipped with acid. His
sense of status was as accurate as his perception of humbug. He
surveyed the tangled webs into which his fellow-humans, by their

vanity and folly, wove their relationships, with a relish which had something of Ben Jonson or Swift about it.

Such a web I found woven in the new play, though the people in it were seen with the compassionate sympathy of its author as well as with his unerring eye for truth. I could not help being troubled by the improbability of the plot, even if the characters brought to it their own genuineness. I also questioned its period: 'Is it set in 1904?' The title suggested the master–servant relationship of that period which was now almost extinct, but which indeed existed between Sir Claude and his 'confidential clerk' Eggerson, from whom young Colby seemed at first ready to carry it on. Could the characters in this play be regarded as living the 'contemporary life' which Tom wanted to depict? The question was particularly pertinent because the post-second-world-war theatre was opening itself to relationships of such a different kind. *Look Back in Anger* was only three years ahead, and many signals of that breakthrough were appearing. Was the poetic drama of today sacrificing its poetry for a contemporaneity which it was failing to attain?

Perhaps though, I thought, that was the wrong question. After all, the play, after a slow start, was entertaining and the complications could add to the fun. With such a plot, it must be seen, not as realism, but as high comedy analogous to that of Oscar Wilde, and the relationships must be presented with his kind of sparkle. The danger was that the author's deep concern for his people kept breaking in. Could the two styles be successfully combined? The verse must help here: it would not be noticeable, the speech hardly ever rose to the intensity of poetry, but it supplied rhythm that unified height with depth, farce with feeling.

This it achieved in its first production, and *The Confidential Clerk* enjoyed a considerable success; but it has very seldom been played since. I cannot help wondering whether, if he had not been living the inward-turning life demanded by a possessive invalid, Tom would have acclimatised himself to the post-war social revolution and let it appear in his work. The scene between Colby and Lucasta in Act II suggests that he would have, for it is full of the loneliness, the restlessness, the longing for love. One is profoundly moved by those two young people: then the incongruities of farce intervene, Lucasta resumes her mask, and Colby, the central figure, retreats into shadow. Perhaps it is this play, rather than *Murder in the Cathedral*, that Tom should have called 'a dead end'.

My 1953 production for Edinburgh, though, was very much alive, and Tom enjoyed it. We worked on the script in his little study at the back of the Chelsea flat in the evenings, both before and during rehearsals. This was the first play of which he attended rehearsals frequently, enjoying the company of some very attractive actors and actresses. Margaret Leighton was playing Lucasta and Isabel Jeans Lady Elizabeth. Alison Leggatt, who had been the London Lavinia, was the 'suburban Pallas Athene', Mrs Guzzard. There was Denholm Elliott as Colby, and Paul Rogers as Sir Claude, Alan Webb as Eggerson and Peter Jones as B. Kaghan. It was indeed a splendid company that Henry Sherek had assembled, and a happy one too. We discovered together the style for the play, and I think this was the most completely integrated production I made of any of the modern plays. Margaret Leighton and Denholm Elliott plumbed the depths of their big scene, and we remained so much aware of them during the ensuing absurdities and tangles that at the end, when Colby goes to Eggerson's garden, we knew that his 'secret garden' would flourish in Joshua Park. The ill-assorted quartet, Lucasta and B., Claude and Lady Elizabeth were left behind: could they learn to live as a family? Well, we knew at least that Claude had accepted his responsibility for the 'dirty public square' in which his illegitimate daughter grew up. Perhaps she would respond to his final appeal: 'Don't leave me, Lucasta.'

This time, thanks to the huge success of *The Cocktail Party*, Henry had no difficulty in finding a London theatre: the Lyric, Shaftesbury Avenue, had already accepted the *Clerk* before its Edinburgh opening. After the London first night, John Hayward arranged on Tom's behalf a party at the Savoy. It was the prelude to a run of over two hundred performances at the Lyric, plus an extra four weeks at the smaller Duke of York's. An American production was offered to Henry under the most lavish conditions; but the most vital one was missing – that unity in the cast which had made the English success. American Equity had obtained a ruling that limited the importation of actors in any company to forty per cent. Henry tried to find an all-American cast, but ended up with a mixture of styles, plus a star-size clash of personalities: Ina Claire (Lady Elizabeth) versus Claud Rains (Sir Claude). They both got fond of me but that didn't stop them hating each other. It began at the first rehearsal, to which Claud came with his lines all pat, while

Ina, notorious for never knowing hers, was fumbling in the garrulously apologetic way that destroys the flow of every passage. By the New York opening, having had a prompter in each wing for the four-and-a-half weeks out of town, she was almost word-perfect, while Claud had been steadily losing his initial confidence and was shaky. Despite all my efforts the antagonism grew, and did great damage beneath the professional surface. The American Colby, too, was subconsciously at odds with the character. So in spite of the opening's glamour, I was surprised that the New York run was as long as four months.

Henzie went over with me while I rehearsed the play over Christmas and New Year, and her letters home show how much we enjoyed ourselves, especially in Boston. That city is the stronghold of the huge Eliot clan. There was even an 'Eliot' telephone exchange. Charles W. Eliot, a remote cousin of Tom's grandfather,

30 *The Confidential Clerk* (T. S. Eliot), Lyric Theatre, Shaftesbury Avenue, London, 1953. Margaret Leighton as Lucasta and Denholm Elliott as Colby

had been President of Harvard when Tom went there, and in his twenty-five years contributed very largely to making the Harvard of the twentieth century. The family was massed to receive us:

Most days we cross over the River Charles to Cambridge (where is Harvard). It is a lovely sight, very wide indeed, frozen over and covered with snow. At sunset with the golden and coloured lights on either bank it is special. These frosty nights have vivid skies, the moon is up while the sun goes down and the snow reflects back all the colours . . . Theresa Eliot (Tom's widowed sister-in-law) in a week has become a real friend. She took us to the Houghton Library at Harvard to see the T. S. Eliot collection now being assembled for posterity. It is all there: a magazine he wrote and illustrated aged 12, MSS, photos, notices, criticisms and all his work in all the stages of preparation. Then back to Theresa's apartment; while she broiled lamb chops we looked at some fine drawings she had made of Tom, some asleep on her couch, one just waking. They are very delicate and perceptive.

Yesterday Tom's cousins Aimée and Rosamond Lamb gave a party. A *Cranford* atmosphere. Here I was told was 'the cream of Boston society'. Mr and Mrs Willie James (a nephew of Henry James), Dr and Mrs Constable (descendant of *the* Constable) . . . they all sounded very English. Martin is a 'Lion' in his own right, but I am a sort of heifer–lioness in as much as I have played in Tom's plays and most of all *know* him . . . Professor Finlay, head of Eliot House, talked a great deal about Eliot and the classics and his understanding of *The Confidential Clerk*. I could have listened for hours.

Imagine wanting all these chance acquaintances to become friends! All talked easily and immediately about ideas and values and art – not eternally about *persons* as most women (and that goes for me) usually do. *All* of us talked, not one 'holding forth', each one contributing.

Tea with Miss Marion Eliot, an older sister, in her small apartment in Cambridge. A charming maiden lady, very thin but most lively. She will fly (first time) to England this summer and spend three weeks with Tom in the Isle of Wight. Here was a little of Aunt Ivy, and the flat might have been in South Kensington. All the echoes of a big family home – her mother's eighteenth-century bureau, family pictures, silver tea equipage – most pleasant and very cosy.

Today we travelled north to Andover, where Emily Hale teaches in a big girls' school. (We met her with Tom at Chipping Camden before the war, when we all discussed *The Family Reunion*.) She drove us round; the houses, mostly white, looked pretty in the deep snow with the dark trees making contrast. We had sherry in her own little room, lunched with the school, and the drama group came to take coffee with us in the parlour . . .

The Signet Society, a Harvard literary club of which TSE was a member, gave a cocktail-party – undergraduates and a few professors. Crowded as the Black Hole of Calcutta, hazy smoky air, loud excited talk. An amazing amount of criticism of the play, drawing most extraordinary conclusions and interpretations: 'Colby stands for the Christ myth . . . Eliot regards himself as God . . . Colby's failure is an interpretation of the Church's failure . . .' A great lack of knowledge of the gospels confounded much of their comparisons, but it was exciting how Eliot stimulated and challenged them. I took up cudgels and was delighted with the spirit in which they took my refutations . . . 'Mrs Guzzard is the Virgin Mary, of course, she wears blue.' 'I bought that dress for her myself; I had to take blue because they were out of grey' . . . Much laughter . . . some decided to consider it again.

Our last afternoon to Theresa Eliot for a quick meal, and then Martin and I gave a reading as a 'thank-you' for all their kindness to us. Forty to fifty relations and friends crammed into the small apartment. We did excerpts from all the plays, especially *The Family Reunion*, and ended with the last Chorus from *The Rock*. Some people said it made so much that had seemed obscure, plain to understand. It was such a happy affair.

It *was* a happy affair: so was the whole Boston fortnight. The family was full of the most attractive and interesting characters: they had given us a great welcome, and their love for, as well as their pride in Tom shone out of every candle that illuminated what was in effect a prolonged party . . . But perhaps this too was something that he had to get away from? In trying to understand the course his life took, I see this possibility. Just as he found himself impelled as a young man to leave his family in St Louis, to their great pain, and face his own hardships and make his own mistakes in the England of the first war, so maybe he had to go on, as an older and famous man, keeping his distance from those loving people. He loved them, and loved to visit them: he was close to Theresa in particular. But these were 'the roots that clutch'.

This New England graciousness, expressed in a precise and exquisite pattern of traditional behaviour and based on a traditional pattern of thought, could insulate a poet against the blasts of the Spirit. Just as the poet of *The Waste Land* had been fashioned by the rasping stresses of a harsh London life, so perhaps the dramatist of *The Family Reunion* could only become the poet of *Four Quartets* by enduring and maintaining the loneliness of another wartime and post-war London.

For our part, we had always felt his need to be separate, his determination to be private: and we knew that our friendship could only be of value to him – would indeed only be possible for him – if we never sought to cross the boundaries within which he kept his personal life. I think it was because he could rely on this respect that he was able to receive our love, and give his in return.

The Drama League, in consenting to my American visit, looked to gain contacts across the Atlantic. The American Educational Theatre Association (AETA), which affiliated college and community theatres throughout the States, held its three-day conference in New York while I was rehearsing, so Henzie manned the League's stall:

The Statler Hotel is immense. A balcony on the mezzanine floor was hung with Christmas wreaths tied with scarlet bows – festive lifebelts in this static ship. For mainmast there stood in the centre a glittering frosted Christmas tree, its branches so thickly hung with coloured balls that the whole vast tree seemed to be made of spangles. It revolved continuously all day while coloured lights of crimson, blue, green and gold played on it in turn. Under the general roar of voices, footsteps, bells and elevators, a remote record played carols.

Theatre Arts Books had a stall on the mezzanine balcony: its directors, Rosamond Gilder and Robert MacGregor, generously shared it with the British Drama League. The news that I was there got round and gradually people found their way to me. I had many happy reunions with friends and acquaintances . . . members of the faculty and student body of Carnegie Tech hailed me across a gap of twenty-three years. *Drama* was the main attraction and many of my visitors became subscribers. I believe there will be many more American callers at 9 Fitzroy Square, and I repeatedly heard of the wonderful welcome and service they had received there in the past.

But I found my visitors were as keen to tell me of their activities as of their needs. This burning need to unburden oneself is a most moving characteristic of humankind. The first visitor I had was an elderly freelance journalist. He paused at my table, told me about his wife's major operation and said that despite the doctor's verdict they both believed she would recover; she had cooked his Christmas dinner. My second visitor's attack was direct: 'Are you a Catholic?' 'Only in the Episcopalian sense of the word,' I replied. But for the most part it was the story, familiar even in Britain but far more frequent in this much larger country, of the drama teacher lonely and cut off from seeing plays or meeting theatre people.

I went back to a full plate in London. The BDL library had far outgrown its space and we had to enlarge it into the next-door house. The Pilgrim Trust met most of the cost, and thanks to this we succeeded in restoring the two fine Adam rooms to their original proportions and revealing their marble fireplaces. The Lord Chamberlain (Lord Scarborough, my friend of the York Festival) reopened the library for us. We sent Frances Mackenzie on a tour across the world, following up our 1951 visit in New Zealand with a series of courses and adjudications, and conducting a school for directors in Australia. Henzie and I took on the main summer school in her absence. At Christmas, lectures for young people were given in professional theatres with a most distinguished team of speakers: Richard Burton and Claire Bloom, George Devine, Athene Seyler and Nicholas Hannen, Sybil Thorndike and Lewis Casson. A junior Drama League was well on the way to establishment. For adults, we launched a Theatregoers' Club. Over three hundred joined in two months, and we were hard put to it to get enough seats! The leading players recognised its value and would come to meet members at a party after the show.

These closer contacts with the professional theatre were given fresh impetus by the chairman I had persuaded to succeed Geoffrey. John Maude, QC was the son of two stars, Cyril Maude and Winifred Emery. He introduced the Christmas lectures and 'chaired' the conferences in a most attractive way. All too soon he became a judge and had to resign, but I was fortunate enough to get Ivor Brown to take his place. Ivor was beloved by the profession as the most honest and stalwart defender of the theatre in print. In the difficult days that were coming, his sure judgement was what the League needed to see it through.

For this flourishing and expanding structure was built upon shifting sand. The League had been founded as a Good Cause; those who worked for it took charity wages, and those who joined it reckoned they were acquiring merit. The truth of the present situation was quite different. Members were receiving substantial benefits for which they were paying a small proportion of the proper cost. Staff in the post-war world could not exist, even if they wanted to, on the salaries that resulted.

I started by getting the subscription raised to two guineas (it had been one guinea in 1919 and one-and-a-half when I came). Additional income accrued from the proportion of our outside earnings which I and the training department tutors paid over to the League. With this I managed to raise all salaries except my own. I also started a pension fund. It was woefully small, but at least it was a beginning, for all except those who deserved it most because they had served longest.

This point came home to me with especial force when Frances Briggs decided to retire early. She had characteristically prepared in good time for a new life in the country, and wanted the years (which still continue) to enjoy it. As a parting gift, the members gave her a new Austin A30. On 17 September 1954 the chairman presented it, and as we all cheered she drove him and Mrs Whitworth round the square, past the GBS plaque, and back to number 9 which she was to leave after twenty years – thirty-five in all with the League. It would change radically with her departure.

For a period of contraction was beginning. Costs were rising faster than income – and in Britain's seemingly permanent financial depression this disparity is still going on. 'Rationalisation' was necessary: what was going to be done must be done with less staff and less space. Much that the League was founded to do has been achieved. The National Theatre is in operation. Civic Theatres have multiplied. State and local authority support is given on a scale Geoffrey, who first launched the Civic Theatre scheme in 1942, never dreamed of. Drama is built into education. The League – or as it has been re-named, The British Theatre Association – has retained its library and its amateur festivals, and found new work in forging links between the many different kinds of theatre.

I remained with the League for over two years more, while re-organisation was worked out. It became clear that there could no longer be a director and a secretary, and that the administrative head must be regularly at his headquarters desk. Ivor Brown and I agreed that that was not where I belonged.

I2

American Seminary

The Confidential Clerk opened at the Morosco on 11 February 1954. Before we left New York, Henzie and I had two public engagements. One was a Sunday night recital of scenes from T. S. Eliot's plays for the Poetry Center. This led, some time later, to our becoming Danforth visiting lecturers to American colleges. In three years we visited about a hundred, and stayed two days in each. Most of them were 'church-related' colleges of every denomination from Catholic to Mennonite. We made friendships which linked people all over the States with the work in Britain and the Religious Drama Society: most treasured of all these friends was Sister Madeleva, President of St Mary's College, Notre Dame. And we learned a great deal of the almost infinite variety of American education.

The other engagement in New York was at Union Theological Seminary (UTS), of which I knew only the rather formidable name. We were asked to speak on religious drama and give illustrative readings. About a hundred students and others were assembled in one of the lecture-rooms. Everyone was then invited to meet us in the president's apartment. One is always somewhat dazed when plunged straight from a presentation into a party: but we noticed ourselves being introduced to several people 'from the Rockefeller Foundation', and we came away with the feeling that 'something was up'.

It was. In March, the president wrote to us in London of

some conversations with the Rockefeller Foundation about our hopes of creating a small training program in religious drama here at Union Seminary . . . They would probably be responsive to a request from the Seminary for a grant for the express purpose of bringing you here to direct such a program.

Over the next two years the plan was worked out, and I was

appointed visiting professor, with Henzie as visiting lecturer, in Religious Drama from September 1956.

When we arrived there, Union was at the height of its fame, 'the world's largest independent and interdenominational Seminary'. It had over six hundred candidates for degrees from some sixty church bodies all over the world, with an equally large number of students in summer courses. The missionary spirit was strong, and alumni kept the Seminary alive to the world's needs which were also represented by present students. The American way of life with its plenty and extravagance came under their searchlight: at the reception for new students after we and they had been there a few days, an Indian was asked what had so far struck him most forcibly: 'The uneaten food on the plates at lunch-time: it would feed my village for a week.'

What struck *us* most was the strength of the corporate life. Considering the infinitely diverse backgrounds from which people came, this was amazing. And it did not depend on a cloistered existence: everyone was exposed to the impact of New York City. The intellectual standard was of the highest – great men like Paul Tillich and Reinhold Niebuhr were among the professors. The battles of wits, ideas and personalities that were always going on were the outward signs of a common inward vitality.

At its centre was worship. In the big chapel there was daily morning service based on the Presbyterian pattern from which the Seminary had grown, but with many variations. On Sundays, Reinhold Niebuhr was among many fine preachers. There was also a small chapel entirely under the students' control, where they conducted two services a day and learned by doing and discussing afterwards. One Sunday morning, Henzie and I were invited to join a group who were making a week-end 'retreat' (from the turmoil of New York) to a hutted camp in the woods. We got there for breakfast: coffee and bread and butter were on the rough table. Everyone sat down in silence. Tom Driver, the leader, read from 1 Corinthians 11:

The Lord Jesus, the same night in which he was betrayed, took bread . . . This do in remembrance of me.

The silence lasted for several minutes. Then we ate and drank and talked. I was reminded of Quaker meals: 'Every meal,' they told me, 'is a sacrament.' As Paul says in the next chapter, 'there are varieties of service, but the same Lord'.

The president, Pitney Van Dusen, and his wife Betty were to become two of our dearest friends. They were the centre-point round which the life of Union moved, because they were open and alert to everything and everybody. Pitney gave the first impression you expect of the head of an American college – a big, authoritative man with a genial manner, an administrator rather than an intellectual. Beneath this lay a profound faith, the quality of which can be perceived in his book on Dag Hammarskjöld, which reveals the underlying unity between his outer and his inner life. Pitney's heart was large enough to embrace not only his own family, not only the hundreds who at any time constituted the resident family of Union, but thousands of alumni and particularly those working on mission and in other theological colleges throughout the world, whom he made long journeys (especially after retirement) to visit. Naturally he was a key figure in the World Council of Churches and the ecumenical movement. Matched with this breadth was a depth from which could erupt a passionate, even violent, expression of his convictions. He had served the Seminary for many years and matured naturally into its president.

Betty was 'an helpmeet for him', a positive and dynamic Scot, witty, downright, a born leader and hostess. She had had two hip operations before we arrived (and the techniques of today had not yet been developed) and had to wear thick glasses, but she would never allow pain or disability to stand in the way of a very full life, of the developments she conceived and persuasively advocated at the Seminary, or of her care for four sons and a huge circle of friends. She had been a Fogerty student, and kept her love of the theatre and of reading poetry aloud.

We were made welcome every year at the family Christmas, as well as at many other occasions, from the prestigious receptions which the job demanded to meals in the kitchen.

We made a circle of friends among the faculty, and as time went on we exchanged homes with some who went on sabbatical leave to London. Union's life had a strong family bias, since it accommodated both married faculty and married students. I looked up 'Seminary' and its first meaning gave me a shock of surprised familiarity. The dictionary says it is 'the original place whence anything is derived, a nursery'. When one used the laundry in the basement, one had to beware of toddlers underfoot!

Our first period at Union was to last from September to the end

of January. I had residual commitments at the Drama League and
was directing the York Mystery Plays in June 1957; so it was
agreed that we should start the Program off, leave it to others for a
year, and return in 1958 to continue work for a further year or
more. The objectives and shape of the Program in Religious Drama
were thus set forth, by Pitney Van Dusen:

Of all the arts, with the possible exception of music, drama has been
perhaps the most intimately linked to the life of religion. Yet for a hundred
years and more, this medium of spiritual education and expression has
suffered something of an eclipse. The time seems ripe for a revival of
religious drama in this country, and it is of utmost importance that the
highest standards be set while the situation is still flexible. We believe that
Union Theological Seminary is in a position to render significant leadership to this end.

The Program will be organised with three groups in mind: first, the
regular students at UTS, to acquaint them with the resources in drama
for their churches and communities; second, active directors of religious
drama who will be encouraged to come to UTS for a year or more; third,
actors, writers and directors, both professional and amateur, who are
interested. The enlarged Program will build upon courses already being
offered and experiments being conducted under Professors John W.
Bachman and Robert E. Seaver of the Seminary Faculty . . .

John Bachman is a 'media man' and didn't teach or direct
drama, but as the Program's chairman, he was responsible for
policy and for fitting its work into the Seminary schedule. Bob
Seaver's regular job was Speech, a compulsory subject for all BD
candidates (Church of England please copy!). He graduated in
theatre at Northwestern University under Lee Mitchell, a student
in our time at Carnegie Tech. Bob had already done some
extra-curricular productions at Union, and their success had
helped to win favour for the curricular Program. Tom Driver, a
Union/Columbia philosophy graduate who had just joined the
faculty, was to contribute especially on the intellectual side.

In order to establish the Program in a single semester, we took
on a very heavy load of work. I gave in weekly lectures 'a
philosophical and historical study leading to the appraisal of
religious drama as a part of the work of the Church', with
discussions to follow. We ran a workshop in acting and directing
with a large student body of very varied experience and talent,
giving a lot of time also to individuals. And we staged no less than
four productions.

The Seminary had then no stage equipped for plays. The alternatives were the chapel, which was also used by the School of Sacred Music, and the social hall which was used for every kind of gathering and had a miserably cramped hole-in-the-wall stage. Both auditoria had flat floors. However, I have always believed that limitations are good for learning. I also wanted these students to discover what a church gives to, and demands of, a director, that a hall does not. So I staged the first play in both hall and chapel. It was the first American showing of what was to become the most popular of modern passion plays, Philip Turner's *Christ in the Concrete City*. Turner wrote it for Pamela Keily, who regularly commissions new plays for her work in the north of England.

To publicise the new Program, each of the first two productions was given an extra invitation performance. The second was already in rehearsal with another group of students. This was the York Nativity Play, given in chapel with the School of Sacred Music supplying a chain of carols to link the scenes. For most, actors and audience alike, this was a first contact with the Mystery Plays.

31 EMB rehearsing in New York, 1958. One of the secretaries at Inter-church Center is taking part in a choral drama by a Union student, Darius Leander Swann. Photo by permission of Hilda Bijur

Brooks Atkinson, the father-figure of American dramatic criticism, wrote in the *New York Times*:

E. Martin Browne has composed a nativity play out of the fourteenth-century York cycle of mystery plays, and staged it in the chancel of a church with music, costumes and lighting. It has grace and beauty. It is also profoundly moving. For there is nothing in art that quite equals the wondrous attitude of the unknown authors of these simple plays toward the story of the Nativity, or of the verse written in the period of Chaucer when the English language was taking form. These plays and this glorious music are our sources. They are pure and humbling, for they mean what they say.

While this was running, Henzie prepared her *Beginning of the Way* (originally written for the Pilgrim Players) with yet another group of students for two performances in the social hall. Most students would afterwards have to tackle the nativity play in 'biblical' costume, and this one gave it a new look.

After working at such pressure, the two-week break at Christmas was more than welcome: and it brought a quite unexpected delight. We heard that the Cassons were coming to play in Graham Greene's *The Potting Shed* on Broadway, and invited them to occupy our second bedroom 'for a few days while you find somewhere to live'. They arrived in time to join the Van Dusens' Christmas dinner-party. After a month, Henzie wrote home:

We have made a lovely job of living together. I do all the meals except that Sybil heats the coffee and makes the toast for breakfast every morning. She generally gets up at 7 a.m., has tea, and then reads her Greek Testament for an hour. Their strength is wonderful . . . Sybil at times looks very tired but Lewis (81) is relaxed and rubicund. Now rather deaf, he reads incessantly, often standing in the middle of the room for long stretches of time like a horse. He had been angry and lost his temper at Friday's rehearsal so on Saturday morning he went out for a long walk over Washington Bridge. He got lost on the subway – so easy to do as there are few direction-posts – and we were all really scared about him and were unsuccessful at concealing our fears! Sybil is very gay and we all laugh a lot.

During that joyful period we were as busy as they. Helen Stout, whom we saw often and who, like all our friends, came to the shows at Union, arranged for me to direct at New Year a 'concert reading' of Christopher Fry's *The Firstborn* at the Poetry Center with a professional cast. Helen had for several years been directing a summer theatre at Sharon, Connecticut, and was able to find me good actors. She introduced me also to this new kind of production, fashionable since *Under Milk Wood*. The actors sit on stools with books in hand, and the focus is on the words they 'read'. But very carefully controlled looks, gestures and occasional changes of place heighten the effect. Henzie, alas, was barred by American Equity from reading Miriam, but passed on her knowledge of the part and of the play. It was well served, thought the *New York Times*:

'The Firstborn' shows Mr. Fry in one of his most serious moods. Only occasionally is there a touch of the humor that characterizes so much of his work. There is evident in the play that great gift of language, of figurative speech and, besides, a vigor that is thoroughly absorbing to hear. Mr. Browne has garnered from a splendid cast a reading that is equal to Mr. Fry's intentions. With only stools, lecterns and a background bathed in blue, the play, static though it is for the most part in its telling, nevertheless succeeds in bounding into life.

Next day, we resumed work at Union, and our last production there was staged a week later. This was of two short plays by Charles Williams, *The House by the Stable* and its sequel *Grab and Grace*. They are much lighter than *Cranmer*, having been written for the Oxford Pilgrim Players to tour in wartime. Their wit was in just the right key for the Seminary audience, but the general public responded with equal relish. Marvin Halverson, head of the Department of Worship and the Arts at the National Council of Churches, in reviewing the production for *The Christian Century*, sums up the significance of the semester's work:

The performances proved an admirable conclusion to the first semester of Union Theological Seminary's new program in drama. Inaugurated last fall, this program was designed to extend the range of theological education. Experience has justified the seminary's conviction that drama is a new area of the church's life.

I confess that my approach to the Williams plays was one of suspicion. I had not read them. My surprise at their clarity and wit and at the psychological immediacy of their characters increased my delight in this production. The audience is not detached. Amid the laughter which ran through the theater, one sensed that each viewer was observing himself.

Theological students and special drama students were cast in the various roles. Despite their amateur status, they brought skill and knowledge to the performance. In fact, the successful production of *The House by the Stable* and *Grab and Grace* with a non-professional cast suggests that drama of this caliber can be produced in many of our churches.

We found ourselves whirled into farewells. The last performance of the Williams plays was to an Alumni Conference (an acid test) on 22 January, and nine days later we sailed. Meanwhile, we saw the opening of *The Potting Shed*; spent the last evening at Jean-Louis Barrault's production of Claudel's *Christophe Colombe*; and at midnight found Sybil and Lewis with Bob Seaver on the dockside to see us aboard the *Queen Elizabeth*. 'Come back!' said everybody at Union.

We did go back in September 1958. The Rockefeller Foundation, who had supplied funds for the first three years of the Program, renewed their grant for another three, so that we worked at Union until 1962. We continued in our visiting appointments, with Bob Seaver as director of the Program. He was the senior member of the regular faculty engaged in drama, and had both the will and the skill to establish it. In the spring of 1957 he had made a production which spoke strongly in the Protestant voice. *The Sign of Jonah* was written by an East German pastor, and brought the Hebrew prophet into the twentieth century as captain of a U-boat. It was received with acclamation.

Now that the Program was more than just an experiment, what should it aim for? A degree for specialists, especially teachers, was required: and we collaborated with our colleagues in Religious Education to set up a Master's (MRE) 'with emphasis in drama'. Past and present students were asked for criticisms and suggestions. The result was that we integrated class-work more closely with productions, which became less frequent, and gave students more opportunities to make their own experiments under supervision. They asked to learn the additional skills of movement and staging techniques. We brought in teachers for both; and Richard Casler, newly graduated from the drama department at Yale, not only taught the techniques of scenery, costume and lighting but created a stage for us in the main lecture-hall, and also designed productions which the students executed under his guidance.

We had by now a keenly interested audience of several hundreds, over and above the strong support of the Seminary community. At least one major play, we felt, should be shown to them each year. But for these we still had to look to European writers. For 1958–9 we did *The Mystery of the Finding of the Cross* by Henri Ghéon. This encases in the historical tale of Helena, mother of Constantine, that devotional *Way of the Cross* which the Pilgrims had acted so often. Henzie directed the 'play within a play', and the Seminary received this Catholic drama with appreciation.

Cranmer was the choice for 1959/60, and the students' reaction to it seemed to me significant:

This viewer and many others (including many who were not theological students) found that the magnificence of the author's poetry carried a power which could not have been achieved in any other way. The force of this play rested upon the speaking and hearing of words that rang and sang and danced in our ears. Running, falling, spinning, dancing are verbs that we hear over and over again. We seek after God, but God chases after us! It is significant that the play ends with the word 'speed', while the actors race from our sight. This concern with motion and movement is a tremendously liberating concept. Our lives and our world are not static and stagnant; and our Creator is one who lives and moves and acts. His love and His grace run constantly before us.

We were fortunate in our actors, especially Jim Alger (soon to be a Lutheran minister in North Dakota) as the Skeleton and Al Carmines as Henry VIII. Al, as a minister at the Judson Memorial Church in Washington Square, has since created several musicals, some to the words of Gertrude Stein, which have won considerable acclaim.

Next year, Al was Harry in *The Family Reunion*. Comparing this with previous experiences, one realises how much it helps the actor of Harry to have 'wrestled with God' in the way that a place like Union compels one to. Henzie as Agatha found Al wonderful to play with. Betty Van Dusen played Amy, and the quarrel-scene between these two made sparks fly!

We knew that if our experiment was to have a future it depended on getting American authors to write new plays. Marvin Halverson had emphasised, in his 1957 review of the Williams bill,

the lack of a comparable body of dramatic literature in the United States. American writing talent is acknowledged as inferior to none. But religious intuitions and apprehensions in American writing are disjoined from a living Christian tradition. If the literature of tomorrow is to be more than a revelation of alienations, bridges must be thrown out for the dramatists, novelists and poets to travel. The initiative lies with the church. Fortunately, that initiative has already been taken in small but significant ways. The program at Union Theological Seminary is one evidence of it.

In May 1958 Bob presented the Program's first 'completely home-grown production'. The cast were all BD candidates, the play written by Bruce Clements, a UTS graduate of 1956, 'in time caught out of the air above a busy church and a young family' and called *The Wedge of Eternity*. Kay Baxter, at that time chairman of RDS in Britain, who as a visiting lecturer had become as much attached to Union as ourselves, worked with the young playwright during rehearsals, clarifying and adapting, so that everyone concerned got an experience of how theatre is really created.

Bob had been pressing for a Christian revue. He got the chance to create *For Heaven's Sake* at the North American Ecumenical Youth Assembly, and showed it afterwards in New York. We found it 'a dazzling stream of entertainment', as one reviewer had said. The satire of numbers like 'A mighty fortress is our Church' and 'Use me, Lord, but not just now' was tellingly stopped in mid-laugh by tiny, thickly compressed sermons:

> He took the rap for me, but I don't see what I ever did to deserve the rap He says He took for me. Or can it be that *that* was the rap pinned on me – that I don't see what I ever did to deserve the rap He says He took for me?

At the other end of the spectrum, Henzie made me a dramatic liturgy, building into the framework of Union's regular morning service a dramatisation of the Presentation of Christ in the Temple. It was called *The Green Wood*. We showed this at the Inter-church Center, and then took it to the National Council of Churches' education conference at St Louis, Missouri. With it went *The Case Against Eve* by Eve McFall from our playwriting class. We held a competition too, but it was not very productive. The winner was a ten-minute play. The two thieves are huddled over a brazier on *A Very Cold Night*; will they give up the one warm spot to the man on the middle cross? The best thing about it was that it extended religious drama to include the language of Didi and Gogo.

The final words of the student review I quoted from above reveal a ferment, which the superlative quality of Union's intellectual life clearly increased:

Cranmer says: 'Can *this life* itself be redemption?' This question could stand a great deal of discussion in these hallowed halls. Williams has been called a theologian of affirmation, yet he never refused to look at, and participate in, the pain and sorrow of this world.

Students were finding the theological church to be an inward-looking institution, as well as far too luxurious (their paper, aptly named *The Grain of Salt*, from which I quote, was repeatedly outspoken about this). A substantial part of the minister's training was 'Field-work'; and when you worked, say in the East Harlem

Protestant Parish which Union had staffed for years, you became acutely aware that you had a secure base outside the poverty and misery of the negro or Puerto Rican population of Harlem. As the sixties went on, Union students and faculty took an active part in the sit-ins, marches and other protests against segregation across the country. Conflict between the academic and the social demands of the Christian ministry was growing towards an upheaval which, after 1968, would change the Seminary almost beyond recognition.

The drama Program as we had created it came to an end. But its influence spread far and wide, across the States and beyond. It still brings forth much fruit.

13

George Bell's Testament

I came in to our London home on 13 January 1958 to find a scrawled message from our cleaning lady:

Bishop Bell would like you to dine with him this evening at the Fenian Club.

I recognised the Athenaeum through the Irish mist. George Bell was retiring that year from Chichester, and had been invited by Archbishop Fisher to propose, at his last appearance in the Upper (Bishops') House of the Convocation of Canterbury, a valedictory motion. He chose to move:

That this House, recognising the Church's concern for contributions of the highest quality by artists and authors in the shaping of modern culture, offers a special welcome to the work done in recent years by poets, writers and producers in the revival of religious drama; expresses its gratitude to the Religious Drama Society of Great Britain; and trusts that the work thus begun may go forward under wise direction.

We spent the evening going through the points of his speech. He traced the developments of the last thirty years in Great Britain, citing both the rediscovery of old plays and the creation of new. He showed that 'this great outburst of poetry and religion mingled in drama had had its effect on the theatre as a whole', and (remembering the International Conference he had chaired, and the Program at Union on which his counsel had been sought and given) that 'the United States looks to England and the countries in Europe look to England'. After a detailed tribute to the work of the Religious Drama Society, he concluded by asking his fellow bishops:

that it should be made more and more widely known that the Church of England, through its bishops and in its dioceses, encouraged that way of presenting religious truth as truth about human life, for its own sake and for kindling, healing and stirring the human imagination.

Bishop George Cockin, a former Chairman of RDSGB, seconded, and after several bishops had supported it the motion was carried by acclamation. We were both invited to attend this, his last testament.

The Bells retired to Canterbury, where I saw them frequently that summer. Margaret Babington's health had been failing and to her distress no Festival play had been produced for three years. She wasn't strong enough to organise one in the Chapter House, so I suggested we ask the civic Marlowe Theatre to house it. We revived *Christ's Comet* by Christopher Hassall. He was pleased with the production: 'One poet is never enough in the theatre,' he said. Miss Babington rejoiced in the play which we had done in her honour; and a few weeks afterwards, sitting at her desk, she died.

Early in October, soon after we had returned to Union, George Bell died also.

Before leaving, I staged *The Elder Statesman*, which proved to be T. S. Eliot's last play. It was not conceived as such, though its starting-point was Sophocles' last play, *Oedipus at Colonus*. Tom had written half of it before his marriage in January 1957 to Valerie Fletcher. He often asked me to work with him at their Kensington home, as he completed the script and we prepared it for the stage. It was a great joy to find him a blissfully happy man. Harry in *The Family Reunion* says to Agatha:

> I feel happy for a moment, as if I had come home.

For Harry, it is only a moment: the next moment he faces the transforming encounter with the Eumenides. Tom, having been through that fire, had come home for the rest of his earthly life.

The play has the mellowness of the 80-year-old Sophocles, but only fitfully displays his strength. Eliot has deliberately reduced the majesty of Oedipus and the mystery which surrounds his death to a domestic scale. It is the secondary characters who have the powerful moments. Lord Claverton himself has, like Becket, to suffer attack for two-thirds of the play and, unlike Becket, lacks the poetic fire to take his chance when it comes in the last act. Yet he is deeply studied as a human being. Paul Rogers, though twenty years too young for the part, made him convincing (and in a 1979 production, when he was the right age, made him even more so). Claverton's dilemma is one of conscience rather than of fate, so his

response to his son's rebellion, instead of Oedipus' curses, is a
guilty reproach; and the son (the young Alec McCowen) is the one
who electrifies the audience with *his* reproach, suddenly wheeling
on Claverton with

> What is my inheritance?

The richest character is Maisie Carghill, now a prosperous widow,
once a musical-comedy actress and Claverton's mistress. Her scene
is the best piece of comedy Eliot ever wrote. She quotes her
fabulous friend Effie:

> 'That man is hollow.' That's what she said.
> Or did she say 'yellow'? I'm not quite sure.

At the end of the scene, she gives Claverton a peep into hell:

> There's a phrase I seem to remember reading somewhere:
> *Where their fires are not quenched.*

Henry Sherek presented the play at Edinburgh, where it was
assured of a welcome. In London, he got the Cambridge Theatre,
but it proved too large and cold for a play with a weak heart. Two
months' run there was quite creditable. The London first night fell
with special appropriateness on the eve of Tom's 70th birthday. At
midnight, in the basement restaurant of L'Ecu de France, we were
all drinking his health and Valerie's. Next morning, Henzie and I
flew to New York.

During the next few summers, for which we came home from
America, we saw them regularly. We were happy in their happiness but sad to see Tom growing progressively frailer as the
emphysema from which he had suffered since 1954 became more
pronounced. On 4 January 1965 we were at Union. Henzie wrote:

On Monday night in bed I turned on our little transistor radio and caught
in a short phrase the death of Tom Eliot. The shock (not surprise) almost
numbed us, and midnight was a difficult time to take it . . . I suppose Tom
and the Bishop of Chichester have formed the pattern of our life and
Martin's work.

So the ones who have formed the pattern have left us: and I find
myself in the position of Elder Statesman! But the pattern remains:
and I can use George Bell's testament to analyse it. This is not,
however, reflection in tranquillity. The pattern is a pattern of life,
and so is constantly changing. And the work does not stop; one

must assess in terms of what is happening now. That is good: work in progress is the stuff of life.

So first, what of the old, the medieval plays? Since I first revived the York cycle of Mystery Plays in 1951, there has been a huge growth of interest throughout the English-speaking world. A new generation of scholars has arisen, adding to the study of texts and their sources an exploration of how they were performed, and an appreciation of their worth as theatre. Many of these scholars insist on putting their work to the test of performance, to discover how the plays affect modern audiences. Productions of every sort and size multiply. But it is still York, in its triennial Festival, which gives its native cycle the most regular showing on the largest scale.

Since 1957 there had been two new directors. Hans Hess was determined that the York 'tradition' which had developed under me should not become immutably set – an obvious danger, since the script was 'given' (though the selection of passages used could alter) and the St Mary's Abbey ruins had taken such a hold of spectators' hearts that every attempt to change the venue was resisted. So change could be made only in the interpretation. David Giles in 1960 and William Gaskill in 1963 had each striven in his different way towards 'realism'. To both, it seemed necessary to detach the plays from the ruined walls with their romantic quality, and they built sets several feet away from them. One description says the set 'did not mask the ruins in any way, it simply ignored them'.

The Festival Society invited me to return for the 1966 production, its only stipulation being

that the whole architectural and scenic possibilities of the Abbey be used in full, and no designer be allowed to obscure or obstruct [its] essential features.

To achieve this, I turned not to a stage designer but to an architect with a strong theatre-sense. Michael Cain is a junior partner of Sir Hugh Casson. I showed him the ruins and my layout, which was essentially the same as before because, though after nine years I could stand back from the plays and the place, they still asked me for the same treatment. Michael carried this out with the utmost simplicity. He described his 'mansions' as 'hexagonal platforms tilted towards the audience, surrounded by heavy rails on which tapestries, banners or hurdles could be placed to dress a particular scene'. The upward path was a stepped ramp 'like a donkey path'. Hell was 'a sort of siege-tower-cum-prison-cum-watchtower'. He used weathered wood: disused railway-sleepers or timbers from a dockside, for instance.

The Abbey received Michael's sensitively chosen materials and skilfully designed stage-areas as if they belonged to it. Alix Stone achieved a like result with costume. Terence Cluderay in *The Tablet* best expresses why I felt fulfilled by this my last production at York:

Within ten minutes of the start, people must have felt a peace moving out from the Abbey gardens and settling over the city. The mystery was back in their famous Mystery Plays . . . The old master, E. Martin Browne, is back – not with the mixture as before, but certainly with the same old magic. Only a fully corporate effort, inspired by good leadership and a common purpose clearly recognised, could have achieved such an excellent production as this is.

I made one innovation which contributed to this unity at 'the still centre'. John Westbrook, who had been in two of my earlier productions, 'doubled' the parts of God the Father and Jesus. I wrote at the time:

This becomes a statement in acting, that these two are one. It states the central tenet of the Christian faith, that God made the world because of love, and because of love came himself to be a man and share man's life and death. On the cross he says

What man greater loving could show than I?

and we recognise the same God who said to the first man and woman

For love made I this world alone . . .
Love me therefore and love me aye:
For my making I ask no more.

But this does not at all take away from his humanity. There will be no doubt of the human sympathy of this Jesus, who is fully sharing the life of the people around him.

Westbrook's Jesus had a sense of humour. He challenged the accusers of the woman taken in adultery:

He that from sin is free,
He first shall cast a stone

and as they slunk guiltily away, Jesus shouted with laughter.

The pattern is still healthily changing at York. Following 1966, the City Council went in for two all-amateur productions. These proved earnestly pretentious, and the Council were wise enough to call in Jane Howell for 1976. In that glorious summer – three weeks of Festival without a cloud – she made a folk-drama of Part I, with children's pictures of the Creation, giant puppets, real animals in the crowded city of the Nativity, music by the city's brass bands and the Kings arriving on horseback. She contrasted with this a stark Passion sequence, culminating in a Harrowing of Hell with all the fireworks. So many interpretations of this great drama are possible, provided they release the fullness of life that is in it.

While we were at Union Seminary, Henzie and I were to give a lecture-recital on the Mystery Plays one evening to a group of musicians. That morning, the telephone rang. 'I am Noah Greenberg of New York Pro Musica. Tonight I have a rehearsal and cannot attend your lecture. Could you show me your slides if I came along?' Of course. He lived only half-a-mile away. This gloriously loveable man, we knew, had come from a poor Jewish home in the drab outskirts of New York and won his way to the

32 York Mystery Plays, 1966: the prison bars fall as Christ harrows hell. Photo: Prospect Photographic Services

creation of the finest early-music ensemble then in existence. 'I am trying something that will interest you,' he said. 'We are going to produce *The Play of Daniel* in The Cloisters. The first rehearsal is Sunday. Can you come?'

I had known *The Play of Daniel* only as a twelfth-century Latin script. So had everyone else: the music had never been performed since the Middle Ages, for it was only recently that scholars had deciphered the notation. The sounds which Noah obtained from his singers-and-players (for most of them did both) with their copies of the ancient instruments on that Sunday morning revealed 'a new-created world', so totally fresh were they to our ears. We urged all our friends – and one came a thousand miles for it – to share in the new glory which was to be revealed at Christmastide; and next year, when we saw the production, it was already famous.

The story has a sequel. Noah longed to bring it to Europe, but the cost could be met only if the State Department adopted the production as a 'cultural export'. Starting at the top, I got Archbishop Fisher of Canterbury to write to his friend John Foster Dulles about it – but Dulles was mortally ill, and nothing happened. The stumbling-block, I discovered, was that *The Play of Daniel* is not an American work. At last, at the 1959 Christmastide Convention of AETA in Washington, Henzie spotted my chance for me. Mr Thayer, who ran the Cultural Exchange program of the State Department, was speaking. Afterwards, I managed to get his ear for long enough to suggest that for American artists to bring to light in Europe a masterpiece which Europe had forgotten would be a triumph of cultural exchange. In ten days, the tour was set for the coming summer of 1960.

Noah asked me to stage the production in the English churches, for of course different dispositions had to be made to suit each building. We opened at Wells Cathedral.

The stage action is of the simplest, but the desire for spectacle is generously satisfied by the processional entrances of each leading character and his or her entourage from all quarters of the building. The original authors certainly knew how to exploit the resources of their own cathedrals in this respect. A rare experience not to be missed.
(*The Times*, 27 May 1960)

At Oxford, since the university church and the college chapels didn't provide enough space, I persuaded the management to risk going to St Barnabas in the red-brick area near the railway. I used

33 York Mystery Plays 1966: Eve (Karin MacCarthy) tempted by 'the Worm' (David Henshaw). Photo: Prospect Photographic Services

to worship there as an undergraduate when I lived in Walton Street. It is 1869 Byzantine, and perfectly suited to the play, which by now was quite well enough known to draw people to an unfashionable neighbourhood. W. H. Auden, who had written the narration to introduce each scene of the Latin text, here delivered it himself. Elsewhere it was done by John Westbrook.

The whole of Whit-week we played in Westminster Abbey. From David Cairns' full-page review in the *Spectator* I take a sample of the reaction it called forth from press and public:

> The tremendous operatic qualities of *The Play of Daniel* leap the centuries and excite us purely as entertainment, as art . . . Mr. Browne's production has a few inventively naïve or spectacular touches – the child angel leading Habbakuk to Daniel's prison by a lock of his long white hair, the formidable procession of Darius' army, lit by flaming torches, up the darkened nave. But mainly he is content, as a good opera producer should, to move with the music.
>
> For, as in all good operas, the music articulates the drama. Simply as sound, *The Play of Daniel* is incredibly exhilarating. Even more remarkable is the flexibility of rhythm, movement and mood that, by imaginative interpretation of the old notation, has been found to lie within the limitations of single-line melody.

The musicologists carried on a controversy about Noah's bold orchestration, while the audiences enjoyed it. What is incontrovertible is that his creative work, based on scholarship and aimed at performance, gave back a masterpiece to the twentieth-century listener.

The seed from which the Mystery Plays grew is the drama of the Resurrection morning. The angel in the York play speaking to the women at Christ's tomb:

> Ye women mourning in your thought,
> Here in this place what have ye sought?

is asking the question which was the first speech of the modern drama:

> Quem quaeritis in sepulchro, O Christicolae?

It was sung, not spoken, in the Latin, for the scene was at first a part of the Easter service. Since I experienced *Daniel* I had wanted to perform this, all the more because I then met W. L. Smoldon. This English scholar had spent half a lifetime deciphering and transcribing the liturgical music-dramas. He was quite unlike the conventional image of a scholar, more like an Essex farmer, endearingly direct in manner, firm in his adherence to his sources as the farmer to his soil. With the young scholar–conductor Roy

Jesson and a group of professional singers headed by Edgar Fleet, I built up an Easter trilogy: *Planctus Mariae* (from Cividale, fourteenth century), *Visitatio Sepulchri* (a twelfth-century Easter morning play from Fleury) and *Peregrinus* (the Emmaus story, from Beauvais at the same date as *Daniel*). I staged them in liturgical style and dressed them in vestments, to be played in a church, and so they were at the 1966 York Festival. The sounds of this music, so simple and so profoundly dramatic, took hold of us all, and for several years we met to present the trilogy in English Cathedrals (Coventry, Guildford, Winchester, St Paul's) and in the USA (St Louis, Washington, New York). Ernest Bradbury, writing in the *Yorkshire Post*, speaks of it thus:

Just as the liturgy itself is these days becoming simpler, more direct, and more especially pointed towards the congregation, so these productions, in their modern-medievalistic way, focus on the most essential and basic elements, becoming indeed in the final play liturgy and music-drama in one. Of the artistic impact it is a joy to speak. The dramas are extremely moving, surprisingly varied, and often, both musically and dramatically, overwhelmingly beautiful.

But how close can the old drama come to the new people of today? In 1962 the new cathedral at Coventry was to be consecrated. The Coventry Theatre Guild, umbrella-organisation of amateur societies (several very good) in the district, appealed to me: could I produce for them an offering to the Consecration Festival?

It was to be in the ruins of the old, bombed cathedral. In 1944, I had done a play there, twice on a Sunday in June, in front of the stone altar with its cross of charred beams and the words FATHER FORGIVE. We had put table-tops on piles of rubble for a stage, and most of the audience stood or sat on other piles. The play itself had no great merit, but it was written to match the moment and called *I Will Arise*.

Should we revive it? No, its moment had passed. We looked now from the old to the new House of God: and we needed something in which was the heart of the Christian faith – and something also which would fill the whole great space of the ruins with drama. I turned back again to the cycle called wrongly, but in this context persuasively, *Ludus Coventriae*. I then conceived an extreme compression of it which would last an hour-and-a-half and move constantly from one part of the ruined building to another, the

34 *The Play of Daniel* (music-drama, 12th century, from Beauvais) in Westminster Abbey at Whitsuntide 1960. Darius' army advancing to overthrow Belshazzar. Photo: Gerti Deutsch

audience following it or finding points of vantage to see it from. The action would flow *through* the audience, with Heralds (modelled on the 'Stytelers' in the morality *Castle of Perseverance*) clearing the way for the actors. For stages, we would plant two or three small free-standing platforms, but mainly we would use what the ruins provided: stumps of pillars, window-frames, side-chapels raised a foot or two above the main floor, a double embrasure ten feet above it. I prepared the script for twenty actors and called it *The Mysteries*.

This added up to a new and thrilling theatrical experience. You would be watching the Fall on a side stage when a voice called from a pillar-stump at the other end of the building – it was Isaiah prophesying the Christ. The Annunciation on one stage led to the journey to Bethlehem, with audience clambering up where the players had been a moment before to see over others' heads. Gabriel cried 'Good Tidings' from a western window-frame to shepherds at the east end, who pushed their way to the side-chapel of the birth. Gethsemane was a ruined pillar in the midst of the people, who found themselves, after the arrest, lining the route to Calvary. The Crucifixion and Resurrection took place in front of a glassless window backing onto a street. Christ 'ascended' into the newly built House of God, 'The gate of Heaven'.

As soon as the play is over [said the programme] the actors will ask for contributions towards the expenses of the production. They will do it in the ancient way, headed by Satan with his rhyme from one of the old mumming-plays:

> Here come I, old Beelzebub,
> Over my shoulder I carry my club.
> And in my hand a frying-pan,
> Pleased to get all the money I can.

The Theatre Guild of Coventry will be grateful if you will give him all you can towards the large burden they have shouldered in presenting this production. All profits will be given to the Cathedral.

The result was a fund of some £600, which after paying production expenses left enough to buy the basic equipment for the drama programme of the new cathedral.

That programme illustrates some of the possibilities, and many of the problems, involved in creating the new, contemporary religious drama that George Bell looked for. His initiative had led to the 'great outburst of poetry and religion mingled in drama' in the thirties and forties. By the sixties, though a number of plays from that period remained very much in currency, the writer's situation was quite different. The theatre itself had radically changed: from the watershed of 1955–6 – *Waiting for Godot* and *Look Back in Anger* – had flowed many rivers, carrying with them new material from human life to be used as subject-matter and new, more varied, means of dramatising it. Christianity was beginning to understand itself anew, and learning to appreciate the other great religions. The writer was exploring rather than celebrating, posing questions not answering them, and treating the religious

35 Coventry 1962: in the ruins of the old Cathedral. *The Mysteries* from the Lincoln cycle is played to celebrate the consecration of the new. The action (and the audience with it) moves all over the building. Here Christ is being tempted in a raised recess on the north side

dimension (whatever he might think that to be) as part of life like the rest.

Coventry began with Porch Plays, for the lunch-hour passer-by on the pedestrian way outside the cathedral. They had to grip his attention at once, pose their question in a direct, hard-hitting way, and take no more than twenty minutes. The first three, which were published and are used elsewhere, may serve as examples. *This Is The End* is a modern *Everyman* with Mr Death in charge of the mike. *The Site* is the field in which is Christ's hidden treasure, and a young man sells all that he has to the property-developer to rescue it, he doesn't know why. *Who Is There To Ask?* is Henzie's: the cry of an adolescent girl with the usual problems forms its title.

When the provost first took us inside the new cathedral, among the forest of scaffold-poles, Henzie suddenly cried 'There's a stage!' It was the entrance to the Chapel of Unity, a platform raised four steps (two feet) above the nave floor and twenty-eight feet wide at the front. With chairs turned to face it across the nave, an audience of three to four hundred people could watch plays there. The one that gained most from being in the cathedral was James Saunders' *A Scent of Flowers*.

It begins with two undertaker's men bringing in the coffin of a young girl whom those related to her in various ways have abandoned to suicide. When they carried it onto *that* stage, the full implications for all the characters and the audience became unforgettably clear.

Saunders doesn't call himself Christian, and the commercial management who presented it at the Duke of York's Theatre in the West End certainly didn't call the play religious. But it's one of the best examples of where we are going, or trying to go, now. The Religious Drama Society, of which I succeeded George Bell as president, had adopted the name Radius: 'Its shorter title reflects the broadening of its aim. This is to encourage drama which throws a true light on the human condition, especially by means of a Christian understanding, and to assist and bring together those who create it.'

Drama is still on the periphery of the Church's work, and no doubt it will stay there. But the last half-century has seen them come together, however 'shyly', and exercise some influence on each other, for each other's good.

14

Canterbury: the centenary *Murder*

1970 was the 800th anniversary of Thomas Becket's martyrdom. The Cathedral Church of Christ in Canterbury, at one of whose altars Thomas was murdered, owes its present character almost entirely to the cult of 'the holy blissful martyr'. His shrine, until Henry VIII destroyed it, was one of the two most popular places of pilgrimage in Europe. The centenary must be celebrated in a fashion dictated not by nostalgia but by the power alive in the cathedral today.

The dean and chapter secured Gerald Peacocke, a master at their King's School who was about to leave for a headmastership elsewhere, to manage the Commemoration for them. He jumped at my suggestion that it should be possible, by reinforcing the modern sound equipment now installed, to produce a play in the nave. *Murder in the Cathedral*, the one great play to have been written for Canterbury, could thus be staged for the first time within the walls of the cathedral where the murder took place.

Becket was a difficult man in life, and has been a puzzle ever since his death. Eliot's Becket, though we see so little of his life, contains the ambiguity, the contradictions of his nature. I had become well aware of this when playing him in another cathedral, Gloucester, in 1955. The nave there, on the floor of which we played (with the audience on a raked stand), is of exactly the same date as the story, and combined with the twentieth-century script to give me a vivid insight. *The Times* reviewer ended his notice with a hope that I would be murdered in as many other cathedrals as possible. But I did not even consider undergoing that fate at Canterbury. The director's problems would be quite enough for me.

Sound was the problem which would condition all the others. The easy solution was that which I had seen adopted for the

Passion Play given in the Place de Notre Dame, Paris: to pre-record the whole text in the actors' voices and let them mime to their own recording. This I absolutely refused to do. It had made the acting completely dead. When the actor has to follow a recording he is not free to think or feel, and the flow of life in and between the characters is destroyed.

Tests showed that lines spoken by live actors could be made audible, if the action were raised and brought as near to the audience as possible. This was in any case most desirable: the steps up to the choir, on which *The Coming of Christ* was played in 1928, are more than fifty feet from the front row. I called in Michael Cain. As at York, an hour's quiet survey told him the solution. He designed a high, gently raked stage built right over the nave stalls,

36 Canterbury 1970: Murder taking place in the Cathedral nave to celebrate the octocentenary of Becket's martyrdom. HB, leader of the Chorus, is standing at the left. Photo by permission of Patricia Cain

its front level with the pulpit, the back leading onto the top step.
Into the stage he sank six tall candles which concealed microphones. The altar at the back had another, and over it hung a great
cross with a grid of 'mikes'. The pulpit had its own.

A control panel was installed from which the operator could see
all the action and constantly switch mikes as the actors moved. I
had to plan so that any speaker was within three feet of a standing
mike. This did not inhibit the actors after a few hard evenings'
rehearsal while they got used to it.

We could not begin until 7 p.m. when the cathedral closed to the
public. We worked till about midnight; and though our attention
was concentrated on the technical problems, the majesty and
mystery of the dark building affected us all, as it continued to do
throughout the three weeks' run.

John Westbrook played Becket. He has the voice and the
authority to command the huge space of the building. And he is as
tall as the historical character: six feet three-and-a-half inches, at a
time when the average man was shorter than now. John found the
experience in the cathedral overwhelming. Weeks after it was over
he wrote to me:

No, it doesn't fade and one is still dazed and curiously empty. I felt
Becket's isolation very strongly and was very desolate after each performance, and that has remained ... Henzie always gives so much to her
fellow-actors in sincerity and concentrated power. I shall never forget
what she gave to me in the crucifixion scene at York.

Henzie had then played Mary the Mother. In Canterbury, she was
the leader of the Chorus. When I saw her off-stage, pulling herself
up steps to make her entrances, the strength with which she met
the challenge on-stage seemed incredible. Her long experience of
the play had deepened her actress' intuitive understanding of it.
Certain aspects of the Chorus were seen as never before in the
group she led. Her opening related it to Greek tragedy:

> Some presage of an act
> Which our eyes are compelled to witness, has forced our feet
> Towards the Cathedral. We are forced to bear witness.

The women's own situation was summed up in her repeated

> Living and partly living.

Their feeling of being involved in the Knights' violence came out in
the frighteningly contemporary speech:

I have consented, Lord Archbishop, have consented.
Am torn away, subdued, violated,
United to the spiritual flesh of nature,
Mastered by the animal powers of spirit,
Dominated by the lust of self-demolition,
By the final utter uttermost death of spirit,
By the final ecstasy of waste and shame.

The still concentration of the group at the very front of the stage, before the Knights hammered at the north-west door, allowed the great building to echo their fear of

Not what we call death, but what beyond death is not death.

During the murder the women lay crouched on the ground and we saw over their heads the Knights butcher the Archbishop at the altar. When the 'curtain of falling blood' had come down, the four men huddled together upstage in dim light, talking over their next move, while the women recalled their vanished 'living and partly living'. Then, as the Knights advanced, rather hesitantly, to attempt their *apologia*, came the climax. The full horror of what had happened burst upon the women: as Henzie said, 'I felt the hydrogen bomb had fallen.'

But this, this is out of life, this is out of time.
An instant eternity of evil and wrong.

The Knights approached and tried to pass, but the women confronted them:

We are soiled by a filth that we cannot clean, united to
supernatural vermin,
It is not we alone, it is not the house, it is not the city that is
defiled
But *the world that is wholly foul*.

And then suddenly, the women rushed from the stage, into the transepts, into the ambulatory, each crying out so that the vaulting re-echoed:

Clear the air, clean the sky, wash the wind . . .
Wash the stone, wash the bone, wash the brain,
wash the soul, wash them, wash them!

In the final scene, Henzie carried the audience's thought forward to the devotion enshrined in the cathedral:

For the blood of Thy martyrs and saints
Shall enrich the earth, shall create the holy places.

For wherever a saint has dwelt, wherever a martyr has given
    his blood for the blood of Christ,
There is holy ground, and the sanctity shall not depart from it
Though armies trample over it, though sightseers come
    with guide-books looking over it . . .

Becket's body was laid on the altar before which he had been killed.
The Chorus moved up to venerate the body and surround it with
candles. They moved away into the choir, beyond which the shrine
of the martyr had once stood, as the cadence of Cooper's *Gloria* rose
to meet them and to give thanks for

    another Saint in Canterbury.

Epilogue

a letter from Henzie to absent friends
25 January 1971

On this day, at 5.30 p.m., Martin became 'D. Litt. Lambeth'. This is literally a rare honour. On 21 October 1970 a letter arrived:

My dear Browne,

Now that the performances of 'Murder in the Cathedral' in Canterbury Cathedral are, for this time, over, I want to make to you a proposal, and your acceptance of it would give not only pleasure to me but widespread pleasure to many people who value the work which you have been doing through the years.

As I expect you know, the Archbishop of Canterbury has power to confer degrees in any subject. This power goes back to the time of Henry VIII, and the recipient of a Lambeth degree may wear the hood and robes of the Archbishop's own University, in this case Cambridge. I invite you to accept the Degree of Doctor of Letters in recognition of your long services to drama, religion and literature. I greatly hope that you may accept this invitation.

The degree is conferred in a short ceremony in the chapel here at Lambeth and you would bring any of your friends to it . . .

With warmest good wishes to you both,

Yours most sincerely,
MICHAEL CANTUAR

Last Thursday, 21 January, about noon, we drove past the Houses of Parliament and over Lambeth Bridge. We had an appointment with the archbishop's chaplain who was to 'show us over the ground', so to speak. Once across the river we turned left under the Tudor gateway and into the great quadrangle of the palace. As we moved slowly in, a small car just ahead of us came to a halt and out stepped Mrs Ramsey, the archbishop's Lady. She greeted us warmly and constituted herself our guide. From the long corridor we moved down steps into the chapel. It is of the Early English style, the walls pierced by triple lancet windows; since it was gutted in the bombing of World War II, most of the walls and all of the glass are new. But here, in 1378, John Wyclif was called to give an account of his heretical opinions. Here, in 1640, Laud 'went to evening prayer in my chapel' before being taken to the Tower. Here, until the congregations grew too large for the chapel to hold them, bishops were consecrated, many to go overseas. In 1787, William White was consecrated Bishop of Pennsylvania and Samuel Provost Bishop of New York . . . At the north-east end of the chapel is a little door into 'Cranmer's Tower', and above it the stone-railed room from which he could watch the service. Just below this, we were to sit on the appointed day.

On *the* afternoon, we dressed slowly and carefully. My legs, a little like paper, were liable to fold, while the valiant heart pounded in wildly syncopated rhythm. We arrived before any of the guests, but only just. The first, in every sense, was our beloved Sybil Thorndike, now 88, very beautiful and her face alight, wearing the white tweed coat we remember from the Thanksgiving Service for Lewis in Westminster Abbey. In the chapel, I sat between Mrs Ramsey and Sybil, whose ever-nagging arthritic pain was for these moments out of mind. Everywhere in the full chapel were known faces: three generations of family, friends, and colleagues all of whose lives had in overlapping circles accompanied Martin's both before and after that day, 30 June, 1930, when he came to meet George Bell. Was Martin, a man of the theatre, willing to devote himself to renewing its alliance with religion? This was the question he asked on that day. Looking back over these years, it is clear how Martin's education, his personal interests, our marriage, our work in the States (at Carnegie Tech) till that time, had been an unconscious preparation for the development which was to follow. The work in the theatre, professional and amateur, the religious drama movement, the association with the poet-playwrights, the renaissance of the Mystery Plays – all this was to stem and flower, expanding from that moment, in Chichester, Canterbury, York, London, and the USA.

We stood as the little procession moved up the aisle through the nave and choir-stalls. The chaplain in black cassock carried the Mace. Martin followed him, resplendent in his scarlet woollen gown of the familiar medieval cut with hanging sleeves lined and faced with taffeta of the same scarlet, and the black velvet Tudor hat (like a soft-crowned beefeater's) with yellow tassel, under his arm. Next, in legal wig and gown, the registrar carrying the documents. Then the archbishop in scarlet but with lavender facings – a great paradox of a man at his mental zenith, but with an outward physical appearance much beyond his 66 years. A suffragan bishop in purple cassock, carrying the Doctor's hood, brought up the rear.

The archbishop seated himself in a chair before the altar, the others ranged on either side.

> *Dominus vobiscum*
> *Et cum spiritu tuo*
> *Oremus:*

A prayer in Latin, and than *Pater Noster*, which was gallantly if unevenly taken up by the congregation, not too certain of the pronunciation.

The candidate was required to swear that he, being admitted to the Doctorate of Letters by (using the massive description) 'the Most Reverend Father in God, by Divine Providence Lord Archbishop of Canterbury, Primate of All England, and Metropolitan', vowed allegiance to the Queen and her heirs and successors. Having repeated the oath, he signed it, then knelt before the seated archbishop who read the 'Instrument'. Addressing his 'beloved in Christ Elliott Martin Browne Master of Arts Commander of the Order of the British Empire' he stated, in terminology presumably framed in the sixteenth century, the 'laudable Usage and Custom . . . with the Approbation . . . of the pure Reformed Churches . . . that they who have with Proficiency and Applause exerted themselves in the Study of any liberal Science, should be graced with some eminent Degree of Dignity . . . *we therefore* . . . have judged it expedient, that you whose Proficiency in the Study of drama and literature, Uprightness of Life, Sound Doctrine, and Purity of Morals are manifest unto Us, be dignified with the Degree of Doctor of Letters'. Here the archbishop hit Martin three times, quite resoundingly, on the head with his reversed academic 'mortar board'.

The purple bishop invested him with the scarlet hood; but Mr Wig pricked the bubble of enthusiasm with the pin of legal caution:

'Provided always that these Presents do not avail you anything unless registered by the Clerk of the Crown in Chancery.' After Martin and the archbishop had signed the Book of Degrees, he concluded with the Latin prayer that all our comings and goings might be filled with the power and mercy of the Trinity, in whose Name he gave us his blessing.

The procession moved out, and we made our way to the drawing-room. I found myself greeting old friends and re-forging links across the years between many who had common connections with our life. The archbishop himself was still, like Martin, wearing his Doctor's robes. Sybil was seated by the fireplace, a queen in her own right.

The archbishop proposed that we drink the health of the new Doctor – adding to the toast my name and Sybil's. Martin thanked the archbishop first for the unique honour done to him:

It is wonderful too that all of you, family, friends, and colleagues from so many phases of our life, are here today to rejoice with us. I am just as much aware of some others who I feel sure are very much with us in spirit. First of all, George Bell, who, just over forty years ago in the Lollards Tower of this Palace, appointed me Director of Religious Drama in his Diocese of Chichester. Next of Geoffrey Whitworth, who introduced me to George Bell, and who was the creator of the British Drama League where I succeeded him as Director. Of T. S. Eliot, whom we met at George Bell's house that same year (1930) and whose widow is with us today: it was his writing that did more than anyone else's to create a new relationship between the Christian Faith and the theatre. Then of the founders of Radius (the Religious Drama Society of Great Britain), Sir Francis Younghusband and Mrs Olive Stevenson (her daughter is here). George Bell was its President until his death in 1958 and I have followed him. Of William Temple, who in 1943 called a conference in this house to plan future ties between Church and Theatre. And so I come to his successor of today who, after the revival of *Murder* in the Cathedral nave of Canterbury in 1970, has so greatly rewarded me, and to his wife who has welcomed with such joy so large a company of guests. I ask you to raise your glasses to our host and hostess.

It was over. The guests went their ways: most were Londoners, but some came from Dorset, Hampshire, Berkshire, Coventry, Birmingham, Edinburgh, Boston, New Zealand. The Primate of All England and Mrs Ramsey came down to the open door and cold night air to see us into our car. To thank them was quite beyond my words.

Index

Plays and books are indexed under their titles